A to Z of
FAMOUS PEOPLE

A to Z of FAMOUS PEOPLE

Edited by
Alan Blackwood

First published by Octopus Books
59 Grosvenor Street, London W1

ISBN 0 7064 1772 0

The publishers gratefully acknowledge the assistance of Alan Jamieson in the preparation of the original manuscript

Printed in Czechoslovakia
50 444

A

ABRAHAM (about 2000 BC)
Jewish patriarch

Abraham is regarded as the founder of the Jewish people. He was born in the city of Ur on the river Euphrates, near the Persian Gulf. He and his family moved north across Mesopotamia, then west and southward to the land of Canaan. According to the Bible, he was told by God to change the form of his name from Abram to Abraham, meaning 'the father of many'. His family and descendants then became known as the Hebrews, which means 'the people from across the river' (the Euphrates); and when they finally settled in Judea the Hebrews were also known as the Jews.

ADENAUER, Konrad (1876-1967)
German statesman

To the people of West Germany Konrad Adenauer was *Der Alter* – 'The Old One'. Old in age and wisdom, he was the man who restored the fortunes of a large part of Germany after the catastrophe of the Second World War. Before the war he had for many years been Mayor of Cologne, until dismissed by the Nazis. Immediately after the war, the victorious Allies divided Germany, creating the Communist-led German Democratic Republic in the east, and the larger German Federal Republic in the west. For a brief period, Adenauer returned as mayor of the devastated city of Cologne, then moved into Federal German politics. As founder and leader of the Christian Democrat Party, he became in 1949 Federal, or West German Chancellor. Adenauer provided the kind of solid and stable leadership needed for a country picking itself up from the ruins of war and the shame of Nazi rule. He brought West Germany back into world affairs, and made her a founder member of the European Economic Community. He established specially close links with Germany's old enemy, France. When Adenauer finally retired at the age of 87, West Germany was secure and prosperous.

AESOP (about 700 BC)
Greek writer and moralist

Aesop created a special type of short story, or fable, using examples of animal behaviour to point out some moral, or illustrate strengths and weaknesses of human character. The well-known story of the Tortoise and the Hare is one of them. Aesop's Fables remained almost unique for over 2000 years, until the French writer and poet Jean de La Fontaine (1621-95) produced another famous set of animal fables. Some of these also poke fun at the customs and habits of his time.

AGRICOLA, Gnaeus Julius (AD 37-93)
Roman soldier and statesman

Agricola played a vital part in the history of Roman Britain, or Britannia. He first saw action helping to put down the revolt of Queen Boudicca (page 34). After service elsewhere, he returned as Governor of the province from AD 78 to 84. During these six years he took his legions into Wales to crush the Celts and Druids. Then he advanced north into Caledonia (modern-day Scotland). He built a line of forts between the rivers Forth and Clyde, and from this base line pushed northwards again deep into the Highlands, where he put to flight the Caledonian tribesmen at the battle of Mons Graupius, near Aberdeen. Back in what is now England, Agricola built new roads, forts and towns, consolidating Roman control over the province. Indeed, he was so good at his job that the Emperor Domitian, fearing a rival for power, recalled him to Rome. Much of what we know of him comes from the Roman historian Tacitus.

AGRIPPA, Marcus (about 63-12 BC)
Roman soldier and engineer

Marcus Agrippa has been called 'Architect of the Roman Empire'. He directed the military campaigns that heralded the greatest period of Roman power, starting with the reign of his close friend, the Emperor Augustus (see page 17). He was also a real architect and engineer, building aqueducts, and the Pantheon in Rome, which remained for centuries the building with the largest dome in the world. Another of Agrippa's achievements was to draw up a map of the world as it was known to the Romans.

AKBAR (1542-1605)
Mogul Indian emperor

Akbar was the most illustrious of the Turkish Mogul emperors who conquered and ruled large areas of northern India. In the early years of his reign (which coincided with that of Elizabeth I of England [page 88]) he was a ruthless warrior. After one battle he is said to have piled up the decapitated heads of thousands of enemy dead. But having enlarged his empire by war and bloodshed he revealed a quite different side of his character. As a Mogul emperor he was a strict Muslim, but allowed freedom of worship among the peoples of his domains, many of whom were Hindus. He introduced new and just laws, opened schools, built roads and encouraged some of the finest art and architecture that India has produced. His own magnificent tomb can still be seen at Sikandra, near Agra.

AKHENATEN (about 1400 BC)
Egyptian king

The civilisation of Egypt, spread out along the banks of the river Nile, was one of the oldest and longest-lasting in history. One of its most remarkable rulers was the Pharaoh Amenhotep IV, who lived over 3000 years ago. Egyptian life centred round religion, and the worship of many gods. Amenhotep suddenly swept all this aside, proclaiming that there was only one god – the sun, symbolised in the sun's disc, called the Aten. To establish this new religious order, he changed his own name to Akhenaten ('All Praise to the Aten') and moved his court from the old capital of Thebes to a brand new city, El-Amarna. There he and his queen, Nefertiti, ruled in the name of the new religion. While Akhenaten lived the religion flourished, together with interesting new styles in art and architecture. But he had deprived the priests of much of their traditional power, and almost as soon as he was dead they restored the old religious order. The great significance of Akhenaten for us today is that, as far as we know, he was the first to create a religion based on a single god – monotheism.

ALCOCK, Sir John (1892–1919)
English aviator

Jack Alcock was an airman during the First World War. As soon as the war was over, he and Arthur Whitton Brown (also later knighted) planned to make the first non-stop flight across the Atlantic ocean. In the summer of 1919, flying a converted twin-engined Vickers Vimy wartime bomber, they took off from an airfield in Newfoundland and over 16 hours later crash-landed on the west coast of Ireland. During their pioneer flight, some of the instruments had failed, and several times the intrepid Brown had to climb out onto the wings to hack off ice. Alcock was killed in a flying accident soon after.

ALEXANDER III, The Great (356–323 BC)
Greek soldier and emperor

Alexander was taught philosophy and wisdom by one of the greatest men in the history of learning, Aristotle (page 13), but a scholarly life was not for him. He became King of Macedon in northern Greece at the age of 20, and by a series of lightning strikes, southward had soon brought all the Greek states under his command. Alexander next turned his eyes eastward, towards the mighty Persian Empire. He and his army advanced through the mountains of Turkey into Syria, crushed the Persian armies of Darius III, took the cities of Tyre, Jerusalem and Babylon, and proceeded southwards into Egypt. Alexander then embarked on his most ambitious campaign of all, an advance right across Persia and into the plains of northern India. There he was halted, not by an opposing army, but by the sheer exhaustion of his own soldiers, many of whom died from hunger and sickness. Alexander himself died from a fever at the early age of 33. He had covered over 30,000 kilometres with his victorious army in less than ten years, an amazing achievement.

Alexander's conquests were spectacular. His influence on the course of history was just as important. He did not destroy the cultures of the people he conquered. Indeed, he built many new cities, including Alexandria in Egypt which was soon to have a famous library of thousands of scrolls. In this way he created valuable links between the civilisations of Greece and those of Asia and Africa. Christianity first spread into Europe from Asia through the cultural links that Alexander forged.

ALEXANDER NEVSKY (about 1220–63)
Russian warrior hero

Alexander held together the land we now know as Russia against attack from the Mongols in the east and the Germans and Swedes from the west and north. He took the name Nevsky after defeating a Swedish army near the river Neva in 1240. Two years later he beat off an invasion by the Teutonic Knights in a battle on the frozen Lake Peipus. Many of the knights apparently were drowned when the weight of their armour and that of their horses caused the ice to crack. This dramatic episode was re-created by the Soviet director Sergei Eisenstein in his film *Alexander Nevsky*, with music by Prokofiev (page 196). The Nevsky Prospect in Leningrad is also named after the Russian hero.

ALFRED THE GREAT (about AD 849–900)
Saxon king

The Saxons from north and central Germany invaded and settled large parts of the British Isles during the 6th and 7th centuries AD. They, in their turn, had to face another wave of invasions, this time by the Danes, a race of people closely related to the Vikings. Their greatest champion against these new invaders was King Alfred. In 878 he won a big victory over them at Edington (or Ethandune) in what is now the county of Wiltshire. By this victory he secured for the Saxons the territories of Wessex and West Mercia (most of southern and central England), while the Danes under their leader Guthrum withdrew to an area called Danelaw (north and east England). Alfred, though, did not relax. He built up both his army and navy, and repelled other Danish attacks on land and sea. He was also a great lawmaker, built churches and monasteries, and attracted scholars from all over Western Europe. He promoted the writing of the *Anglo-Saxon Chronicle*, a marvellous source of information to us about his life and times.

AMUNDSEN, Roald (1872–1928)
Norwegian explorer

The North-West Passage from the Atlantic to the Pacific oceans across the top of Canada had haunted explorers' minds for centuries. In a three-year voyage, starting in 1903, Amundsen, with six brave companions, was the first man to navigate the icy waters of the Passage. He next planned an expedition to the North Pole itself, but was beaten to this objective by the American explorer Admiral Peary (page 187). Undaunted, he turned his attention to the even colder, unexplored South Pole. Here he had a rival in the person of the British explorer Captain Scott (page 215). But by taking a better route and using teams of husky dogs, Amundsen was the first to reach the South Pole, on 14 December 1911. In 1926 he also became the first man to fly over the North Pole, in an airship. He was killed, trying to rescue companions whose airship had crashed during another Polar expedition a fitting death for one of the greatest explorers of the twentieth century.

ANDERSON, Elizabeth Garrett (1836–1917)
English pioneer woman doctor

Elizabeth Garrett was inspired by the fact that Elizabeth Blackwell in America had become the world's first woman medical doctor. In the face of bitter opposition from all those people who thought that a woman's place was in the home, Elizabeth Garrett determined to become a doctor. She qualified, and after more years of struggle against anti-feminine prejudice, opened her own hospital for poor women and children in London. A similar institution is now named after her. In this and other ways, Elizabeth Garrett Anderson – her married name – was a pioneer in the fight for equal opportunities.

ANNE (1665–1714)
British queen

Queen Anne, daughter of James II, was the last of the Stuart monarchs. She was a docile, easy-going woman, but her reign from 1702–1714, was filled with events. There was the War of the Spanish Succession, in which Britain sought to maintain the European balance of power with a series of victories by Churchill, the Duke of Marlborough (page 55), over Louis XIV (page 151). At home the Act of Union of 1707 politically united England and Scotland, and the two political parties known as the Whigs and the Tories – very important for the future of Britain – came clearly into being.

ANTONIUS, Marcus (about 82–30 BC)
Roman soldier and politician

Marcus Antonius, or Mark Antony as he is often called, rose to prominence and power through his support of Julius Caesar (page

42). He helped Caesar defeat his political rival Pompey (page 195) at the battle of Pharsalus in 48 BC; and after Caesar's murder four years later, Antonius took the lead in pursuing and defeating his chief assassins, Brutus and Cassius, at Philippi. Antonius was then in a very strong position, and with Caesar's adopted son Octavian, and the general Aemilius Lepidus, he shared the government of the Roman Empire (the Triumvirate). He married Octavian's sister. Antonius's love for Queen Cleopatra of Egypt (page 59) was his undoing. He deserted his wife for Cleopatra. Octavian, smarting at this insult to his sister, and suspecting Antonius of selling out to Cleopatra, followed him east. There he destroyed the combined navies of Antonius and Cleopatra at the sea battle of Actium in 31 BC. Antonius killed himself soon after.

ARCHIMEDES (about 287-212 BC)
Greek inventor and mathematician

Archimedes lived in Syracuse on the island of Sicily, which was then a Greek colony; and several of his most famous inventions or discoveries were connected with problems set for him by the King of Syracuse. Apparently the king asked him to find a way of removing bilge water from the hold of a ship. Archimedes's solution was the Screw – a device which raised the water as a spiral screw turned inside a tube. Another problem was to find out whether the king's crown contained the right amount of gold. Archimedes was already interested in the effect on weight of objects immersed in water, and of displacement of water in relation to volume and weight, and used his observations to solve the matter. The story goes that he hit upon the answer while taking a bath, and ran through the streets shouting *'Eureka!'* ('I've solved it!'). Archimedes discovered other principles of mechanics and mathematics, including the use of levers and the formula for calculating the area of a circle. He lived during the time of the Punic Wars between the Roman Republic and Carthage, and is also said to have invented a giant concave mirror that focused the sun's rays on the sails of invading Roman galleys and set fire to them.

ARISTOPHANES (about 448–380 BC)
Greek dramatist

Classical or Hellenic Greece is now seen as the starting point for so many branches of European or Western culture: architecture, music, philosophy, mathematics – and drama. Early Greek plays were based largely on the Chorus, a group of players who commented upon the drama rather than taking part in it themselves. Aristophanes gradually reduced the importance of the Chorus, so that his plays had more freedom of action. He wrote comedies, which often poked fun at Greek society, and sometimes at the work of fellow dramatists. Among these comedies are *The Birds, Lysistrata, The Frogs* and *The Parliament of Women.*

ARISTOTLE (about 384–322 BC)
Greek philosopher and teacher

Aristotle, who lived nearly 2500 years ago, is one of the greatest figures in the history of learning and knowledge. He joined Plato's (page 193) Academy in Athens, first as a student and then as a teacher. Aristotle taught and wrote on many subjects – mathematics, medicine, biology, astronomy, history, government and law. Above all, he contributed to the equally important question of *how* we should train and use our minds to think clearly. To Aristotle we largely owe the branch of philosophy now called Logic (or Analytics as he called it), which uses a disciplined, step-by-step method of establishing what may be true or false in any line of thinking – similar to proving a theorem in geometry.

ARKWRIGHT, Sir Richard (1732–92)
English inventor and industrialist

In the early period of the Industrial Revolution – the second half of the 18th century – one of the chief industries was the manufacture of cotton. Several men invented ways of improving the spinning and weaving of cotton, notably James Hargreaves, Samuel Crompton, and Richard Arkwright. He was born in Lancashire, the centre of the English cotton industry, and with help from others developed the first successful mechanically-powered cotton spinning machine. He set up his own factory at Cromford Mill in Derbyshire, where his machines were driven first by water and then by steam. On one occasion cotton workers broke in and destroyed the machinery, fearing that it would put them out of work. In the event, Arkwright's machines increased production, and the factory methods he introduced created more employment.

ARTHUR (about AD 500)
British king

Was there a real King Arthur? Some historians believe him to have been a soldier named Artorius, the descendant of a Roman officer, who organised resistance against the invading Saxons. A 12th-century chronicle (already 600 years later) mentions a victory by Arthur over the Saxons at Mount Badon, and his defeat and death at the battle of Camlan in AD 537. But there is little or nothing that is certain about him. The Arthurian legends, on the other hand, are world-famous. The medieval French poet Chretien de Troyes and the 15th-century English author Thomas Malory made Arthur the central figure in a mythical world of chivalry and magic, with their stories of the Knights of the Round Table, Merlin the Wizard, the sword Excalibur and the Search for the Holy Grail.

ASOKA (about 264–220 BC)
Indian emperor and religious leader

Asoka was a warrior king who became disgusted with the bloodshed and suffering of war and became a Buddhist. Three hundred years earlier, in the same land of India, Gautama Buddha (page 103) had preached kindness, toleration and a respect for all forms of life. Asoka himself built homes and hospitals for the poor, sent missionaries to the nearby lands of Sri Lanka (Ceylon) and Burma, and had the principles of Buddhist teaching carved on stone buildings and rocks throughout his domains. His own Buddhist kingdom did not long survive him, but he had greatly helped the spread of Buddhism in Asia.

ATATURK, Kemal (1881-1938)
Turkish soldier and statesman

'The Sick Man of Europe' was the name given to Turkey in the early years of this century. Though not strictly a part of Europe, Turkey controlled the old Ottoman Empire that had covered most of the Balkans. By 1900 this empire was crumbling fast, and Turkey was a poverty-stricken and backward country. Ataturk did much to change this state of affairs. In the First World War, when Turkey was allied to Germany, he commanded the troops that repulsed the British and Commonwealth landing on the Gallipoli peninsula. Soon after the war, he defeated the Greeks, and swept away the old Muslim rule of the Sultan. As President of the new Turkish Republic, Ataturk did everything he could to turn his country into a modern 'westernised' state – much as Peter the Great (page 190) had tried to do for Russia two hundred years before. He substituted the Latin for the Arabic alphabet, and released women from the bondage they had known in the old days of the Sultans. New industries and better education were other ways by which Ataturk eventually changed the customs and habits of centuries.

ATTILA (about AD 400-53)
Hun warrior king

The Huns were one of the barbarian races that came out of Asia, over-running large areas of Europe and hastening the collapse of the Roman Empire. They were brilliant horsemen, and their leader was Attila, known as 'The Scourge of God'. He first led his wild cavalry southward, as far as Constantinople, forcing the Emperor

Theodosius to pay him a huge amount in gold and silver to spare the city. He then moved swiftly westward and invaded Gaul (France). At Chalons-sur-Marne in 451 he suffered his only defeat, at the hands of a Roman and Visigoth army. Consequently he turned back and headed for Rome itself, where Pope Leo I also managed to buy him off. Attila was planning further campaigns when he died.

ATTLEE, Clement Richard, Earl (1883–1967)
British statesman

Clement Attlee looked too meek and mild to make a good politician, but he led one of the most radical and dynamic governments ever elected by the British people. Attlee studied law, but gave up the chance of a comfortable, well-paid career to take up social work in east London. Then he joined the Labour Party and was elected to parliament. He served in Ramsay MacDonald's two short-lived Labour governments of 1924 and 1929, and was elected Party Leader in 1935. During the Second World War, when a coalition government was formed, he was appointed Churchill's (page 56) deputy. When the Labour Party won a sweeping election victory in 1945, Attlee at last became Prime Minister. Mild-mannered but a shrewd judge of people and events, he headed a government that included such strong personalities as Ernest Bevin, Aneurin Bevan and Sir Stafford Cripps. It was a government that nationalised road and rail transport, the gas, electricity, coal and steel industries, set up the National Health Service, and granted independence to India. The Labour Party narrowly won the next election in 1950, but were voted out of office the following year.

AUGUSTINE (about AD 560–604)
Italian missionary and saint

Saint Augustine was a Benedictine monk, whom Pope Gregory I sent to Britain to convert the Anglo-Saxon invaders to Christianity. Augustine landed in Britain with 40 other monks. In their missionary travels some of the monks were killed, others disappeared, but they did succeed in converting many people in southern England to their faith, including the Saxon King Ethelbert of Kent. Augustine built a church at Canterbury and became the first Archbishop.

AUGUSTUS CAESAR (63 BC-AD 14)
Roman soldier and emperor

'Augustus' means 'Exalted', and the man who took that title ruled the Roman Empire as it was nearing its greatest extent and power. His name at birth was Octavian. Julius Caesar (page 42) was his great uncle and adopted him as son and heir. When Julius Caesar was assassinated in 44 BC, Octavian at first joined two other leading Romans, Aemilius Lepidus and Marcus Antonius (Mark Antony) (page 11), to form a ruling Triumvirate. With their support he defeated the chief conspirators involved in Caesar's killing, Brutus and Cassius, at the battle of Philippi in 42 BC. He then stripped Lepidus of his power, dividing the Empire between himself and Antonius. The famous love affair between Antonius and Cleopatra of Egypt (page 59) soon made Octavian act again. He suspected Antonius and Cleopatra of conspiring against him, and moved east to bring about their downfall at the sea battle of Actium in 31 BC. That left him, at the age of 33, sole ruler of Rome and its empire. In 27 BC he took the titles of Imperium, or Emperor, and of Augustus.

The reign of the Emperor Augustus Caesar was noted for firm government, a further expansion of the Empire, prosperity and the construction of many fine buildings. After his death, the Romans elevated him still further, almost to the status of a god, and named the month of August after him.

AUSTEN, Jane (1775-1817)
English novelist

Jane Austen was the daughter of an English country clergyman, and led a pleasant, uneventful life centred round family and friends. This kind of life – among comfortably-off people in provincial Regency England – was exactly what she wrote about. There is not much drama or real excitement in her work, but she was a shrewd observer of human character and frailty, which she recorded with a good deal of wit. In *Pride and Prejudice, Sense and Sensibility, Emma* and her other novels, she made a fine art of writing about what might at first glance seem quite ordinary people and events.

B

BABBAGE, Charles (1792–1871)
English mathematician and inventor

Babbage worked out the principles of the computer well over a hundred years ago. He often found inaccuracies in calculation tables for such things as the movements of the Moon and planets. Since they were due to human error, he decided to try and devise a machine that could make all such calculations. His first device, built as early as 1827, compiled and printed sheets of logarithms. Babbage went on to construct an 'analytical engine' that was intended to make any sort of mathematical calculation. Its principles were perfectly sound, but it never worked properly because it was too far ahead of the general level of technology of the time. The first really workable, electronic computer was not produced until 1946.

BACH, Johann Sebastian (1685–1750)
German composer

Johann Sebastian Bach belonged to a long line of musicians. Many of his ancestors had taken up music, and two of his own sons – Johann Christian and Carl Philipp Emanuel – became famous composers in their turn. J. S. Bach was born in Eisenach, a small town in the region of Thuringia (now in East Germany), and he never moved far from home. He held a series of musical posts, the last and longest of these being as Cantor, or musical director, at the Church and School of St Thomas in Leipzig. He was recognised as a fine organist, but was seldom praised as a composer – a fact that sometimes made him bitter, stubborn and irritable.

Bach wrote different types of music to suit his various employers.

For the organ he composed fantasias (fairly free-sounding pieces that give us a good idea of how Bach himself might have improvised at the organ), chorales, and preludes and fugues. For the harpsichord, he wrote suites of dances, *The Goldberg Variations*, and another group of Forty-eight Preludes and Fugues, known as *The Well-Tempered Clavier* (or Well-Tuned Keyboard), because they were inspired by a new system of tuning keyboard instruments. For other instruments he wrote pieces ranging from suites and partitas for solo violin and cello to the *Brandenburg Concertos* for different combinations of instruments. For solo voices and chorus he wrote nearly 300 church cantatas (the melody called 'Jesu, Joy of Man's Desiring' comes from one of these), the *St John* and *St Matthew Passions* (dramatic settings of Christ's arrest and trial taken from the gospels) and the huge Mass in B minor.

Bach was not a revolutionary composer, like Beethoven (page 24) or Wagner (page 242). He wrote mainly in the polyphonic style – the weaving together of strands of melody – which went back hundreds of years. Even before he died he was considered an old-fashioned composer, and much of his vast output of music was soon forgotten. Mendelssohn (page 163), nearly a hundred years later, was among the first to rediscover some of his greatest music, and to show people how wonderfully expressive, grand and powerful it really is.

BACON, Francis (1561–1626)
English statesman and philosopher

Francis Bacon lived during the reigns of Elizabeth I (page 88) and James I. He was one of the most eminent political figures of his time, rising to the positions of Attorney General and Lord Chancellor, until he was charged with bribery and disgraced. Today we remember him mainly for his writings. Bacon's Essays are his thoughts about life in general and are full of good common sense and insight. His larger treatises are about science and learning. In them he writes of the importance of checking ideas and theories by experiment, so making him a founder of modern scientific thinking.

BACON, Roger (about 1214–1295)
English scholar and scientist

Roger Bacon was one of the greatest scholars of his time, who prepared an encyclopedia of knowledge for the Pope. He was also an interesting mixture of the old and the new in what he believed and thought. He held to many of the ancient notions and ideas of alchemy, long since rejected by science, and he put his faith in the Scriptures. On the other hand, he had a restless and inquiring mind, which led him into many experiments. Gunpowder and the telescope are just two of the many things people have said he invented, though without real proof. As a Franciscan monk, Roger Bacon was a man of the Church. As a man who constantly questioned the nature of things he was a true scientist.

BADEN-POWELL, Robert (1857–1941)
English soldier and youth leader

Lord Baden-Powell was a soldier who served with the British army in the South African Boer War of 1899–1902. He organised the defence of Mafeking against the Boers, and when the town was finally relieved he found himself a national hero. Soon after he started the Boy Scout movement, based on his own experiences as a scout in the army. His idea was to train boys to be alert and self-reliant, by sending them out into the country and getting them to fend for themselves. That, he believed, was the best way to shape their character. In time, his Boy Scout movement spread all over the world, with himself as Chief Scout. With his sister he founded the Girl Guides, based on the same ideas.

BAIRD, John Logie (1888–1946)
Scottish inventor

Baird was an electrical engineer who was one of the first people to think about the possibility of television. He was a sick man with very little money, but doggedly went ahead with experiments, working mainly in a dingy back room in London, until he had developed a television system. This he triumphantly demonstrated in 1926, and three years later the British Broadcasting Corporation began experimental television transmissions with his equipment. Sadly for this brave and determined pioneer, his particular method of scanning objects and scenes was soon overtaken by other developments in electronics, and his system was never widely used.

BAKUNIN, Mikhail (1814–76)
Russian revolutionary

During the last century, in Europe, the poverty and hard lives of working people in the new industrial cities, and the pressing need for reforms of all kinds, produced many uprisings and revolutions. The Anarchist movement, dedicated to the overthrow of existing forms of government and society, played a big part in all this. The most famous anarchist was Mikhail Bakunin. He was a Russian aristocrat and Tsarist officer, but came to hate the repressive rule of the Tsars. From then on he worked for revolution, as a kind of active counterpart to revolutionary thinkers like Karl Marx (page 160) with whom he quarrelled. In 1848 – 'The Year of Revolutions' – he was involved in uprisings in Paris and Prague, and the next year was in the thick of another uprising in Dresden. Bakunin was arrested, handed over to the Russian government and sent to Siberia. He escaped and continued his revolutionary activities for the rest of his stormy life.

BALZAC, Honoré de (1799–1850)
French novelist

Balzac was a big man with a constitution like an ox, and his output of work matched his size and strength. Much of it is contained in a series of nearly a hundred novels, collectively titled *La comédie humaine.* By 'comedy' Balzac meant the whole range of human character and behaviour, and the novels of this huge series are studded with vivid portraits of human types. He lived during the French equivalent of the Industrial Revolution, when money and capital played an increasing part in the society around him. Balzac himself had very little money and was often in debt, and the corrupting effect of money is another big theme running through his work. Despite his strength, he died relatively young, exhausted by his ceaseless labours as a writer of life as he saw it.

BARNARDO, Thomas (1845-1905)
English philanthropist

Dr Thomas Barnardo was one of the great philanthropists of the 19th century – people who took individual action on behalf of the poor and downtrodden of the new industrial towns and cities. He planned to go to distant "China as a medical missionary, but found as much poverty and misery in east London as he was likely to find anywhere. He was especially moved by the plight of homeless children, and set up a small home of his own for them. With help and support from friends, he was soon able to establish more havens for abandoned children. Where possible he organised them into 'family groups' with a woman, in place of a real mother, in charge. His ideas and methods were taken up elsewhere, and there are now Dr Barnardo Homes for orphaned children all over the world.

BAUDELAIRE, Charles (1821-67)
French poet

Baudelaire's most famous group of poems is called *Les Fleurs du Mal* (Flowers of Evil), and when he published them in 1857 he was prosecuted for obscenity. They and some of his other poems are now appreciated for the subtle way the words and phrases conjure up other ideas or sensatins deep in the reader's mind. This fascinating new kind of poetry had a big influence on other French writers of the 19th century, who formed what is called the

Symbolist Movement, and on the music of such composers as Debussy (page 73). Baudelaire was also a noted art critic, and admirer of the work of Edgar Allan Poe, many of whose writings he translated into French.

BEETHOVEN, Ludwig van (1770–1827)
German composer

Beethoven's family came from the Netherlands and settled in the Rhineland town of Bonn, where Ludwig was born. His father was a local musician, but also a drunkard, and the boy's childhood was not happy. His talents, though, were encouraged. He went to Vienna, where Mozart (page 170) promised great things of him, and soon settled in that city. Beethoven began his career as a composer-pianist, and though he was a rebellious young man, the Viennese aristocracy liked him and gave him their support. The big crisis in his life was caused by the onset of deafness, and from the age of 30 he withdrew more and more from public life, to concentrate on composition. In his last years, his deafness was total, and he suffered from many illnesses, including dropsy. As doctors drew the watery fluid from his body he is supposed to have muttered defiantly, 'better from my belly than from my pen', and he went on working almost to the end. He died in squalor, but was already famous, and thousands turned out for his funeral.

Beethoven grew up during the period of the French Revolution, and his own life and work matched the revolutionary spirit of the age. He was a fiercely independent man, who never accepted a job as a court or church musician, as most composers before him had done. Thus he was free to build up the main styles and forms of music of his time – the symphony, sonata, string quartet – and make them express thoughts and feelings with a new depth, drama and intensity. Composition was often long and laborious, but the end result – music that is both emotionally powerful and intellectually very strong and controlled – makes him for many the greatest of all composers. Beethoven's principal works are nine symphonies (no 3 *Eroica*, no 6 *Pastoral*, no 9 *Choral*), the Mass in D (*Missa Solemnis*), the opera *Fidelio*, five piano concertos, 32 piano sonatas and 17 string quartets.

BECKET, Thomas à (about 1118-70)
English churchman and saint

The tragic relationship between Thomas à Becket and Henry II (page 118) was part of the long dispute between English monarchs and the Roman Church about who had most authority. For many years Becket was Lord Chancellor and a close friend of King Henry. Then Henry appointed him Archbishop of Canterbury, and they started quarrelling about such matters as the Church's right to administer its own system of justice. For several years Becket went into exile in France. When he returned to Canterbury his quarrels with Henry soon flared up again. In a moment of rage, the King is supposed to have declared, 'Who will rid me of this turbulent priest?' Four knights acted on his words, rode off and murdered Becket in his own cathedral. Even in those violent times this was regarded as a shocking crime, and Henry had to beg the Pope's forgiveness. Not long after, Becket was made a saint.

BELL, Alexander Graham (1847-1922)
Scottish-American inventor

Bell's experiments with hearing aids for deaf and dumb children led to one of the biggest inventions of our age – the telephone. His original telephone apparatus dates from 1876, when he used it to call his assistant Thomas Watson from another room with the famous words, 'Mr Watson, please come here, I want you'. Thomas Edison then helped to improve this very first telephone, so making it a tremendous commercial success. Bell, for his part, helped Edison (page 84) to develop the phonograph, another of the 19th century's sensational inventions. Edison Bell Records was one of the earliest recording companies. Bell Telephones is still one of America's biggest electronics companies.

BENEŠ, Eduard (1884–1948)
Czechoslovak statesman

In 1918, at the end of the First World War, the old empire of Austria-Hungary was broken up and Czechoslovakia was created a free and independent state. Eduard Beneš became foreign minister, and in 1935 he took over as president. But by the terms of the Munich Agreement of 1938 between Germany, Britain and France, Nazi forces moved into the country and Beneš was forced to resign. During the Second World War he formed a Free Czechoslovak government in London, and in 1945 returned home as president. However, Czechoslovakia was by then within the post-war Soviet sphere of influence, and in 1948 a Communist government was formed. Beneš once more resigned, and died soon after.

BEN-GURION, David (1886–1973)
Jewish-Israeli soldier and statesman

David Ben-Gurion did more than anyone to create the modern state of Israel. He was born in Poland and joined the Zionists, a world-wide movement among Jews to establish a new nation in Palestine, ancient homeland of their race. Palestine was then a Turkish possession. Ben-Gurion first went there in 1906, was expelled in 1915, but returned soon after to fight with the British, who pushed the Turks out of the country. After the First World War, Palestine remained under British control, but Ben-Gurion stayed there, helping Jews to settle in the land. At last, in 1948, the state of Israel was created, and Ben-Gurion became prime minister. This was a great triumph for him and for the Jewish people, but it left the Arabs living there in a difficult situation, and soon there was conflict between Israel and neighbouring Arab nations. Ben-Gurion, prime minister from 1949 to 1953 and again from 1955 to 1963, held Israel firmly together. But when he died the problems between Jews and Arabs were as serious as ever, and they are with us still. The Israeli state still feels threatened by many of her Arab neighbours and is quick to take action if it sees any danger of attack.

BENZ, Karl (1844–1929)
German inventor and industrialist

Many people helped to develop the internal combustion engine. The German inventor Nicholaus Otto made one of the first really successful engines of this type in 1876. Karl Benz built his own version of the internal combustion engine three years later. Benz was not satisfied to leave things there. He wanted his engine to drive a vehicle, and in 1893 produced his first four-wheeled 'horseless carriage'. He then became the first man to manufacture and sell such vehicles to a standard design. So Benz was one of the pioneers of the automobile, or motor car. He later teamed up with the Mercedes company, and Mercedes-Benz is still one of the most illustrious names in the motor industry.

BERNHARDT, Sarah (1844–1923)
French actress

'The Divine Sarah' she was called all over the world. Sarah Bernhardt specialised in tragic parts, notably in the title role of Racine's play *Phedre*, and the Queen of Spain in Victor Hugo's *Ruy Blas*. Almost unique among actresses, she also performed some of the greatest male roles, including Shakespeare's Hamlet. Real-life tragedy struck in 1915 when she was involved in a bad accident and had to have a leg amputated. But she went on acting almost up to the time of her death. A famous Paris theatre is named after her.

BESSEMER, Sir Henry (1813–98)
English scientist and industrialist

Iron and steel were the two mightiest products of the Industrial Revolution. Bessemer's part in all this was to find a way of rapidly converting large quantities of the one into the other. He designed a convertor, looking rather like a giant iron coffee pot, in which the chemical impurities in molten pig iron were burnt off and removed by a stream of air. Other chemicals were then added in the right proportions to complete the change to steel. Bessemer built his own works in Sheffield to mass-produce cheap steel, and became a millionaire. He went on inventing: a new metal type-setting machine for printers, a new braking system for trains, and a machine to roll out sheets of plate glass.

BISMARCK, Otto von (1815–98)
German statesman

Bismarck was called the 'Iron Chancellor', and most portraits show him looking very stern beneath his helmet with a spiked top. He was the man who forged Germany into a single nation. When Bismarck entered politics, Germany was still a loose confederation of 39 states, of which Prussia in the north was the largest and strongest. Bismarck himself came from an old Prussian Junker family – people who believed in discipline and hard work. To these qualities he added political cunning, and for a few years manipulated half the other statesmen of Europe like puppets.

In 1862 the King of Prussia, William I, appointed Bismarck chief minister of state. So he began his task of uniting Germany. He persuaded Austria-Hungary to join him in an attack on Denmark, by which he gained the territories of Schleswig and Holstein. He then turned the tables on the Austrians by provoking them into a war which enabled him to gather the other German states into a much closer federation under Prussian leadership. He next provoked war with Napoleon III of France (page 173). The Franco-Prussian War of 1870–71 was not only a military triumph for Bismarck. It set the seal on a united Germany, with William as Emperor or Kaiser. He was crowned in the Palace of Versailles, near Paris, which was a terrible humiliation for the French.

From 1871 to 1890 Bismarck was chancellor of the new German Empire. He was now very careful to preserve peace in Europe, while gaining for Germany overseas possessions. At home, though not much in favour of social democracy, he greatly improved conditions for the workers in Germany's big new industrial towns and cities. He left office in 1890, when Kaiser William II (page 248) came to the throne. Bismarck did not like the new Kaiser's arrogance. He warned angrily that William II would ruin everything he had achieved. The First World War, with its defeat for Germany and all the misery that followed, proved him right.

BIZET, Georges (1838-75)
French composer

Bizet composed beautifully for the orchestra, and had a fine gift for melody. The incidental music he wrote for Alphonse Daudet's play *L'Arlésienne* (The Maid from Arles) is especially attractive in both these ways. His masterpiece is the opera *Carmen*, a passionate tale of the loves, life and death of a Spanish gipsy girl. Bizet died at the fairly early age of 37, just before *Carmen* became a real success. It has ever since been one of the best-loved operas and is performed throughout the world to this day. The lyrical qualities of Bizet's music were not recognized in his lifetime.

BLAKE, Robert (1599-1657)
English soldier and sailor

Admiral Blake was one of the most successful fighting men in history, though he knew nothing of warfare until he was over 40! At the outbreak of the English Civil War in 1642 he joined Cromwell's Parliamentary army and fought first as a soldier. In 1649 he was appointed General-at-Sea. Blake's first action was to pursue and destroy the Royalist fleet of Prince Rupert off the Spanish coast, capturing 17 Portuguese treasure ships for good measure. With the start of the Dutch Wars in 1652, he proved more than a match for Admiral Tromp (page 231) in engagements off Dover and Portland. Then he sailed into the Mediterranean and cleared it of pirates that menaced British merchant shipping. War with Spain saw this audacious man take his ships into the heavily fortified harbour of Santa Cruz in the Canary Islands, to sink a Spanish treasure fleet.

BLAKE, William (1757–1827)
English poet and artist

William Blake lived during the Romantic period in literature and art; but he was completely individual as a writer and artist and really belongs to no period or movement. His mystical ideas about heaven and hell and the struggles of the soul inspired most of his work. Among his poems, the best-known is the one that has been made into the hymn known as 'Jerusalem'. His drawings and watercolours, one important group illustrating the Book of Job in the Old Testament of the Bible, are even more remarkable. They owe almost nothing to the style of any artist before him, and no one has tried to imitate them since. Blake invented his own process for printing his poetry and illustrations – just one more side to the life of this strange and visionary man.

BLÉRIOT, Louis (1872–1936)
French aviator

The first landmark in the history of modern aviation was the Wright Brothers' brief but epoch-making powered flight in 1903 (page 253). The second was made six years later, when Louis Blériot flew across the Channel. Blériot set up an aircraft factory in 1906 and produced a monoplane (an aircraft with a single pair of wings) far in advance of the Wright Brothers' machine. It was in this that he took off from Calais on 25 July 1909, and crash-landed near Dover just over 35 minutes later. In another five years, powered aircraft were going to be climbing, diving, turning and shooting at each other high above the trenches in the First World War.

BLIGH, William (1754–1817)
English sailor

Captain Bligh is popularly remembered as the brutal sea captain who provoked a mutiny on board his ship HMS *Bounty*. There was much more to his career than that. Early on, he sailed as master of the *Resolution* on Captain Cook's (page 63) last voyage to the Pacific. The notorious voyage of the *Bounty* was also to the Pacific, to collect samples of breadfruit that Bligh himself had earlier discovered. After the actual mutiny, led by the mate Fletcher Christian, Bligh and 18 other members of the crew were cast adrift in an open boat. Without compass or chart, he navigated the boat over 6400 km (4000 miles) to the nearest land, the large island of Timor. The voyage lasted 48 days, and ranks as one of the great survival stories of history. Bligh returned home, to fight with Nelson (page 176) at the battle of Copenhagen in 1801, and then to be sent as governor of the territory of New South Wales in Australia. He was also promoted to Vice-Admiral. Christian and his companions, meanwhile, had sailed on to the remote South Pacific island of Pitcairn, where they stayed until they died or were recaptured.

BOCCACCIO, Giovanni (1313–75)
Italian writer and poet

The Renaissance period was notable for the freedom of thought and action among artists, writers and thinkers, after the long period of the Middle Ages when the Church controlled nearly every aspect of European life. Boccaccio lived right at the beginning of the Renaissance, but his work already expresses this new spirit. His masterpiece is *Il Decameron*, a collection of one hundred short stories about many different types of people and situations. The theme binding them all together is that they are supposed to be told by a group of noblemen taking refuge in the country from the plague.

BOHR, Niels (1885–1962)
Danish scientist

Niels Bohr was a pioneer in the field of atomic physics. He investigated with Rutherford in Cambridge (page 212) the structure of atoms, presenting them as electrical particles containing a central nucleus and one or more revolving electrons – like infinitesimally small versions of the solar system. With the German invasion of Denmark in 1940, Bohr went to the United States to join the international team of scientists working on the production of the first atomic bomb (the Manhattan Project). After the Second World War he returned home, to work on the peaceful uses of atomic or nuclear energy.

BOGART, Humphrey (1899-1957)
American film actor

The golden age of the cinema, when sound and then colour were added to vision, was during the 1930s and 1940s; and the place where most films were made was Hollywood, California. Hollywood stars like Fred Astaire and Ginger Rogers, Bette Davis, Clark Gable and Judy Garland were idolised all over the world. The star that now stands for that whole period in many peoples' minds is Humphrey Bogart. With his lisp and his cigarette he had one of the most distinctive of all screen personalities. He was also a very versatile actor. He began by playing thugs and gangsters, moved over to the right side of the law, and went on to play such different parts as a mentally disturbed naval captain in *The Caine Mutiny* and the broken down skipper of an old river boat in *The African Queen*. Some of his other films, as popular today as they ever were, are *The Maltese Falcon, Casablanca* and *The Big Sleep*.

BOLIVAR, Simon (1783-1830)
South American revolutionary hero

When Simon Bolivar was born in Venezuela it was still part of the huge Spanish colonial empire that stretched the length of South America. His own parents were Spanish, and he was sent back to Spain to study law. It was there that he learnt about the French Revolution, with its call for liberty. Fired by this ideal, Bolivar returned to Venezuela, resolved that the natives of the country should govern their own lives. He organised an uprising against the ruling Spaniards in the capital city of Caracas. This failed, and Bolivar fled to the West Indies. But in 1818 he returned with a new force and drove the Spanish out of Venezuela for good. He then marched his army of freedom fighters down the long backbone of the Andes mountains, liberating the territories of Columbia, Ecuador, Peru, Bolivia (named after him), Chile and Argentina. By 1824 the Spanish had been driven from almost the whole of South America. Bolivar was acclaimed a great hero, but his dream to make Latin America one strong and united nation did not come to pass.

BOOTH, William (1829-1912)
English religious leader

Young William Booth worked in a pawnbroker's shop, where he saw many cases of hardship. This experience, and his own strong Methodist religious faith, roused him to action. He first set up the East London Revival Society, intended both to help the needy and spread the Methodist word. In time he wanted to extend his social and missionary work, and decided to go about it as though he were fighting a military campaign. The result was the Salvation Army, founded in 1878. It had uniforms and ranks, banners, bands and parades, and it took its mission out into the streets. General Booth's Salvation Army at first came in for a lot of knocks, and sometimes its members were actually knocked about. Early recruits to the ranks, especially the women, were in truth as brave as any soldiers. Gradually its aims and methods came to be admired. It grew in numbers and strength, and today it is a world-wide organisation for the relief of poverty and distress, and still also for religious teaching.

BOTTICELLI, Sandro (about 1445-1510)
Italian artist

Botticelli worked mainly in Florence, where the rich and powerful Medici family were patrons of the arts. This was one of the centres of the Italian Renaissance, when artists were inspired afresh by the art and architecture of Classical Greece and Rome. Several of Botticelli's own paintings were inspired by themes from the mythology of those earlier civilisations. *The Birth of Venus* is one of these. The chief feature of this and his other great paintings is the marvellously flowing lines of the figures, their clothing and hair. To emphasise these lines, Botticelli painted in delicate, sometimes almost transparent colours. He also produced a complete set of drawings to illustrate Dante's (page 69) *Divine Comedy*.

BOUDICCA (about AD 15-61)
British warrior queen

'She was,' wrote a Roman historian, 'a huge woman, with a piercing glance and a loud voice. A mass of red hair hung below her waist, and around her throat she wore a golden necklace. She grasped a spear, to terrify everyone.' Queen Boudicca was one of the few Celtic Britons to resist the Roman occupation. The trouble started with the death of her husband King Prasutagus of the Iceni tribe in East Anglia. The Romans demanded repayment of money loaned to the king, and ill-treated Boudicca and her family. The formidable queen immediately led an uprising by the whole Iceni tribe. With most of the Roman army in Britain at that time campaigning in Wales, Boudicca and her followers sacked and burnt the Roman townships of Camulodunum (Colchester), Verulanium (St Albans) and Londinium (London). However, she and her tribesmen were no match for the disciplined Roman legions that hurried back to meet her under the command of the British Governor Seutonius Paulinus. They were soon routed in battle, near Fenny Stratford, and Boudicca killed herself.

BOYLE, Robert (1627-91)
English scientist

Boyle's best-known work was to do with the properties of gases, and a famous law of physics stating the relationship between volume and pressure as applied to gases is named after him. Boyle was also among the first to regard substances in terms of elements, either mixed together or combined in fixed proportions to form compounds. In this respect, he was a key figure in the scientific revolution that finally rejected the ancient ideas of alchemy and put in their place the modern science of chemistry. Boyle was a founding member of the Royal Society (1660), which has since promoted much other valuable scientific research.

BRAHMS, Johannes (1833-97)
German composer

Brahms came from Hamburg. He was given much encouragement by composers Robert and Clara Schumann, then settled in Vienna where he became a rather gruff old bachelor. He was a conservative composer. Others of his generation, such as Franz Liszt and Wagner (page 242), were leading the Romantic movement in music with their revolutionary new symphonic poems and music-dramas. Brahms preferred to go on writing sonatas and string quartets, concertos and symphonies, in the Classical tradition of Haydn, Mozart (page 170) and Beethoven (page 24); and sometimes fugues and other types of composition of even earlier times. But there was a warm, lyrical side to him, so that his finest works are a blend of the Classical style and the more expressive mood of Romantic music. In addition to his works for orchestra and his chamber music, he wrote many songs or *Lieder*, and a noble setting of passages taken from the Lutheran Bible called *A German Requiem*. Brahms was very self-critical and destroyed a good deal more music that he was not satisfied with.

BRAILLE, Louis (1809-52)
French innovator

Louis Braille had a bad accident as a little boy and lost his sight. He was sent to an institution for the blind, learnt as much as he could and became a teacher there. But without books, blind people were denied a proper education. So Braille devised a form of alphabet or code for the blind to use. This was a system of raised dots on a page for blind people to feel with their fingertips. Braille's original sets of dots stood for the letters of the alphabet. He later extended his code to represent numerals, and even music.

BRAUN, Wernher von (born 1912)
German scientist

Wernher von Braun is one of the most important names of the Space Age up to the present time. During the Second World War, he directed work at Germany's Rocket Research Centre at Peenemunde on the Baltic coast. There he produced the revolutionary V2 rocket used to bombard London from launching sites across the Channel. The V2 rocket came too late to change the outcome of the war, but for von Braun it was only a start. Soon afterwards he went to the United States, which was involved in the 'space race' with the Soviet Union. For the Americans he largely designed the booster rocket for their first space satellite in 1958. He was then employed on the Apollo space programme, helping to build the colossal Saturn V rocket that projected the first men on their way to the Moon in 1969.

BRINDLEY, James (1716–72)
English engineer

James Brindley never learnt to read or write, but he knew all about the machinery of his day and was soon improving it. He built an engine to pump water from some coal pits, and designed a mill for making silk. This way he came to the notice of the Duke of Bridgewater who in 1759 employed him to plan a canal to transport coal from his estates to nearby Manchester and Salford. Without notes or drawings, Brindley constructed the Bridgewater Canal, which included the massive Barton aqueduct over the river Irwell. This was the first industrial canal in Britain. It was an immediate success, proving by far the best way to transport heavy goods before the advent of the railways. Brindley went on to construct other canals which made a big contribution to the Industrial Revolution.

BRITTEN, Benjamin (1913-76)
English composer

Beginning with Elgar (page 87), this century has given us a whole generation of important British composers – Ralph Vaughan Williams, Frederick Delius, Sir William Walton, and Benjamin Britten. Britten was not an 'advanced' composer for his time, but developed a style that appealed to music lovers the world over. He composed a number of operas – a type of music that hardly any English-born composer had succeeded in before him. *Peter Grimes*, set in a Suffolk fishing village, and *Billy Budd*, a drama about the British navy of Nelson's day, are two of these. Britten also wrote very effectively for children's voices in several other stage works. A popular work for the concert hall is his *Young Person's Guide to the Orchestra*, being a set of variations and a fugue on a theme by Purcell (page 198).

BRONTË, Charlotte (1816-55), **Emily** (1818-48) **and Anne** (1820-49)
English novelists

The Brontë sisters lived in a lonely Yorkshire vicarage, but their lives were far from dull. Their clergyman father was a rather eccentric man. Their brother Branwell was a talented artist, but took to drink and died young. Two other sisters died as children. This quite eventful home life, and a close acquaintance with the bleak and stormy Yorkshire Moors, drew from them two of the 19th century's most remarkable novels: Emily Brontë's *Wuthering Heights*, and Charlotte Bronte's *Jane Eyre*. These are both love stories, but in their different ways written with a kind of passion and grimness that made them literary landmarks. Anne, too, wrote a fine novel, *The Tenant of Wildfell Hall*, though this has been overshadowed by her sisters' more powerful works.

BRUEGEL, Pieter (about 1525-69)
Flemish artist

Pieter Bruegel (the Elder) was one of the most important artists of what is called the Northern Renaissance period. His best-known paintings are those depicting scenes from Flemish life, such as harvesting, a wedding dance, and hunters in a snowy landscape. Because they are executed with such a fine eye for observation, these paintings are also a valuable commentary upon the life of those times. Bruegel painted many other scenes taken from the Bible, among them *The Tower of Babel*, as described in the Book of Genesis. For him religion also had a darker side. He lived when the Netherlands were occupied by Spain, and there was savage religious persecution. *The Triumph of Death* is one of the paintings he produced in response to this grim situation. Like his compatriot Hieronymous Bosch before him, Bruegel worked into these paintings many strange and morbid images.

BRUNEL, Isambard Kingdom (1806-59)
British engineer

'A genius working in iron' is how people described Brunel. His father was a famous engineer from France, and one of his own first projects was an iron suspension bridge to span the Avon Gorge near Bristol. He had more to do with Bristol when he was appointed chief engineer of the Great Western Railway. He planned the rail route from London to Bristol and beyond, with all its bridges, tunnels and stations, and laid the tracks to a very broad gauge so that trains could run safely at speed. Paddington station in London and the Royal Albert Bridge at Saltash in Cornwall are two monuments to this chapter of his career. In fact, he saw the railway as only the first step in a rail-sea link between London and New York, and built ships to accomplish this. The *Great Western* was the first true ocean-going steamship. The *Great Britain* was the first large ship to be driven by screw propellors. The *Great Eastern* was an iron colossus with five funnels that remained the largest ship afloat for fifty years. There seemed no end to Brunel's vision and invention. For the Crimean War he designed new guns, and a hospital of prefabricated parts that could be shipped to the Crimea and re-assembled. Another of his ideas was for an 'atmospheric' railway whose coaches were drawn along by vacuum power.

BUNYAN, John (1628-88)
English religious teacher and writer

John Bunyan was a Puritan who fought in Cromwell's Parliamentary army during the Civil War of 1642-9. When the fighting was over he started preaching, but after the Restoration of the Monarchy in 1660, Puritans were not allowed to preach in public. Bunyan repeatedly disobeyed the law, and spent many years in prison. It was there that he wrote much of *Pilgrim's Progress*, one of the most famous books with a religious theme. It is an allegory about the problems and dangers of trying to be a good Christian in an evil and corrupt world.

BURNS, Robert (1759-96)
Scottish poet

Robert Burns was often called in his time 'the ploughman poet', because he came from a farm. He did not care for the nickname, nor did it suit him. Though born in a country cottage in Ayrshire, Burns was no humble toiler of the soil. He was a hot-blooded young man, radical in his opinions, also a drinker and a womaniser; and as soon as he began to have some success as a poet, he was off to Edinburgh. Later he did return to the country, but ended his days as an excise officer. Burns's greatness as a poet lies in the way he used the dialects mainly of the Scottish border country to create a rich and lyrical new kind of poetry. Some of his poems express tenderness and love. Some, like *Tam O'Shanter* are wildly exciting. Others again, such as *Holy Willie's Prayer*, are bitingly satirical. Most famous is his song *Auld Lang Syne*, now traditionally sung by people all over the world on New Year's Eve. To the Scots themselves, 'Rabbie' Burns is a hero, and Burns's Night, celebrating his birthday, is an occasion for the kind of carousing he so much enjoyed himself.

BURTON, Sir Richard (1821-90)
English explorer

Richard Burton was one of the 19th century's most intrepid travellers and explorers. Disguised as an Arab, he travelled to the city of Mecca in Arabia, the most holy shrine of Islam and forbidden to non-believers. He wrote a fascinating account of this very risky pilgrimage. His big ambition was to find the source of the river Nile, somewhere in the heart of 'Darkest Africa'. The Royal Geographical Society sent Burton and another explorer, John Speke, on such an expedition. Together they discovered Lake Tanganyika. After both men had been ill, Speke went on to discover Lake Victoria, true source of the Blue Nile. Burton, angry at being left behind, refused to believe this, and the two men had a famous quarrel about it.

BYRD, William (1543-1623)
English composer

Elizabethan England was a wonderful time and place for music, and William Byrd was one of its leading composers. He wrote pieces for early keyboard instruments, and madrigals – part-songs for small choirs – which were a very popular type of composition during Elizabeth's reign. He also wrote much church music. They were troubled times where religion was concerned, with Catholics,

Protestants and Anglicans often at each other's throats. Byrd was a Catholic, but such a fine professional musician that he wrote equally beautiful music for both his own church and for the newly-established Church of England. As a mark of his distinguished position, he was granted, with another great musician of the time, Thomas Tallis, a monoply over the printing of music.

BYRON, Lord George Gordon (1788-1824)
English poet

Lord Byron is one of the most romantic figures in literature. Even his limp, caused by a deformity, has become a glamorous part of his image. He did indeed lead a colourful and romantic life. He was titled and he enjoyed a huge overnight success with the publication of his narrative poem *Childe Harold's Pilgrimage*. He lived for some years in Venice, and died in Greece, where he had gone to help the people in their fight for freedom against the Turks. But although he also lived during the Romantic period of literature, much of his own poetry is closer in style and spirit to that of the 18th century. His finest work, the long poem *Don Juan*, is, in turn, very witty, satirical and sometimes quite despairing over the follies of mankind.

C

CABOT, John (about 1450–98) **and Sebastian** (about 1476–1557)
Anglo-Italian explorers

John Cabot was born in Venice, but emigrated to England, from whence he made two big voyages of discovery. Inspired by Columbus's epoch-making voyage across the Atlantic of only a few years before, John Cabot set out with his son Sebastian and a crew of only 18 other men. They reached the North American continent at Cape Breton Island, just off Nova Scotia, though John believed they had sailed far enough to have reached the coast of north-east Asia. In a second voyage, he reached the coast of southern Greenland – almost certainly the first European to set eyes on that desolate land since the Vikings – then turned south and followed the coast all the way down to what is now Delaware.

Sebastian was even more adventurous. He first sought a North-West Passage through to Asia that took him as far as the Hudson Bay. Then he was attached to the Spanish navy and explored the coast of South America. He also believed there was a North-East Passage round the top of Russia, and as Governor of the Merchant Adventurers, organised an expedition to the Arctic ocean. One of the captains of this expedition, Chancellor, reached Archangel and signed a trade agreement with Ivan the Terrible (page 128).

CAESAR, Gaius Julius (102–44 BC)
Roman soldier and statesman

Veni, Vidi, Vici – 'I came, I saw, I conquered'. Thus did Julius Caesar sum up his triumphs as a military commander. He conquered Gaul (modern France); led two expeditions to Britain; routed

General Pompey who was a rival for power at the battle of Pharsalus in Greece (48 BC); and led his invincible legions on other campaigns in Syria and North Africa, where he also had his famous love affair with Queen Cleopatra (page 59). Caesar's exploits in the field made him master of the whole Roman world. They also made him dangerous enemies among other leading politicians, who considered that he had too much power for the good of Rome. A conspiracy was hatched against him, led by Brutus and Cassius, and on a date in the Roman calendar known as the Ides of March he was stabbed to death, by each conspirator in turn, in the Senate House. Some people see Julius Caesar as a power-hungry politician who deserved his fate. Others think of him as a visionary statesman, who tried to impose firm rule after years of a corrupt and discredited form of republican government. No one questions his military genius, and his own accounts of his campaigns are considered fine works of literature and of history. Caesar was his family name. So great did his reputation soon become, that his successor Octavian (page 17), and other emperors, added his name to their own as a special title.

CALVIN, John (1509-64)
French religious leader

The Reformation was the religious revolution in Europe that broke away from the Roman Catholic Church and created new churches in its place. John Calvin was one of its leaders. He came from northern France and was an early convert to the new Protestant faith. Because the French Protestants – the Huguenots – were being persecuted by King Francis I, he escaped to Switzerland. There he made Geneva his headquarters, and one of the most important Protestant centres. In hundreds of books, articles and letters, Calvin spelt out a very strict new form of religion, based on the individual's own conscience and on the severe punishment of sin. This religious life-style spread to many other parts of Europe: back into France, where the Huguenots regarded Calvin as their own leader, to the Netherlands, and to England and Scotland, where Puritans then conveyed it across the Atlantic to the new American colonies.

CANALETTO, Antonio (1697-1768)
Italian artist

In the 18th century, many wealthy British people went on a Grand Tour of Europe. Venice was one of their favourite cities, and it was there that Antonio Canaletto, or Canale, was working. Visitors eagerly sought his wonderfully clear, bright and detailed views of the city and its buildings – one of the finest records of a time and place captured by any artist. Canaletto was later invited to England, where he produced many more painted views of Georgian London.

CANUTE, or KNUT (about 994-1035)
Anglo-Danish king

Canute invaded England with his father, King Sweyn of Denmark. When Sweyn died, Canute uneasily shared the English kingdom with the Saxon Edmund Ironside. Upon Edmund's death in 1016, Canute was elected king of all England by the Witan, the Saxon parliament. A few years later, he defeated a Norwegian sea attack on his homeland and by so doing became king of Denmark and Norway also, and ruler of a north European Empire. Canute ruled well, became a Christian and went on a pilgrimage to Rome. There is a famous story that he sat by the edge of the sea, commanding the tide not to come in. If the story is true, what he was probably doing was showing his court that he was only a man and not a god, and had no power over the waves.

CARAVAGGIO, Michelangelo (1573-1610)
Italian artist

Caravaggio, whose real name was Michelangelo Merisi, painted in a style noted for what is called in Italian 'chiaroscuro' – dramatic contrasts of light and shade. This was a revolutionary development in painting that had a big influence on many later artists, especially in the Netherlands. No less revolutionary was the way Caravaggio represented his many big religious paintings. He depicted people and places with a down-to-earth realism that sometimes shocked the church dignitaries of his time.

CARLYLE, Thomas (1795–1881)
English historian

Carlyle's most celebrated work is his *History of the French Revolution.* In this and his other books and articles he wrote in a very dramatic, rhetorical style, as though he were intending his words to be read out loud at large assemblies or open-air meetings. To this extent, Carlyle's work is not only about other times and events. It also expresses his own Victorian Age.

CARNEGIE, Andrew (1835–1919)
Scottish-American industrialist

Andrew Carnegie was a shrewd, hard-working man who made a huge fortune from the almost limitless resources and booming industries of 19th-century America. He went there with his family from Scotland, starting out as a messenger for a telegraph company. He worked hard, saved money, then began investing in the rapidly expanding railroads, in companies making iron and steel during the Civil War, and in the first oil companies. He ended up one of the richest men in the world and a great philanthropist.

CARROLL, Lewis (1832–98)
English writer

Charles Dodgson was his real name, and he was a mathematician. Under the pen name of Lewis Carroll he wrote two of the best-loved children's books: *Alice in Wonderland* and *Alice Through the Looking Glass.* These can be enjoyed simply as the adventures of a little girl in a fantasy dream-world peopled by such characters as the

Mad Hatter and the Red Queen. At a deeper level they are remarkable examples of a form of surrealism – making apparent nonsense of many accepted ideas and associations, in order to show how nonsensical real life can sometimes be!

CARTIER, Jacques (1491-1557)
French explorer

Cartier first sailed across the Atlantic in 1534, hoping to find the North-West Passage – the sea route that would lead to the Pacific ocean and the rich lands of Asia. He arrived at the broad estuary of the St Lawrence river, not at first realising that it was a river at all. On a second voyage of discovery he sailed further up the great waterway, landing by Indian villages that were later to be the sites of the cities of Quebec and Montreal. The Indians also told him that the land was called 'Canada', which was simply their word for 'village'. So Cartier opened the way for the French colonisation of Canada, along the St Lawrence river to the Great Lakes.

CASTRO, Fidel (born 1927)
Cuban revolutionary leader

In 1959 Fidel Castro and his guerilla army overthrew the dictatorship of President Batista on the large Caribbean island of Cuba. He set up a communist regime in its place – the first true communist state in the American continent. Most people in the United States did not like this at all, and in 1961 President Kennedy (page 138) backed an attempted invasion of the island by Cuban exiles at a place called the Bay of Pigs. The invasion failed, and Castro's position was made stronger. The revolutionary leader, already a familiar sight with his bushy black beard and combat uniform, was not out of the news for long. In 1962 United States reconnaissance aircraft picked out Soviet missiles on the island. For a few very tense and nerve-wracking days it looked as though this 'Cuban Crisis' might spark off a major war. Then the missiles were withdrawn.

CATHERINE DE MEDICI (1519-89)
French queen

The Medicis were an Italian family of rich bankers who ruled over Florence for most of the Renaissance period. Through marriages they spread their influence abroad. Catherine Medici married Henry II of France, and when he died she governed the nation on behalf of her sons. France was at that time badly divided by quarrels between Catholics and Protestant Huguenots. Catherine tried to hold a balance between the two sides by political intrigue – something the Medicis were good at. Then fearing that the Huguenots might become too strong, she connived at the murder of one of their leaders. Events suddenly got out of hand, leading to the St Bartholomew's Day Massacre of 1572, when thousands of Huguenot men, women and children in Paris and elsewhere were put to the sword. This dreadful event led to civil war inside France, and deepened the hatred between Catholics and Protestants throughout Europe.

CATHERINE THE GREAT (1729-96)
Russian empress

Catherine was a German princess who was married at the age of 16 to the Grand Duke Peter of Russia. Catherine was clever, cunning and ambitious. Her husband was vain and stupid. In 1762 he became Tsar, but within a year she had him deposed, and may also have arranged his murder. For the next 34 years, she ruled Russia virtually alone. Catherine admired the art and architecture of Western Europe, especially that of France, and wished the capital of St Petersburg to rival Paris for beauty and culture. She was also impressed by industrial progress in Britain, and set up new industries at home. Her failure to end the slavery of the serfs, however, brought about a serious revolt led by a Cossack chief named Emil Pugachev, which it took several years to put down. Despite these internal troubles, Catherine annexed large areas of Poland and fought two successful wars against the Turks, so pushing Russia's frontiers hundreds of kilometres westward and southward to the Black Sea and the Caucasus. Altogether, Catherine the Great left her adopted country far stronger and richer than she found it.

CAVENDISH, Henry (1731–1810)
English scientist

Cavendish made discoveries and carried out experiments in many areas of science. He analysed water, so proving it to be a compound of hydrogen and oxygen, and not an element, as most chemists still believed. He discovered the main components of air. His electrical experiments brought him remarkably close to the discoveries of more famous men in that field of research, such as the Frenchman Coulomb and Faraday (page 91). Turning to Newton's (page 177) work on gravity, he calculated the Earth's density and mass. As a man Cavendish was extremely shy. He also inherited a fortune, which he cared little about, so that people called him 'the richest of philosophers and the most philosophical of the rich!' A famous laboratory in Cambridge is named after him.

CAVOUR, Count Camillo (1810–61)
Italian statesman

Il Risorgimento (The Resurrection) was the name of a newspaper published by Count Cavour which campaigned for democracy in his north Italian kingdom of Piedmont. From this beginning, Cavour strove to create a single united kingdom of Italy out of many separate states. Piedmont itself was a small, unimportant country by the standards of European power politics. Once he was in the government, Cavour turned this weak position into a strong one by brilliant political stratagems.

His first objective was to free other regions of north Italy from the Austrian Empire. Piedmont sent a small military force to fight alongside the French and British in the Crimean War of 1854–56.

Cavour used this fact to gain the support of Napoleon III (page 173) and in 1859 got French troops to help him push Austria out of north Italy at the battles of Magenta and Solferino. The other great Italian patriot of the time, Giuseppe Garibaldi (page 101), had meanwhile taken Sicily and Naples in the south, and was advancing with his famous 'Redshirts' on Rome. The position of Rome, as the centre of an international church, had been a delicate political matter for centuries. To avoid a big crisis, Cavour sent King Victor Emmanuel of Piedmont and an army south to meet Garibaldi, and head off any move against Rome itself. By this manœuvre, he also managed to unite Garibaldi's conquests with his own under the sovereignty of Victor Emmanuel. So this very shrewd and clever man brought about his goal of a united Italy, just a few months before he died.

CAXTON, William (about 1422-91)
English printer

William Caxton was a cloth merchant who went to Flanders and Germany on business. There he learnt of the new process of printing from movable type, developed by the German Gutenberg (page 112). With this invention, books no longer had to be laboriously copied out by hand. Caxton was so impressed that he took up printing as well. In 1474 he set up a press in Bruges, where he printed the first book in the English language – a long poem which he had translated from the French. Two years later he came home, and started printing in a shop near Westminster Abbey in London. At his death, Caxton had produced some 90 printed books, including an edition of Chaucer's *Canterbury Tales* (page 53).

CEZANNE, Paul (1839-1906)
French artist

Cezanne's father was a wealthy banker, and he had no money problems to worry him as he worked on his revolutionary new way of painting. Early on, he was influenced by the work of the

Impressionists. Soon, though, he lost interest in their effects of light and atmosphere, and turned to a study of what he felt was the deeper and more permanent shape and form of the natural world. He viewed this as a kind of geometry, and worked with infinite care, using each brush stroke to build up the shape and substance of objects and scenes as he saw them. One of Cezanne's famous paintings in this style is a study of the huge rocky mass of Mount St Victoire near his home town of Aix-en-Provence. In these paintings he paved the way for Cubism and other major developments in the art of our century.

CHAMPLAIN, Samuel de (1567–1635)
French explorer

Jacques Cartier was the first Frenchman to explore Canada. He was followed in the next century by Samuel de Champlain, who began to colonise the land. Champlain made his first voyage to Canada in 1603. He sailed a good way up the St Lawrence river and made friends with the Algonquin and Huron Indians. In 1608 he returned with some of the first French settlers and founded the city of Quebec. He made more voyages to and fro across the Atlantic, bringing French people to the huge new lands of Canada. He also founded a second city, Montreal, discovered the lake that bears his name, and mapped out lakes Huron and Ontario. In 1629 the new settlement of Quebec was attacked by the British, Champlain was captured and sent back to England. He used his captivity to write a fascinating account of his explorations and adventures that was later published. In 1633 he was allowed to go back to his beloved Canada, where he died.

CHAPLIN. Charles Spencer (1889–1977)
English film actor, director and screen writer

The history of the cinema as popular entertainment dates from the early years of this century. It created a new generation of entertainment stars – Mary Pickford, Buster Keaton, Rudolph Valentino, and most celebrated of all, Charlie Chaplin. He was born in London, appeared in music halls from the tender age of eight, then joined Fred Karno's famous travelling circus (along with Stan Laurel of Laurel and Hardy fame). This took him to America and to Hollywood, California, where most films were being made. By 1914 he had joined Mack Sennett's studios, which specialised in slapstick comedy, and created the character of the Tramp – the little man pushed around by everyone but always managing to survive. These were all silent movies. Chaplin went on to make much bigger sound pictures, such as *The Great Dictator* and *Limelight*, showing how versatile and gifted he was as director, scriptwriter and composer, as well as actor. But it is as the Tramp, as seen in *The Gold Rush*, with bowler, baggy trousers and cane, that he is immortalised on film.

CHARLEMAGNE (AD 742-814)
Holy Roman Emperor

Charlemagne, meaning 'Charles the Great', began as King of the Franks, a race of people who settled in an area stretching westwards from the river Rhine into France. From this starting point, Charlemagne crossed the Rhine to conquer most of what is now Germany and Austria, and subdued the Lombard people of northern Italy. In another great campaign he moved southwards into Spain, to do battle with the Moors and Saracens. In the process he created an empire that covered most of western and central Europe. Charlemagne, though, was not just a conqueror. He was a devout Christian and a patron of learning and the arts. He built churches and monasteries in the Romanesque style, and brought to his palace at Aachen, near the Rhine, some of the finest scholars and artists of his time. By these deeds, he did much to end the period of European history known as the 'Dark Ages' – the centuries of disorder and barbarism that followed the break up of the earlier Roman Empire.

In the year 800 Pope Leo III rewarded Charlemagne by crowning him Emperor of what was then named the Holy Roman Empire.

This confederation of Europe united under the Church of Rome did not survive Charlemagne for long; though the Holy Roman Empire, in various forms, continued for hundreds of years.

CHARLES I (1600–49)
English king

The seeds of Charles's downfall were sown by his father, James I (James VI of Scotland). He had upset the English Parliament with his strong belief in the Divine Right of Kings – the notion that monarchs could do no wrong. Charles also insisted on this. Then he was pushed into wars he could not pay for, and tried to get the money from Parliament. The quarrel between King and Parliament over money and the right to rule went on for years. It reached its crisis when Charles one day arrived in Parliament's midst and tried to arrest those members who most strongly opposed him. Soon afterwards, in 1642, Civil War broke out. Charles was a gallant soldier, but he was no match for Oliver Cromwell (page 66), who commanded Parliament's army. He lost the crucial battle of Naseby (1645) and with it the war. He escaped to Scotland, then to the Isle of Wight, but was finally captured. Cromwell and Parliament put him on trial for his life, and he was executed on 30 January 1649.

Charles I was a noble man, but in some ways a weak one who took bad advice. His son, Charles II, was restored to the throne in 1660. He showed far more political sense than his father and so made the Restoration of the Monarchy a success.

CHARLES V (1500–58)
Holy Roman Emperor and King of Spain

Charles was a Hapsburg – one of the family who ruled the Holy Roman Empire for hundreds of years, and by marriage gained control of other parts of Europe also. Through this complicated arrangement of marriages between the royal houses of Europe, Charles inherited the Netherlands, Spain with its rapidly expanding colonies in central and south America, and the Holy Roman Empire itself (the German states, Austria and a large part of Italy). He was a taciturn, able and strong-willed man, but the task of governing all these possessions was almost too much for him. He had to combat the rivalry of Francis I of France, whom he defeated at the battle of Pavia (1525); deal with the Reformation and the militant spread of Protestantism within the Holy Roman Empire; put down an uprising in the Netherlands; and fight off attacks from the Turkish Ottoman Empire in the east. As a result, Charles V spent most of his life on the move, trying to hold his domains together. In 1555, exhausted by it all, he divided rule among his heirs and relatives and retired to a monastery in Spain, where he died.

CHARLES MARTEL (about AD 689-741)
Frankish king

Charles Martel, or Charles 'the Hammer', brought under his role most of the territory of what is now France, and parts of Germany. So he prepared the ground for the Holy Roman Empire created by his grandson Charlemagne (page 51). At Poitiers – the first important cavalry battle in history – he also defeated the Moors of North Africa who had advanced through Spain and over the Pyrenees. By his victory Charles Martel halted the spread of the Islamic Empire into Western Christian Europe.

CHATHAM, Earl of *see* **Pitt**

CHAUCER, Geoffrey (about 1340-1400)
English poet and story writer

Geoffrey Chaucer had a very full and active life. He fought in the Hundred Years War, was held to ransom by the French, served in the English court of Edward III, and travelled far and wide in Europe as a royal ambassador. He had already started writing, and on his travels got to know the work of such great literary figures of his time as Dante (page 69) and Boccaccio (page 31). All these influences enriched his own style. It was then that he began writing *The Canterbury Tales*, a collection of stories supposed to be told among a band of pilgrims on their way to the shrine of Thomas à Becket in Canterbury. In a Prologue, Chaucer describes the character of each pilgrim. The stories themselves are wonderfully varied, some romantic, some comic and quite rude, some religious or philosophical. To read *The Canterbury Tales* in their original early English needs special study. Nevertheless, the work is the real start of English literature, as something distinct from the literature of continental Europe.

CHEKHOV, Anton (1860–1904)
Russian dramatist and novelist

Chekhov first made his name as a short story writer. His early plays were a failure, and he was about to give up play writing when the Moscow Arts Theatre decided to revive *The Seagull*. The director of the theatre was Konstantin Stanislavsky, whose new ideas about acting brought out the real beauty of *The Seagull* – the way its situations and characters hover the whole time between tragedy and farce. Chekhov went on to write *Uncle Vanya* (a revision of an earlier play), *Three Sisters* and *The Cherry Orchard*. Each play conveys something of the air of helplessness felt by many Russians in the years leading up to the Revolution, and maintains the same marvellous balance between laughter and tears. The modern theatre owes a great deal to them.

CHIANG Kai-shek (1887–1975)
Chinese soldier and statesman

A Chinese republic was created by Sun Yat-sen (page 224) in 1911. When he died in 1925 Chiang became leader of the main party, the Kuomintang, or Nationalist Party, and assumed also the nation's leadership. He was never properly in control of events. He turned against the communists, who united against him under Mao Tse-tung (page 157). Then in 1931 Japan invaded Manchuria and advanced into other parts of China. From then on Chiang was caught between the Japanese invaders and the Chinese communists. He was commander-in-chief of China's forces on the Allies' side during the Second World War, but did almost nothing to help. He was more worried about the communists, with whom he was soon fighting a civil war. By 1949 Mao controlled almost the whole of mainland China. Chiang fled to the offshore island of Formosa (Taiwan). The Americans at first supported his claim still to be China's true leader. But after the admission of the People's Republic of China to the United Nations in 1971, nobody took him seriously.

CHOPIN, Frederic (1810-49)
French-Polish composer

'Hats off, gentlemen, a genius!' was Schumann's famous verdict on the young Chopin. Chopin was born and brought up in Poland, but his father was a Frenchman, and he lived most of his life in Paris. He had a celebrated love affair with the writer George Sand (pen name of Aurore Dudevant) and gave many concerts. His work and public appearances taxed his frail health too far and he died quite young. Chopin wrote two piano concertos, otherwise nearly all his compositions are short pieces for the solo piano: polonaises and mazurkas (based on Polish dances), studies (*études*), preludes, ballades, nocturnes, waltzes and scherzos. He lived during the Romantic period, and his music is sometimes stormy and passionate, sometimes dreamy and reflective.

CHURCHILL, John, First Duke of Marlborough (1650-1722)
English soldier

The Duke of Marlborough is one of England's great military heroes – the man who never lost a battle. Yet during his own lifetime he was often in disgrace. James II promoted him to the rank of general, but when William of Orange landed in England in 1688 he deserted James for the sake of the Protestant faith. William, though, did not trust him either, stripped him of his rank and put him in prison. Marlborough's great years as a soldier began with the reign of Queen Anne in 1702. This year also saw the start of the War of the Spanish Succession, in reality a power struggle between Louis XIV (page 151) and an alliance of Britain, the Netherlands and Austria. Marlborough was given command of the Alliance. With valuable support from Prince Eugene of Savoy, he won a brilliant victory at Blenheim in Bavaria (1704), and followed this with other decisive victories at Ramillies, Oudenarde and Malplaquet in the Netherlands. During these campaigns he also looked after his soldiers well, and they fondly called him 'Corporal John'. When he returned from the wars, though, his troubles started again. His wife, Sarah, had lost her earlier influence over the Queen, and political enemies accused him of making money out of the war. So he was once more dismissed. George I reinstated him, and he was rewarded with the building of Blenheim Palace, but illness wrecked his last years.

CHURCHILL, Sir Winston Leonard Spencer (1878–1965)
British soldier and statesman

The world remembers Winston Churchill as a valiant wartime leader, with his bulldog expression, big cigar and victory sign. In fact, he had already done more than most other people by the time he became Britain's war leader in 1940. His father was Lord Randolph Churchill, a prominent British politician, and his mother was American. He hated school and joined the army as soon as he could. In the Sudan, at the battle of Omdurman (1898) he took part in the last cavalry charge made by the British army. Soon after he went to South Africa as a journalist to report on the Boer War, was captured by the Boers, and escaped. In 1900 Churchill entered politics and was elected as a Conservative MP. Four years later he switched to the Liberal Party and was soon a cabinet minister. One of his achievements at this time was the setting up of Labour

Exchanges. During the First World War he devised a plan to attack Turkey and so try to break the deadlock on the Western front. When this Gallipoli campaign failed he resigned from the government, but was soon back as Minister of Munitions.

Churchill rejoined the Conservative Party in 1922, and served several years as Chancellor of the Exchequer. He was in the centre of a political storm when he wanted to use troops to break the General Strike of 1926. During the 1930s he was out of office because of his opposition to Prime Minister Neville Chamberlain's policy of trying to reach an agreement with Hitler (Appeasement). When war came in 1939 he was proved right, and a year later, with Britain close to defeat, he was made Prime Minister. Churchill rallied the people with his famous speeches, in which he echoed their determination to fight on, and spoke of the nation's 'Finest Hour'. When first the Soviet Union and then the United States had joined the fight against Nazi Germany, he conferred often with Stalin (page 220) and Roosevelt (page 209), though aware of big differences between them. He wished to preserve the British Empire, and distrusted Stalin. With post-war policy already in mind, he was shaken when in 1945 the British people voted him out of office. Yet in 1951 he served one more term as Prime Minister.

Churchill also found time to write several books, including a long account of the Second World War in which he himself had played such a big part. On his death he was given a state funeral, as a national hero.

CICERO, Marcus Tullius (106–43 BC)
Roman orator, philosopher and politician

Cicero was probably the finest orator among a race of people noted for their speech-making. He was also a Greek scholar, and through his own books and letters preserved many Greek ideas that might have been forgotten. Our own language and vocabulary owe much to Cicero. He was not so clever as a politician. He lived through turbulent times, culminating in the assassination of Julius Caesar. Very soon after this event, Cicero, too, was murdered by political enemies. His head and hands – seen and heard so often in debate – were severed from his body and mockingly placed on display.

CLAUDIUS (10 BC–AD 54)
Roman emperor

Claudius was the nephew of the Emperor Tiberius, who had been a good soldier. This was one reason why the Praetorian Guard – the élite of the Roman army – picked him as emperor after they had done away with the half-crazed Emperor Caligula in AD 41. Not that Claudius looked the part of leader of a mighty empire. He was weak and sickly, walked with a limp and stuttered badly. Yet he proved able and popular. He rebuilt parts of Rome, extended Roman citizenship to people in many other parts of the Empire, and presided over the conquest of Britain, which he visited. He could still not escape the violence of his times. He was poisoned, probably by his wife Agrippina.

CLEMENCEAU, Georges (1841–1929)
French statesman

The French people called Clemenceau 'The Tiger' because of his fierce and fearless speeches. He was one of the staunchest defenders of Captain Alfred Dreyfus, a Jewish army officer whose trial in 1894 on a charge of treason raised political feelings in France almost to the point of civil war. During the First World War, Clemenceau was equally outspoken in his criticism of the French leadership, and in 1917, at one of the blackest moments in the struggle, he himself became prime minister. He rallied the nation and did much to bring about the final Allied victory in November 1918. Many French people then criticised him for not being hard enough on the defeated Germans at the peace conference, and he resigned as premier in 1920. He, in his turn, repeatedly warned his fellow countrymen against a new rise in German militarism. He even predicted 1940 as the year of the next German attack. But few people listened to him.

CLEOPATRA (about 69-30 BC)
Egyptian queen

Queen Cleopatra was descended from the Macedonian Greek general Ptolemy who marched with Alexander the Great (page 8). She is remembered as one of the world's most beautiful women, and she certainly bewitched two of the greatest men of her age. The first was Julius Caesar (page 42), who went to Egypt in pursuit of the Roman general Pompey, his rival for power. Cleopatra had been driven from Egypt by her brother. Caesar restored her to the throne, then took her back with him to Rome, where she stayed until his assassination in 44 BC. On her return home she met Marcus Antonius (Mark Antony) (page 11), commander-in-chief of the eastern part of the Roman Empire. Their love affair has been immortalised by Shakespeare (page 216). Marcus Antonius dreamed of creating a separate kingdom for himself and Cleopatra; but Julius Caesar's adopted son Octavian (Augustus Caesar) (page 17) shattered these plans by defeating their combined galley fleets at the sea battle of Actium in 31 BC. Marcus Antonius promptly killed himself. Cleopatra tried to charm Octavian, and when this failed took her own life with the bite of a poisonous snake which legend claims to have been an asp.

CLIVE, Lord Robert (1725-74)
English soldier

The 18th century was a time of great rivalry between Britain and France, with their growing empires. Britain's hero in India was Robert Clive. He was an unruly and hot-tempered young man, sent to India as a clerk for the East India Trading Company. He hated the job and joined the army. As the clash of interests in India between Britain and France flared up into open war, he soon had the chance to prove himself as a soldier. In 1751 he captured the town of Arcot with only 500 men and held it for 53 days against a French and Indian army nearly 10,000 strong. His greatest triumph came in 1757 when against even more enormous odds he defeated the army of the Indian ruler Surajah Dowlah at Plassey, near Calcutta. This established British supremacy in India. As Governor of Bengal, Clive also did much to stamp out corruption. Nevertheless, when he returned to England he himself was accused of dishonesty. Parliament pardoned him because of the services he had rendered to his country. But the whole affair depressed him and made him ill, and he took his own life.

COCKCROFT, Sir John (1897–1967)
English scientist

Sir John Cockcroft made one of the biggest breakthroughs in atomic physics. With his fellow scientist Ernest Walton in Cambridge, he made a 'particle accelerator' that used very high electrical voltages in a vacuum tube. With this apparatus Cockcroft and Walton demonstrated in 1932 that they could break up the nucleus of atoms. For this 'splitting' of the atom they were awarded the Nobel Prize for Physics. Also in 1932 one of their colleagues, Sir James Chadwick, discovered the neutron, another kind of atomic particle.

COCKERELL, Sir Christopher (born 1910)
English inventor

For a long time, ship designers have tried to find ways of reducing the friction, or drag, of a ship's hull as it moves through water. Sir Christopher Cockerell's answer to this problem was to raise a vessel completely clear of the water. He did this by using high-powered fans to produce a cushion of air on which the vessel could float. This is the principle of the hovercraft. Cockerell made his first experimental model hovercraft out of a treacle tin and a vacuum cleaner. His first working prototype, SRN 1, successfully crossed the Channel in 1959. Today's hovercraft can transport big loads of cars and passengers across water, or level land, at speeds of up to 100 kph (over 60 mph) and have made it easier and quicker for Frenchmen and Englishmen to visit each other's countries.

COLUMBA (AD 521-97)
Irish missionary

Saint Columba brought Christianity to Scotland. He founded a monastery in his native Ireland, then with a small band of fellow monks set sail for Scotland. They landed at Iona, an island off the west coast, where they built another monastery. From there Columba crossed to the mainland to convert the Picts and Scots.

COLUMBUS, Christopher (1451-1506)
Italian explorer

Christopher Columbus came from Genoa. He believed the Earth was round and that if he sailed in a westerly direction across the Atlantic ocean he would eventually reach Asia. He spent many years trying to interest kings and princes in his bold plan and to give him the money to put it to the test. At last he obtained the backing of King Ferdinand and Queen Isabella of Spain (page 92), and in 1492 set sail on the *Santa Maria*, with two other ships, the *Nina* and *Pinta*, in support. Thirty-six days out from the Canary Islands he and his men sighted land. Columbus, who had underestimated the size of the Earth's circumference, thought they had indeed reached a point off the mainland of China or India. It was, in fact, one of the Bahama islands on which they landed. Columbus named it San Salvador. Thus he had discovered the Americas – the New World – although he did not know it.

Columbus returned to Spain, where honours were heaped upon him. He made three more voyages, discovering Jamaica, Trinidad, Honduras and Panama. He died peacefully back in Spain, convinced to the last that he had been exploring the 'Indies' of Asia.

CONFUCIUS (about 550-479 BC)
Chinese philosopher

Confucius, or K'ung Fu-tzu, did not preach about matters of the soul or spirit like most religious leaders. Nor did he delve into the problems of existence and the meaning of life, like many philosophers. He was quite conservative in his outlook, saying that each person should accept his or her own station in life and make the best they could of it, while those born to rule should set an example in terms of justice, honesty and tolerance. By these precepts lay the best hope of happiness and harmony among men. His many sayings were gathered into a collection called the *Analects*. His whole approach to life and society profoundly influenced Chinese civilisation for over 2000 years.

CONSTABLE, John (1776–1837)
English artist

Constable was born in East Anglia, that part of England closest to Holland. He studied the Dutch landscape painters of an earlier century, and started painting his own East Anglian countryside. The fairly flat country, with views stretching into the distance and wide open skies, inspired him to paint in a way that gave a special new beauty to cloud and light. In some of his sketches he concentrated solely upon cloud formations and sunlight. Constable had a very successful exhibition in Paris, and the techniques he used to create his effects had a big influence on the French Impressionists.

CONSTANTINE I, The Great (about AD 280–337)
Roman emperor

Constantine was a Roman general, first acclaimed emperor by the legions stationed in Britain. He had to defeat several rivals in battle before actually taking the title of Emperor in AD 314. Soon afterwards he was converted to the new religion of Christianity. Before this event, Christians had been regarded as a threat to Roman law and order and often savagely persecuted. With Constantine's conversion, Christianity became the most important religion in the Western World. Constantine also moved his capital city from Rome to Byzantium, by the shores of the Bosporus, which he thought was better placed in relation to the Empire as a whole. He rebuilt the city and re-named it after himself as Constantinople (now Istanbul). The other major event of his reign was the Council of Nicae (325) which laid down the basic doctrines and rules for the Christian Church throughout the Roman Empire.

COOK, James (1728-79)
English sailor

Captain Cook worked his way up from humble deck hand on a collier taking coal from Whitby to London, to commander of three great voyages of discovery. In 1768 he set sail in the *Endeavour* to explore *Terra Australis* – the 'Southern Land' – in the vast Pacific ocean. He discovered and charted the two main islands of New Zealand and went on to explore the eastern coast of Australia, landing at Botany Bay, not far from Sydney. During his second voyage to the Pacific, Cook sailed farther south into Antarctic waters than any man before him. On his third expedition in the ships *Discovery* and *Resolution* he sailed north across the Pacific looking for the North-West Passage across the top of Canada. Returning to warmer waters, he was killed by natives on one of the Hawaiian islands. Captain Cook also discovered that a diet of fresh fruit and vegetables prevented scurvy, a disease that had previously killed hundreds of sailors on long sea voyages.

COPLAND, Aaron (born 1900)
American composer

Aaron Copland is one of this century's composers who has still wished to write music that many people can enjoy. He has also wanted to convey something of the spirit of America. The result has been such compositions as the ballets *Rodeo* and *Billy the Kid*, and *Appalachian Spring* which includes some of the old folk-melodies of the early settlers. Copland is now the most popular 'serious'

American composer, though he has also written music that is much harder for most people to listen to and enjoy.

COPERNICUS, Nicolaus (1473–1543)
Polish mathematician and astronomer

For over a thousand years before Copernicus, going back to the time of the Greek Ptolemy (page 197), it was accepted nearly everywhere that the Earth was the centre of the universe. Copernicus, however, discovered other ancient Greek teachings that had placed the sun at the centre of the Solar System, of which the Earth was one of the revolving planets. Copernicus believed this to be the truth, and set his own ideas down in a Latin treatise called *De Revolutionibus orbium coelestium* (On the Revolution of the Celestial Spheres). This truly epoch-making document provided the basis for the work of such other great scientists and thinkers as Galileo (page 100), Kepler (page 138) and Newton (page 177), and for our whole knowledge of the universe as we understand it today.

CORTÉS, Hernando (1485–1547)
Spanish soldier and explorer

Cortés was one of the long line of Spanish explorers and *conquistadors*, or conquerors, who colonised most of central and south America in the century after Columbus. Cortés was the conqueror of Mexico. In 1519, with a tiny force of only 500 men, plus guns, horses and mastiff dogs, he landed on the coast and advanced inland, literally burning his boats so that there should be no turning back. His boldness was rewarded. The principal race of people already living in Mexico were the Aztecs. They had never before seen guns, horses or mastiff dogs, and were overawed by Cortés' expedition. Their king, Montezuma, actually believed him to be a god called Quetzalcoatl. Cortés took swift advantage of the situation, moved into the Aztec capital of Tenochtitlan (now Mexico City), made Montezuma his prisoner and started to rule the country. When he later returned to the coast, the Aztecs rebelled. Cortés hurried back, crushed the rebellion, during which Montezuma was killed, and enslaved the Aztec people. He then governed the great new Spanish colony of Mexico for several years, until the king of Spain grew jealous of his success and power and stripped him of all authority, a sad end for so proud a man.

CRANMER, Thomas (1489-1556)
English churchman and statesman

On a March day in 1556, Archbishop Cranmer was burnt at the stake. His last conscious act was to thrust his right hand into the flames – the hand that had signed a confession denying his Protestant faith. The scene grimly reminds us of the bitter religious struggles that wracked Tudor England. Cranmer was appointed Archbishop of Canterbury by Henry VIII (page 118), and went along with the king's desire to break with the pope in Rome. During the young Edward VI's brief reign, he moved the new Church of England closer to the Protestant faith by issuing the Book of Common Prayer in English. When Edward died, Cranmer tried, with good reason, to prevent Henry's daughter Mary from coming to the throne. He failed, and his fate was sealed. Mary was a staunch Catholic. She had Cranmer put on trial for treason and sent to the stake.

CRICK, Sir Francis (born 1916)
English scientist

Sir Francis Crick worked with James Watson and Maurice Wilkins during the 1950s to discover one of the basic secrets of life – how physical features are passed on from generation to generation in animal species. They found that the secret lay in a giant molecule called DNA (deoxyribonucleic acid), which is organised like two interlocking spirals, or a double helix. For their work on this vital aspect of genetics they were awarded the Nobel Prize for Medicine.

CROMWELL, Oliver (1599-1658)
English soldier and statesman

Oliver Cromwell was a gentleman farmer from Huntingdon and might well have remained so had times been different. He was elected to Parliament, but during the eleven years when Parliament was not called, continued to live quietly at home. When, however, the so-called Long Parliament assembled in 1640, he soon emerged as leader among the Puritans who opposed what they regarded as King Charles I's high-handed ways (page 52); and when the quarrel between King and Parliament came to civil war in 1642, he was made Parliament's military commander. He trained his soldiers well and formed them into what was called the New Model Army, one of the best equipped and disciplined bodies of fighting men since the days of the Roman legions. At Marston Moor (1644) and at Naseby (1645) his 'Ironsides' roundly defeated the Royalists, and the king was put to flight. In 1649 Charles was executed, but Cromwell was not satisfied. He crushed all further Royalist resistance in England and Scotland, and as an ardent Puritan, persecuted the Catholics in Ireland. With the backing of his all-powerful army, he then took over the government of Britain with the title of Lord Protector.

In the next few years Cromwell's name became feared and respected abroad. His army was victorious in France, his navy beat the Dutch and Spanish. Upon his death, his son Richard succeeded him as Lord Protector, but for a few years only. Oliver Cromwell's severe Puritan rule had become unpopular, and most British people welcomed the restoration to the throne in 1660 of the likeable Charles II. Cromwell, though, had changed many things for good. He had shown that kings could no longer behave like gods, and so paved the way for constitutional monarchy.

CURIE, Marie (1867-1934) **and Pierre** (1859-1906
French scientists

Marie Sklodowska was born in Poland and married the Frenchman Pierre Curie, who taught physics at the Sorbonne University in

Paris. They became the most famous husband and wife team in the history of science. When they began life together, the German Wilhelm Röntgen (page 208) had just discovered X-rays, and another Frenchman, Antoine Henri Becquerel was investigating a similar form of radiation found in uranium materials. The Curies eagerly followed up these developments. Working in an old woodshed, they isolated from several tons of the uranium ore pitchblende tiny quantities of two new elements, polonium (named after Marie's native country) and radium. The radium gave off the concentrated form of radiation they had been looking for, which Madame Curie called radioactivity. For their work, Becquerel and the Curies were jointly awarded a Nobel Prize.

Pierre Curie is remembered on his own account for work on the connection between heat and magnetism. When he was killed in an accident in 1906, Marie continued her researches into radium and radioactivity, for which she was awarded a second Nobel Prize. She eventually died from leukaemia, ironically caused by radioactivity.

CUSTER, George (1839-76)
American soldier

As the American nation grew during the 19th century, and more and more settlers moved west, the government gave the Red Indians – the original inhabitants – their own reservations of land. The Sioux Indians had a reservation in South Dakota, but when gold was found in the area, white men flooded in. The Sioux took up arms, and there was war. One of the American soldiers on the spot was General Custer of the US cavalry. He had a good record as a soldier during the Civil War of 1861-5, but the Sioux hated him as a ruthless man who killed defenceless Indian women and children. In 1876, without waiting for reinforcements, he led his cavalry column against what he thought was a small Indian encampment near the Little Big Horn river. It turned out to be the main Sioux warrior force, led by Chiefs Sitting Bull and Crazy Horse. They surrounded and massacred Custer and his men, and 'Custer's Last Stand' became a legend of the Wild West.

D

DAGUERRE, Louis (1789–1851)
French inventor

Louis Daguerre is one of the big names in the story of photography – the process of preserving images through the action of light on chemically sensitive surfaces. In 1826 he teamed up with Joseph Nicéphone Niepce, another Frenchman working in the same field, and just over ten years later perfected a method which produced photographs called daguerreotypes. Many pictures taken during the 1830s and 1840s are daguerreotypes, including a famous portrait of the composer Chopin.

DAIMLER, Gottlieb (1834–1900)
German inventor and industrialist

German scientists and inventors blazed the trail in the development and early production of the automobile. Nicholaus Otto and Karl Benz (page 27) were two of these men. Gottlieb Daimler was another. In 1885 he constructed a kind of motorcycle, by fitting an internal combustion engine to a vehicle with a wooden frame and solid wooden wheels. From this rather cumbersome beginning, he went on to found the Daimler motor company, producing tramcars and trucks as well as motor cars, and other types of internal combustion engine designed for boats. Daimler, like Mercedes-Benz, is still one of the great names in the motor industry. Today, Daimler cars are manufuctured by the Jaguar company in Coventry, England, which is part of the giant British Leyland Group. Daimler limousines are used by important people all over the world as befits such splendid and handsome motor cars.

DALTON, John (1766-1844)
English scientist

The notion that matter consists of tiny individual parts, or atoms, was considered by the ancient Greeks. John Dalton put the atomic theory on a firm scientific basis, and so helped to lay the foundations of modern chemistry. He defined atoms as the smallest, or 'ultimate' particles of matter, and distinguished between the atoms of different elements. He also proposed a scale of atomic weights, starting with the lightest hydrogen atoms as unit one on the scale. Dalton took a keen interest in other scientific matters, including the problem of colour blindness, which he suffered from himself.

DAMPIER, William (1652-1715)
English sailor and explorer

William Dampier has gone down in history as one of the first men to reach the continent of Australia. In 1699 he charted a long stretch of the north-west coast, giving his name to several locations. For much of his seafaring life, however, Dampier was a buccaneer, raiding Spanish ports in the Caribbean, or chasing after Spanish treasure ships. It was on one of these adventures that he helped to rescue the castaway Alexander Selkirk, soon to be immortalised as Robinson Crusoe by Daniel Defoe (page 73).

DANTE, Alighieri (1265-1321)
Italian poet

Dante is regarded as Italy's greatest poet, and beyond that as one of the greatest figures in world literature. He was born in Florence, but because of an unfortunate involvement in politics was exiled from the city for many years. The other big event in his life was his love for a woman called Beatrice, who died young. Most of his poetry flowed from these upsets and sorrows. His masterpiece is an epic poem called *The Divine Comedy* – 'comedy' in this older dramatic sense of the word suggesting the whole range of human thought and experience. The work is in three parts – Hell (or Inferno), Purgatory and Paradise – which Dante imagines he visits in turn, with the shade or soul of the Latin poet Virgil (page 240). The awesome and terrible inscription he reads over the gate of Hell is famous in many languages: 'Abandon All Hope, Ye Who Enter!'

DANTON, Georges (1759–94)
French revolutionary leader

'The kings of Europe would challenge us. We throw them the head of a king!' So Danton roared after the execution of Louis XVI (page 151) in 1793. Georges Danton was a lawyer, used to public speaking, and he became the greatest orator of the French Revolution. He was a member of the radical Jacobin Party, and in 1792 was made Minister of Justice in the new revolutionary government. He voted for the death of King Louis and Marie Antoinette after their attempted escape from France, and by his stirring speeches roused the mass of French people to resist and defeat the armies of other European monarchs when they invaded France. Danton, though, was not in favour of the wholesale slaughter of aristocrats and political enemies that began with the Reign of Terror. It was mainly because of this moderation that he fell out with Robespierre (page 206) and the more extreme revolutionary leaders, and was himself guillotined.

DARIUS I (about 550–486 BC)
Persian emperor

Darius succeeded Cyrus the Great as the sole ruler of the Persian Empire. For their time, these Persian emperors were humane men. Darius followed Cyrus's example, with his tolerant attitude towards the many different races that lived within the empire. He also revelled in the pomp and ceremony of his own position, and started work on a magnificent new palace and city at Persepolis – one of the architectural wonders of the ancient world. He also wanted an even bigger empire. He advanced eastwards across India, then northwards into the Steppes of Russia, until the winter cold made him turn back. His next plan was to subdue the Greek city-states in the west, whose growing power and prosperity he saw as a threat. Darius raised a large army and advanced on Athens, only to be stopped dead in his tracks at the famous battle of Marathon (490 BC). He was preparing another campaign against the Greeks, when he died.

DARWIN, Charles Robert (1809-82)
English scientist

Charles Darwin was a naturalist who in 1831 sailed in HMS *Beagle* on a scientific expedition to the Pacific ocean and South America. He was fascinated by all the new and exotic forms of life he saw in remote places like the Galapagos islands; and impressed also by the way similar species appeared to change their form according to differences in their surroundings. Darwin pondered long and hard upon all this, then in 1859 published his book *On the Origin of Species by Means of Natural Selection.* This was a comprehensive theory about the way animal life was constantly changing its form, or evolving. Ideas about evolution in plants and animals had been put forward by other naturalists, including the Frenchman Jean Baptiste Lamarck. But it was Darwin's thinking that attracted public attention, and caused so much anger because it denied the account of life as presented in the Bible. He stirred up more trouble with a second book, *The Descent of Man*, in which people thought he was saying that mankind was descended from apes and monkeys instead of being made in the image of God.

DAVID (about 1050-932 BC)
Hebrew king

The story of how the young shepherd boy David killed the giant

Philistine warrior Goliath is one of the most famous in the Bible. David served at the court of King Saul, then became king of Judah and of Israel, capturing Jerusalem and fighting off the Philistines and other enemies of his people. Though his rebellious son Absalom was killed, his descendants ruled Judah and Israel for nearly 400 years. David is also famous as a psalmist and musician, and many medieval illuminated church manuscripts and stained glass windows depict him playing the harp or some other musical instrument.

DAVIS, Jefferson (1808–89)
American soldier and statesman

Jefferson Davis was the champion and leader of the Southern Confederate states in the American Civil War. He had been a soldier and a cotton planter in Mississippi for many years before Abraham Lincoln's (page 147) anti-slavery policies drew him into American politics. As a senator he spoke up for the right of the southern states to retain slavery and, if need be, to leave the United States and form their own nation of confederate states. Upon the outbreak of war in 1861 he was elected President of the Confederacy and made Commander-in-Chief of their forces. Davis threw himself heart and soul into the task of winning the war, but the forces of the Union eventually proved too strong. Just before the end of the fighting in 1865 he was captured and imprisoned. He was released after only two years, but had nothing more to do with politics.

DAVY, Sir Humphrey (1778–1829)
English scientist

Two hundred years ago the greatest danger in coal mines was from explosions caused when poisonous and inflammable gases were ignited by the flame from a miner's lamp. In 1815 Sir Humphry Davy designed a lamp in which the flame was protected from the outside air by metal gauze. This greatly reduced the risk of explosions, and the Davy Safety Lamp became his most celebrated achievement. In fact, Davy was most interested in electricity and how it could be used to break up chemical compounds by electrolysis. This way he discovered the elements potassium and sodium. He also discovered nitrous oxide, or laughing gas.

DEBUSSY, Claude-Achille (1862-1918)
French composer

Debussy has been called a 'musical impressionist', because in many of his compositions he conveyed such effects as wind and sunlight, mist and rain, as did the Impressionist painters. His orchestral masterpiece *La Mer* is a marvellous sound picture of the sea in all its moods; and the piano pieces *Claire de Lune* (Moonlight), *Jardins sous la pluie* (Gardens in the Rain) and *Brouillards* (Mists) are other fine examples of this kind of impressionism. Debussy also composed an opera, *Pelléas et Mélisande*, set in a legendary land of long ago and full of a strange, shadowy atmosphere. In these works, Debussy developed new ideas about harmony, rhythm and musical form that made him one of the most original of all composers.

DEFOE, Daniel (1660-1731)
English novelist and journalist

Daniel Defoe's own life was packed with incident and adventure, as merchant, traveller, soldier and secret agent in Scotland for William III (page 248). He was a political pamphleteer, which earned him a spell in the pillory and another in prison. It was while he was publishing a periodical – an early form of newspaper – that Defoe interviewed a Scottish sailor named Alexander Selkirk who had been shipwrecked for several years on the remote Pacific island of Juan Fernandez. This was the inspiration for *Robinson Crusoe*, one of the earliest and most famous of English novels. Defoe wrote several other novels after that, including *Moll Flanders*; also *A Journal of the Plague Year*, which was a fine example of imaginative writing, since he was only a small boy during the plague in question.

DEGAS, Edgar (1834–1917)
French artist

Degas belonged to the Impressionist school of painters; but while most of the other impressionists concentrated on landscapes and outdoor scenes, Degas was more interested in people. He was especially attracted to the world of ballet, with its stage lighting and movements of the dancers, using pastels as well as paints to achieve some of his effects. He also made wax models, cast in bronze, of ballet dancers, that are as remarkable as his paintings for the way they capture a sense of motion.

DE GAULLE, Charles (1890–1970)
French soldier and statesman

In June 1940 General De Gaulle broadcast over the French language service of the BBC in London. 'The flame of French resistance,' he declared, 'must not and shall not be extinguished. Vive la France!' The day before, France had surrendered to the German army. Only a handful of Frenchmen had the will to fight on. De Gaulle was there to lead them.

Twenty-five years earlier, De Gaulle had fought in the First World War, and afterwards put forward ideas about the way tanks could be used to spearhead attacks and keep battles on the move. His ideas were largely ignored, and it was German tanks that ran rings round the French and British armies in 1940 and brought about their defeat. De Gaulle escaped to England, gathered together those other French soldiers and sailors that had also escaped, and created the Free French Forces. In June 1944 he landed on the Normandy beaches with the other Allied forces, and a few weeks later entered Paris in triumph. The next year, De Gaulle became head of a provisional government, but soon lost patience with other politicians and retired scornfully to his country home.

His greatest days were yet to come. In 1958 France was waging a bitter and costly war against her large North African colony of Algeria. With the existing government on the point of collapse, De

Gaulle was recalled to the Presidency. He ended the war, then reorganised the French constitution into the Fifth Republic. Under his leadership France had stable government and grew economically strong. De Gaulle, so proud and independent as a man, also made France strong and independent in world affairs. He ended military alliance with the United States and vetoed British entry into the European Community, but worked closely with Chancellor Adenauer (page 5) of West Germany to end the long years of bitterness between the French and German people. A wave of strikes and riots in 1968 forced his resignation the next year, but he had by then done all he could for his country.

DESCARTES, Rene (1596–1650)
French philosopher and mathematician

Cogito ergo sum – 'I think, therefore I am' – wrote Descartes in *Discourse on Method.* In this celebrated book he presented his case for accepting nothing as fact until it can be proved beyond doubt, and then using that fact to deduce other truths. This method of clear, careful, reasoned thinking was his basis for the philosophy of Rationalism, which had a profound influence on thought and action in the 18th century – The Age of Reason. In connection with his work, Descartes also devised a new kind of mathematics, called analytical geometry. He was a famous man in his own lifetime, counting among his friends and admirers such eminent contemporaries as Cardinal Richelieu (page 204), Charles I of England (page 52), and Queen Christina of Sweden. The adjective 'Cartesian' is sometimes used to describe his work and methods.

DIAGHILEV, Sergei (1872–1929)
Russian ballet impresario

Ballet as we know it started in France, with the court dances and entertainments of Louis XIV (page 151). In 1907 Sergei Diaghilev first brought a Russian ballet company back to France. It was a big success, and for the next few years Paris and Diaghilev's *Ballets russes* became the focus for all that was new and exciting in the world of the performing arts. As an impresario – someone who promotes theatrical productions – Diaghilev had a genius for getting the best out of other people of genius. Among those who worked for him were the dancers and choreographers Vaslav Nijinsky, Anna Pavlova and Michel Fokine; the composers Stravinsky (page 222), Debussy (page 73), Ravel (page 202), Falla and Prokofiev (page 196); and the artists Picasso (page 191) and Henri Matisse. *The Firebird, Petrushka, The Rite of Spring, The Three-Cornered Hat* were four of the ballets that he and his company first staged.

DIAZ, Bartholomew (about 1450-1500)
Portuguese explorer

In 1487 Diaz was sent by the King of Portugal to find the southern limits of the African continent. After rounding the coast of West Africa, strong winds and storms carried Diaz further and further southward into uncharted waters. Finally, he was able to turn north, and it was then that he found the land he had been sent to discover – the southern tip of Africa. Though there is no definite record of this, historians believe that Diaz originally named it the Cape of Storms, and that it was the king who re-named it Cape of Good Hope, to encourage people to settle there.

DICKENS, Charles (1812-1870)
English novelist

The man who created such marvellous characters as Wackford Squeers, Ebenezer Scrooge, Uriah Heep, Mr Podsnap and Mrs Gamp, was born in Portsmouth. Young Charles's first and not very happy taste of life was working in a boot polish factory. He escaped from this as soon as possible and began his real career as a newspaper reporter. His first ventures into fiction were short stories which he wrote under the pen name of 'Boz'. His first book was really a collection of individual episodes, now known as *The Pickwick Papers*. Indeed, many of Dickens's novels first appeared as weekly or monthly instalments in periodicals, holding in thrall millions of readers. The earlier ones, *Oliver Twist, Nicholas Nickleby, The Old Curiosity Shop*, still have a fairly loose plot. Later novels, *Dombey and Son, David Copperfield* (which is partly autobiographical), *Bleak House, Hard Times, Great Expectations*, have much more strongly woven themes. Dickens felt strongly about the wrongs and abuses of Victorian society, and often used his novels to bring them to public attention. At the same time, he had the keenest eye for characters and situations, which inspired him to write some of the funniest passages in any language. He also loved acting, and gave dramatic readings from his own works that were immensely popular both in Britain and America.

DIESEL, Rudolf (1858-1913)
German inventor

In 1898 Rudolf Diesel first displayed a new kind of internal combustion engine. It was designed so that the compression of the pistons inside the cylinders was high enough to ignite the fuel without the need of an electric spark. Once the engine was working, it drove itself. Such an engine had two big advantages: it was relatively simple, because there was no electrical system to go wrong; and it used low-grade fuel oil instead of refined petrol, which made it cheaper to run. Diesel's engines, known by his own name, are used all over the world, usually as large motor units to drive buses, trucks, tractors, railway locomotives and ships.

DISNEY, Walt (1901-1966)
American film cartoonist and producer

Animated cartoons – made up from hundreds or thousands of drawings on film – were an early form of cinema entertainment. The man who made them into big business was Walt Disney. He produced the first animated cartoon with sound in 1928. It was called *Steamboat Willie*, and featured a little character called Mickey Mouse, whose high-pitched voice was supplied by Disney himself. Mickey Mouse was soon known all over the world, and joined by such other favourites as Donald Duck. In 1937 the Disney Studios in Hollywood produced *Snow White and the Seven Dwarfs*, the first full-length animated cartoon film in sound and colour. Another interesting creation was *Fantasia*, a kind of animated cartoon ballet set to famous pieces of music. Though much of his work now looks dated, Disney's creations are sure of a place in the cinema's history.

DISRAELI, Benjamin, Earl of Beaconsfield (1804–1881)
British statesman

Benjamin Disraeli was a Jewish novelist and witty speaker, who dressed in rather foppish clothes. Each of these things was against him as a politician in the stuffy, straight-laced atmosphere of Victorian Britain. Yet he became one of Britain's outstanding leaders at the time of the nation's own greatest period of wealth and power. Disraeli entered Parliament in 1837 as a member of the Tory Party. Just under ten years later, through his brilliance as a speaker and clever political manoeuvring, he became Party leader. He was three times Chancellor of the Exchequer and twice Prime Minister (in 1868 and from 1874 to 1880). In general, Disraeli's policy was to bring about social reform at home, while strengthening Britain's empire and influence abroad. Among his achievements were the Reform Act of 1876, which gave more people the vote, and other acts to improve housing, health and working conditions; also the purchase of shares in the newly opened Suez Canal and a dominating role at the big international Congress of Berlin in 1878. In all these ways, Disraeli helped to change the old Tory Party, which stood for the landed gentry, into the modern Conservative Party with a far wider appeal. His great political rival for many years was Gladstone (page 105). Disraeli had Queen Victoria (page 239) on his side. He flattered her with the title Empress of India. She made him the Earl of Beaconsfield.

DONNE, John (about 1572-1631)
English poet

Donne belonged to a group called the 'Metaphysical Poets' – poets who were always searching for new knowledge or meaning behind words and ideas. He was a clergyman and scholar with a most penetrating mind. He wrote mainly of love and religion, filling his verses with odd and unusual ideas, and clever, sometimes obscure puns. During his last illness, Donne had a painting done of himself wrapped in a funeral shroud. An effigy in white marble was made from it, and this strange piece of work can be seen in St Paul's cathedral, London, where Donne had been dean. Many of the lines he wrote are familiar today, and Ernest Hemingway used one of them for the title of one of his best known books – *For Whom the Bell Tolls*.

DOSTOEVSKY, Fyodor (1821-81)
Russian novelist

Dostoevsky's life reads like one of his own magnificent but gloomy novels. His strict and cruel father was murdered. As a young man, he joined a revolutionary party, was arrested and sentenced to death. He was actually facing a firing squad when his reprieve came through. He still served several years in a Siberian prison camp. For some years after that he was poverty-stricken, until his books at last brought him some reward. Dostoevsky's most famous novel, *Crime and Punishment*, is about a young student who murders for money and of the policeman who plays upon his conscience until he confesses to the crime. *The Brothers Karamazov* is also about a murder, this time committed by one of the brothers against their brutish and tyrannical father. In these and in his other major novels, *The House of the Dead, The Idiot* and *The Demons*, Dostoevsky looked deeply into the great moral and religious problems of life. Through them he added a new dimension to the novel as a means of thought and expression, and did much to make the 19th century such a rich period for Russian literature.

DRAKE, Sir Francis (about 1540–96)
English sailor and explorer

Sir Francis Drake was for many years a buccaneer, sailing the Spanish Maine – the sea route from the Caribbean to Spain – in search of treasure ships to attack and rob. In 1577 he set out with a small fleet of four ships on his biggest venture of this kind. He crossed the Atlantic, sailed down the length of South America and round the storm-tossed Strait of Magellan into the Pacific ocean. From there he proceeded up the west coasts of south and central America, attacking Spanish ports and shipping. He continued as far as the coast of California (which he called New Albion), then turned westward again, across the Pacific and Indian oceans and on round the Cape of Good Hope, so becoming the first Englishman to sail round the world. On his return, Elizabeth I (page 88) knighted him on board his ship, originally named *Pelican* and re-named *Golden Hind*. When war broke out with Spain, Drake sailed into Cadiz harbour, setting fire to the ships at anchor – an incident popularly known as 'singeing the King of Spain's beard.' The next year, 1588, Drake was on hand to harrass the Spanish Armada as it struggled up the Channel before coming to grief by fire and storm. England's best-loved sea captain was not so successful in his last years. When he died and was buried at sea, which is what he would have wished.

DUMAS, Alexandre, father (1802–70), and **son** 1824–95)
French novelists

Alexandre Dumas, the father, wrote two of the most popular historical adventure novels: *The Three Musketeers* and *The Count of Monte Cristo*. Stories like these, written with dash and daring against a colourful historical background, are often called 'swashbuckling', and have given rise to many more books, plays and films of the same basic type. Alexandre Dumas, the son, was a fine writer too. His best-known work was the romantic novel *The Lady of the Camelias*. This was turned into a play, and then into Verdi's (page 238) famous opera *La Traviata*.

DUNANT, Jean Henri (1828–1910)
Swiss reformer

Dunant was a Swiss banker who visited the battlefield of Solferino in 1859. He was so distressed by the suffering of the wounded that he wrote a book proposing an international organisation to look after the wounded and protect the rights of prisoners in time of war. His initiative led to the Geneva Convention of 1864, signed by 26 nations, which set down basic rules for the treatment of all wounded soldiers and prisoners. Coupled with this was the founding of the International Red Cross Society to take the necessary action. The Red Cross adopted its name and emblem by reversing the white cross on a red background of the Swiss flag.

DUNCAN, Isadora (1878–1927)
American dancer

Isadora Duncan loved dancing, but scorned Classical ballet with its special shoes and frilly skirts, and its many other rules and conventions. For her, dancing should be free, natural and spontaneous – the most beautiful thing both to do and to look at. She danced barefoot, in long, filmy, flowing clothes, looking like some pagan goddess from ancient Greece. Isadora Duncan's dancing created a sensation at the time, and has had a lasting effect on modern forms of ballet. She also led a liberated private life and spoke up for the rights of all women to live as they pleased. By a terrible twist of fate, she was riding in a car when one of her long flowing garments caught in a wheel and strangled her to death.

DUNLOP, John Boyd (1840–1921)
Scottish inventor

John Dunlop was a veterinary surgeon who began experimenting with air-filled rubber tyres, to help his young son ride his bicycle over rough cobbled streets. The results were so good that in 1888 he patented his idea for a pneumatic tyre, which gave vehicles far better road-holding ability, allowing them to travel safely at faster speeds, and giving passengers or goods a much smoother ride. Dunlop never made much money from his invention, but he lent his name to one of the world's biggest rubber tyre companies, and versions of his pneumatic tyres are used on nearly all road vehicles.

DÜRER, Albrecht (1471-1528)
German artist

Albrecht Dürer's home town was Nuremberg, then famous for its trades guilds and pageantry. Dürer visited Italy, saw the wonderful work of Renaissance artists there, and determined that he would make Nuremberg and Germany a great home of the fine arts as well. He painted a number of striking self-portraits, but his finest work took the form of woodcuts and engravings. From a purely technical point of view, these are superb. They mostly depict religious subjects, like the Passion and the Apocalypse, and share with the work of such other northern Renaissance artists as Hieronymous Bosch of Holland and Pieter Bruegel (page 38), a serious, sometimes quite morbid outlook on life. Though not so important as his woodcuts and engravings, Dürer also did some water-colour paintings of landscapes, which was a rare form of art in his day.

DVOŘÁK, Antonin (1841-1904)
Bohemian-Czech composer

When Dvořák lived Czechoslovakia did not yet exist as an independent nation, but he dreamed of the day when it would. Like his compatriot Smetana, he wrote music that expresses these hopes and aspirations. Dvořák, though, was not quite so intense and nationalistically-minded as Smetana. He composed symphonies, concertos and instrumental pieces in the manner of Brahms (page 35) and other German-speaking masters, but filled them with fresh, sunny music that is unmistakably his own. He was honoured abroad, especially in the United States, where he composed his best-loved work, the Ninth Symphony, entitled 'From the New World'. This was partly inspired by Negro spirituals and folk tunes – the music of another (at that time) oppressed people for whom Dvořák felt deep sympathy.

DYCK, Sir Anthony Van (1599-1641)
Flemish artist

Van Dyck began his career as an assistant to Peter Paul Rubens (page 211) in Antwerp. He then travelled to Italy, quickly gaining a reputation as the most gifted and stylish portrait painter of the time. In 1632 he was invited to England, to become court painter to Charles I (page 52), and one of his best-known paintings is his portrait of the king standing by his horse. Through paintings like this, Van Dyck established a tradition of English portrait painting continued by Sir Joshua Reynolds, Thomas Gainsborough (page 100), and others.

E

EASTMAN, George (1854–1932)
American inventor

Before George Eastman's time photography was an expensive and quite complicated business. In 1884 he invented a flexible roll of film that could be fitted into a camera and simplified the actual taking of a picture. Four years later he produced a small new camera specially designed to take this type of film. He thought up a catchy name for his camera – Kodak – and marketed them with the equally catchy slogan, 'You press the button – we do the rest!' In this way Eastman made photography cheap and easy for millions of people. It made him a millionaire.

EDISON, Thomas Alva (1847–1931)
American inventor

Thomas Alva Edison took out patents on more than a thousand inventions. Many of these might be regarded as improvements on other people's ideas rather than entirely new discoveries, but in the history of science and technology this has often been the case. One of his own finest achievements was the invention of the phonograph in 1877 – the first device for recording sound. One of his biggest technical advances on other men's work was his making of the first practical electric light bulb in 1879. A few years later he built a generating station and provided electric lighting for a whole section of New York City. Edison made other big contributions to wireless telegraphy, the telephone and cinematography – all this, and much more, from the man who had only a few months at school and had to find out everything for himself.

EDWARD, 'The Black Prince' (1330–76)
English soldier

Edward probably received the title of 'The Black Prince' because of his distinctive black armour. He was the eldest son of Edward III, and when the Hundred Years' War with France began, took the field at his father's side. Still only 16, he commanded a wing of the English army at the victorious battle of Crécy (1346). He won another famous victory at Poitiers (1356), so gaining control of the large French province of Aquitaine.

EDWARD, 'The Confessor' (about 1002–66)
English Saxon king

Edward the Confessor was brought up in Normandy in France, while the Danish King Canute (page 44) held the English throne. In 1042 Canute's own son died, and Danish rule in England came to an end. Edward was then chosen to be king. He was a very religious man who preferred prayer and contemplation to the life of a ruler, and began the building of Westminster Abbey. The significant thing for the future of England was that Edward was related to Duke William of Normandy (page 247). Upon his death in 1066, William invaded England, so making Edward the last of the Saxon kings.

EIFFEL, Alexandre Gustave (1832–1923)
French engineer

Gustave Eiffel was one of the first engineers to use iron and steel in a really big way – in the construction of bridges and viaducts spanning deep ravines and broad valleys. He also designed the steel framework for the Statue of Liberty in New York harbour, and giant lock gates for the Panama Canal. Above all, there is the great tower, named after him, which he built for the Paris World Exhibition of 1889. With a height of 300 metres, it was for many years by far the tallest structure in the world.

EINSTEIN, Albert (1879–1955)
German-American scientist

In the 17th century, Isaac Newton (page 172) revolutionised men's understanding of the universe with his facts and theories about gravitation. In the early years of this century, Albert Einstein in Germany created another scientific revolution with his own theories about Relativity: how the dimensions of time, space and velocity are related to each other throughout the universe. He began this stupendous line of thought while still working as an office clerk, but by 1914 was Professor of Physics at Berlin University and already one of the greatest names in the world of science.

The latter part of Einstein's career was dramatically tied up with politics and war. He was a Jew and left Germany when the Nazis came to power, to continue his work in the United States. One aspect of his studies, concerning the equation between mass, velocity and energy, was closely connected with other work going on in the field of atomic or nuclear physics. In 1939 he wrote a momentous letter to President Roosevelt (page 209), pointing out that his theories could lead to the making of an atomic bomb. The result of Einstein's warning was the manufacture of the atomic bombs dropped on Hiroshima and Nagasaki in 1945 and the start of what we now call the Nuclear Age.

EISENHOWER, Dwight David (1890–1969)
American soldier and statesman

General Eisenhower ('Ike') was the most popular military commander among all the Allies of the Second World War. In 1942 he directed the American forces in the combined invasion of French North Africa (Operation Torch). His likeable personality, and his skill in getting men from different countries and armed services to work together, led to his appointment as Supreme Allied Commander for the main invasion of Europe in June 1944 (Operation Overlord), and for the advance across France and Belgium and into the heart of Germany.

At the end of the war, Eisenhower became American Chief of Staff in Washington, but returned briefly to Europe in 1951 as Supreme Commander of the North Atlantic Treaty Organisation (NATO). The following year, the Republican Party nominated him as their presidential candidate. 'I like Ike' was his famous campaign slogan, and he won easily. He was re-elected four years later. President Eisenhower believed in delegating work to others. This was especially the case with foreign affairs, which he left largely in the hands of Secretary of State John Foster Dulles. At the time of the Korean War (1950-3), relations between the Western and Communist parts of the world were very bad. Dulles followed a policy of 'brinkmanship' – apparently taking the world to the brink of new wars, as a means of strengthening the Western alliance.

EL GRECO (1541-1614)
Greek-Spanish artist

El Greco – 'The Greek' – was how the Spanish people referred to Domenikos Theotocopoulos from the island of Crete. He studied and worked in Italy for some years, then moved on to the city of Toledo in Spain, where he remained for the rest of his life. Spain at that time was an intensely religious country, under the influence of such reforming teachers and mystics as Ignatius Loyola (page 127) and St Theresa of Avila. El Greco's paintings are full of movement and dramatic effects of colour, light and shade, in the new Baroque style of the age. Beyond that they seem almost to burn and flicker like the visions of some religious mystic. Among his greatest works is the altar piece for Toledo cathedral.

ELGAR, Sir Edward (1857-1934)
English composer

For two hundred years, since the time of Purcell (page 198), there had been no really important English-born composer. Elgar himself was over 40 before his *Enigma Variations* – portraits in music of his friends, based on an original theme – made people realise that at last England had another great composer of her own. Elgar, who lived near Worcester and was largely self-taught, composed in the manner of Brahms (page 35) and other 19th-century German composers, but the sound of his music, sometimes rich and noble, sometimes wistful and sad, was very much his own style. He also wrote oratorios, two big symphonies, concertos and other orchestral works. At the time of the First World War, the melody from one of his *Pomp and Circumstance* Marches was given the words 'Land of Hope and Glory', and soon became a kind of patriotic hymn, though Elgar did not like its jingoistic tone.

ELIZABETH I (1533-1603)
English queen

Elizabeth was the daughter of Henry VIII (page 118) and Anne Boleyn. Her unhappy mother was executed when she was still only three years old, and when Henry died she was third in line for the throne, after her half-brother Edward and half-sister Mary Tudor. Upon their deaths she became queen in 1558. At that time, England was deeply divided and weakened by strife between Catholics and Protestants. It was also very much in the shadow of more powerful European nations like Catholic Spain and France. Elizabeth's great achievements were to calm religious feeling at home and unite the people (despite the fact that she imprisoned and finally executed the Catholic Mary, Queen of Scots); and to lay the foundations of English sea-power across the world, by challenging Spain and bringing about the defeat of its great Armada in 1588.

Elizabeth was highly intelligent and had a strong personality. She inspired many brilliant men to serve her, notably her chief minister William Cecil (Lord Burghley), and such great sea captains as Sir Francis Drake (page 80), Sir Martin Frobisher (page 98), Sir John Hawkins and Sir Walter Raleigh (page 201). Her Elizabethan Age was a golden one in literature and the arts as well. It was the time of William Shakespeare (page 216), Ben Jonson (page 134) and Christopher Marlowe in drama and poetry; of William Byrd (page

40), John Dowland and Thomas Morley in music. Surprisingly, Elizabeth never married, which is why she is sometimes called 'The Virgin Queen'. With no heir, the Tudor period ended when she died.

ERASMUS, Desiderius (about 1466–1536)
Dutch scholar

Erasmus was a priest and theologian, like nearly every other scholar of his time. He was also a man of the Renaissance in the way he travelled about Europe, including England, exchanging ideas and broadening his mind. He produced a famous edition of the New Testament of the Bible taken directly from the original Greek texts, which shed new light on the meaning of the scriptures. In other works, such as his treatise *In Praise of Folly*, he ridiculed and attacked what he saw as wrongs and abuses within the Church. When, however, Martin Luther (page 154) openly rebelled against the pope and the Church, Erasmus was troubled. As a true scholar, he believed in argument and persuasion rather than open rebellion as the way to change things.

ERICSSON, Leif (about 1000–50)
Norse explorer

Historians believe that over 400 years before Columbus (page 61), Norsemen, or Vikings, discovered the American continent. A Viking chief, Eric the Red, led an expedition to Greenland some time round AD 985, and founded a small colony there. According to accounts in some of the Norse sagas, Eric's son Leif sailed south from Greenland and came upon new lands which he named Helluland ('Land of the Flat Stones'), Markland ('Land of Forests'), and Vinland ('Land of the Vine'). These places were probably Labrador, Newfoundland and a part of New England, respectively. Archaeologists have found evidence on a site in Newfoundland suggesting that all this may well have been true.

EUCLID (about 300–250 BC)
Greek mathematician

Euclid established the mathematics of geometry as we still understand it, over 2000 years later. In a long treatise called *The Elements* he presented his theorems – statements of fact about the relationship between lines, angles, distances and areas – deduced from axioms, or self-evident truths. Through the ages, this great treatise has been translated into many other languages, including Arabic and Latin. One of the valuable things about Euclid's geometry is the way it trains the mind to think and reason clearly.

EYCK, Jan Van (about 1390–1441)
Flemish artist

This early master of the Northern Renaissance school or style of painting is associated with one of the big technical advances in art – the use of oil paints instead of paints based on such substances as egg yolk or egg white, called tempera. He showed what could be done with oil paints, building up the colours and bringing a new strength and light to his own masterpieces. Many of these are religious works, like the altar piece called *The Adoration of the Lamb* in a church in Ghent. But Van Eyck also helped to break more new ground by painting portraits of the people around him – a major branch of the art of painting in the centuries to come.

F

FARADAY, Michael (1791–1867)
English scientist

Michael Faraday had very little schooling, but was fascinated by anything to do with science. He attended some lectures given by Sir Humphry Davy (page 72) at the Royal Institution in London, and persuaded Davy to take him on as an assistant. Such is the background of the man who first demonstrated the principle of electro-magnetic induction – the direct relationship between electricity and magnetism. Faraday showed how this great scientific principle could be used, first to generate electricity, and then to convert it from energy into motion. From these discoveries came the generator and the electric motor, the two pieces of equipment that have done as much as anything to shape our modern way of life.

FAWKES, Guy (1570–1606)
English political conspirator

The Gunpowder Plot of 1605 was hatched by a group of English Roman Catholics who hoped to restore their faith throughout the British Isles. The plan was to blow up King James I and Parliament, as the start of a general Catholic uprising. The ringleader was not Guy Fawkes but Robert Catesby. Fawkes, however, was discovered guarding the barrels of gunpowder that had been smuggled into a cellar beneath the Palace of Westminster on 4 November – the day before the planned explosion. He held out bravely under torture and did not give away any names. But by then the whole conspiracy had been uncovered, and Catesby and the others were all either killed outright or arrested and executed.

FERDINAND (1452-1516) and **ISABELLA** (1451-1504)
Spanish monarchs

King Ferdinand of Aragon married Princess Isabella of Castile, so uniting the two largest kingdoms of Spain. Ferdinand went on to conquer the other large province of Granada in the south, which was the last stronghold of the Moors in Spain, and Navarre in the north, so bringing most Spanish territory under one rule. Isabella, for her part, backed Christopher Columbus (page 61) in his voyage of discovery, so opening the way to the mighty Spanish empire in the Americas. Together they made Spain the most intensely Catholic nation of Europe, expelling Jews and Moors who would not join the Church, and setting up the Inquisition.

FERMI, Enrico (1901-54)
Italian-American scientist

Among those working on atomic or nuclear research before the Second World War, Fermi's name stands high. Together with Cockcroft (page 60) and Walton in England, and Otto Hahn in Germany, Fermi in Rome was bombarding atomic particles and bringing about changes in the fundamental structure of matter. For this work he received the Nobel Prize. In 1938 he left Fascist Italy for the United States, and in 1942, in Chicago, built the world's first atomic pile or nuclear reactor. With this he successfully controlled the process of nuclear fission and tapped the stupendous new source of energy that scientists knew existed within the atom.

FLAUBERT, Gustave (1821-80)
French novelist

Flaubert's first and most famous novel was *Madame Bovary*. It is the powerful story of how a woman's search for love ends in degradation and destruction, and it brought a new kind of honesty and realism to novel writing. Flaubert and his publisher were charged with an offence against public morals, but acquitted, and the novel is now considered a masterpiece of world literature. Another of his novels is *Salammbô*, which sets out with the same aim of realism and truth to describe life in ancient Carthage.

FLEMING, Sir Alexander (1881-1955)
Scottish scientist

Alexander Fleming was a bacteriologist – a scientist who studies the minute organisms called bacteria in living things. In 1928 he was carrying out research in a London hospital when he noticed that a fungus called *penicillium notatum* had accidentally grown on a culture of germ bacteria. More importantly, he noticed that the fungus mould had killed the bacteria around it. Fleming published the results of his discovery, but ten more years went by before two other bacteriologists, Howard Florey and Ernst Chain, isolated the penicillium mould and began using it to treat germ bacteria infections in humans and other animals. Penicillin, as they called it, was the first really effective antibiotic, saving the lives of many wounded servicemen during the Second World War, and of millions more people since. Fleming, Florey and Chain were together awarded a Nobel Prize for their work.

FORD, Henry (1863-1947)
American industrialist

Soon after Karl Benz (page 27) and Gottlieb Daimler (page 68) started making automobiles in Germany, Henry Ford set up his factory in Detroit. In 1908 he introduced a revolutionary design of car called the Model T, and a revolutionary new way of making it. The parts were made in different workshops and brought together for rapid assembly. This was the first assembly-line method of production in industry, turning out Model Ts at a price millions of people could afford. By 1927, his factories were producing 10,000 cars a day, and he had sold over 15 million of them. During the

Second World War, Ford applied his methods to aircraft production, building giant four-engined Liberator bombers at the rate of one an hour. Today there are Ford industrial plants around the world. His own vast fortune was turned into the Ford Foundation for welfare programmes.

FOX, Charles James (1749-1806)
English politician and radical

Charles James Fox was one of England's greatest champions of freedom and liberty. As a leading member of the Whig Party, he spent many years opposing George III and the Tory government of Lord North. As a matter of principle, he opposed the powers of the British monarchy as they existed at that time. On particular issues, he supported the American colonists in their War of Independence, and, more bravely still, supported the French Revolution and opposed war with France. He also fought against the slave trade – shipping Black Africans to America – and campaigned for full social and political rights for British Catholics and others not belonging to the established Church of England.

FOX, George (1624-91)
English religious leader

When George Fox was once arrested for disturbing the peace and brought before a magistrate, he shouted, 'Ye shall quake [tremble] at the Word of the Lord'. That, at least, is the explanation as to how his new Puritan religious movement became known as the Quaker movement. The official name was The Society of Friends. Its members disapproved of all ritual or ceremony in religious worship. They did not even have churches, but joined together for silent prayer and contemplation in Meeting Houses. They also dressed very soberly, lived simply and avoided all forms of violence. Many of the first Quakers, including William Penn (page 188), emigrated to the American colonies, where they might set up new communities without fear of persecution. Quaker people today still live by the principles of George Fox and his original Society of Friends.

FRANCIS-JOSEPH (1830-1916)
Austrian emperor

The Hapsburg family had played a major part in European politics since the election of Rudolph I as Emperor of the Holy Roman Empire in 1273. The long reign of Francis-Joseph, or Franz-Josef, brought 600 years of Hapsburg rule to a close. He became Emperor of Austria in 1848 and King of Hungary in 1867. He refused any freedom to the Czechs, Hungarians, Germans and other peoples within the Austro-Hungarian Empire, and continued to rule like an old-time absolute monarch. History, though, was not on his side. Events were moving against him. He lost a part of his domains to Italy under the growing leadership of Cavour (page 48) and suffered defeat at the hands of Prussia under Bismarck (page 28). The final catastrophe, for him and for the whole of Europe, was the assassination of his nephew and heir to the throne Francis Ferdinand at Sarajevo in June 1914. This triggered off the First World War. Stubborn, lonely 86-year-old Francis-Joseph died in the middle of the war. At the end of it, with the defeat of Germany and the Central Powers, his empire ceased to exist and the Hapsburg dynasty was ended.

FRANCIS OF ASSISI (about 1182-1226)
Italian religious leader and saint

His full name was Francis Bernardone, the son of a rich merchant in the small town of Assisi. Francis was a rather spoilt and selfish young man, until a serious illness changed his whole outlook on life. He became a devout Christian, gave up all his worldly possessions and started working for the poor and sick. Others joined him, and together they founded the order of friars called the Franciscans, or Grey Friars. Francis himself went to Egypt, to plead for better treatment of Christians in Muslim lands. He is especially remembered for his kindness to animals, and is nearly always shown in pictures, or described in books, surrounded by birds and beasts.

FRANCO, Francisco (1892–1975)
Spanish soldier and statesman

Francisco Franco became his country's youngest general and Army Chief of Staff. This meteoric rise in his own career coincided with even bigger events in Spain as a whole. The king, Alphonso XIII, abdicated in 1931, and a left-wing Republican regime took his place. Franco was bitterly opposed to this. The government dismissed him to the Canary Islands, but he soon crossed back to Spanish Morocco, gathered together a large part of the army, and invaded the homeland. The Spanish Civil War, between the Republican government forces and Franco and the army, lasted from 1936 to 1939. An International Brigade, including some famous writers and intellectuals, fought with the Republicans. Franco received armed help from Hitler (page 122) and Mussolini (page 171). Franco won the war, and established a right-wing dictatorship, with himself as 'El Caudillo', or Leader. In 1940 Franco shrewdly refused to enter the Second World War on Germany's side. After the war he was helped by the United States, which wanted to include Spain in its Cold War strategy against the Soviet Union; and by a great wave of tourism, which brought more money into the country. Standards of living gradually improved for the Spanish people, and Franco ruled to the end of his long life. A more democratic form of government took his place, with Juan Carlos as a constitutional monarch.

FRANKLIN, Benjamin (1706–90)
American scientist and statesman

Benjamin Franklin was born in Boston, but Philadelphia became his home. There he published a very successful newspaper, and took charge of the city's administration, giving it well-paved streets and lighting, an efficient fire brigade and police force, a college and public library. Still bursting with energy and ideas, Franklin took up science and geography. He carried out some extremely dangerous experiments, flying kites in thunderstorms, to prove that lightning is created by an electrical discharge in the atmosphere; investigated the geology of eastern America; and plotted the course of the Gulf Stream across the Atlantic ocean. All this time, the American colonies were still part of the British Empire. Turning then to politics, Franklin went to England to present the American colonial case against such issues as taxation. As the situation worsened, he helped to draft the Declaration of Independence, and soon after war broke out between Britain and the American colonies in 1775, was sent to Paris to seek French military aid. After the war was won, he became President of Pennsylvania and helped to draft the other founding document in American history – the Constitution of the United States.

FREDERICK II, The Great (1712–86)
Prussian king

Young Frederick loved music and books, and hated war. His father, Frederick William, beat and bullied him into becoming one of Europe's most valiant military commanders. With grim determination, Frederick II entered European power politics, involving Prussia in two big wars, The War of the Austrian Succession (1740–8) and The Seven Years' War (1755–63). In the second of these he won brilliant victories at Rossbach and Leuthen, then came very close to defeat against an alliance of Austria, France, Sweden and Russia. At the end of the fighting, he had secured the territory of Silesia for Prussia. One last time, in 1772, he ventured forth again, to capture a large area of Poland. Within Prussia, Frederick the Great was a good example of a benevolent despot. He used his strict personal rule to help farmers grow more food, to establish new industries, and generally to increase the prosperity of his country. So Frederick, who still made music and read poetry and philosophy whenever he could, made Prussia the strongest German state – the one which, under Bismarck's (page 28) leadership, would lead the fight for German unity.

FREUD, Sigmund (1856-1939)
Austrian psychiatrist

Psychology is the whole area of study dealing with animal, especially human, behaviour. Psychiatry is the specialised study of mental illness. Its founder was Dr Sigmund Freud of Vienna. He believed that mental disturbance was caused by some anxiety or complex which the patient would not admit to, or was probably not even aware of, because it was pushed back (repressed) into the mind below the level of consciousness. Moreover, he believed that these complexes were probably created during the early years of the patient's life, when he or she failed to adjust to the different stages of growing up. To cure the patient, he argued, the psychiatrist must find the complex and bring it out into the open. Freud began by hypnotising his patients in an attempt to discover the cause of their troubles. Later he developed the special technique of talking to them and urging them to open their minds more and more – the technique of psychoanalysis. Several other pioneer psychiatrists, notably Alfred Adler, also of Austria, and Carl Jung of Switzerland, followed Freud's lead. They modified, or even disagreed with some of the latter's ideas. But Freud's own pioneering work still dominates the modern medical science of psychiatry.

FROBISHER, Sir Martin (1535-1594)
English sailor

Frobisher was one of the many explorers who tried and failed to find a North-West Passage that would lead them from the Atlantic to the Pacific oceans round the northern limits of Canada. On two expeditions he got as far as Baffin Island and to the bay that now bears his name, before being turned back by ice floes. In the war against Spain that broke out soon after, Elizabeth I (page 88) affectionately called him one of her 'sea-dogs'. He commanded a squadron that harassed the Spanish Armada in 1588, and died from wounds fighting another Spanish attack against the French port of Brest.

FROEBEL, Friedrich (1782–1852)
German educationalist

Froebel believed, like the Swiss reformer Johann Pestalozzi and the famous Swiss-French philosopher Jean-Jacques Rousseau, that children would learn best if they were encouraged to think and act for themselves. He believed this process should start as early as possible, and created 'kindergarten', or 'children's gardens', in which the very young could play in interesting surroundings and so start to take a spontaneous and happy interest in the world about them. Froebel's kindergarten schools, and his ideas in general, have had a big influence on the whole world of education as we know it today.

FULTON, Robert (1765–1815)
American engineer and inventor

Robert Fulton came to Britain to study canal building, and in 1802 saw William Symington's pioneer steamboat the *Charlotte Dundas* at work on the Clyde Canal in Scotland. This inspired in him a life-long fascination with boat and steamship design. One of Fulton's own early, and most remarkable designs, was for a kind of submarine, called the *Nautilus*. He built this while still in Europe, and it functioned well, but attracted very little interest. He had far more success back in America. In 1807 he built the first passenger paddle steamboat, the *Clermont*, which travelled up and down the Hudson river; and in 1815, for the American government, he built the *Fulton*, the world's first steam-powered warship.

G

GAINSBOROUGH, Thomas (1727-88)
English artist

Thomas Gainsborough and Sir Joshua Reynolds (page 00) were the two most fashionable portrait painters in Georgian England. Gainsborough worked for some years in Bath, where wealthy and titled people spent their time taking expensive cures and relaxing. Apart from his brilliant technique, Gainsborough often portrayed his subjects within a broader landscape, which gives his paintings their special charm and beauty. He also painted landscapes on their own account.

GALILEO, Galilei (1564-1642)
Italian scientist and astronomer

'But it does move!' Galileo is supposed to have muttered as he signed his confession of heresy for saying that the Earth moved round the Sun. Copernicus (page 64) had suggested the same thing a hundred years before, but it was Galileo who gave the idea a wider circulation. Since the teachings of the Church still insisted that the Earth was the centre of the universe, Galileo got into serious trouble. Earlier, he had built one of the first successful telescopes, through which he had observed details of the Moon's surface, and the orbits of the planets Venus and Jupiter. He had made other important discoveries about the physics of motion and gravity, by relating the swing of a pendulum to time, and proving that objects of different weight still fall at the same rate of speed. He demonstrated this latter fact by dropping weights from the top of the leaning tower of Pisa. It was a striking example of Galileo's belief in the need to prove all theories and suppositions by experiment – a basic principle of science that he did much to establish.

GANDHI, Mohandas Karamchand (1869-1948)
Indian religious leader and statesman

In 1947 India – once the proudest possession of the British Empire – was granted independence. This was a personal triumph for Mahatma (Saint) Gandhi, who had been campaigning against British imperial rule since 1915. The significant thing about Gandhi's long campaign was his methods. As a devout Hindu, he did not believe in violence of any kind. His policy was one of 'passive resistance' – the boycotting of British goods, quiet disobedience of British rules and regulations, and, if need be, hunger strikes. Gandhi himself went to prison several times. By his example, he and his movement gained such respect that in 1931, dressed only in his humble loin cloth and sandals, he came to London to talk to political leaders and to King George V. So in 1947 Gandhi's passive resistance movement achieved its principal aim. Tragically, his own pacifism did not prevent bloodshed between Hindus and Muslims, leading to the division of the new nation into India and Pakistan. The saintly man was himself killed by a religious fanatic only a year after Indian independence.

GARIBALDI, Giuseppe (1807-82)
Italian soldier and patriot

Garibaldi, with Count Cavour (page 48), fought for and won the unification of Italy. After he had led an early and unsuccessful uprising in Genoa, Garibaldi fled to South America and became a guerrilla fighter. He returned to Italy in 1848 – 'The Year of Revolutions' – but again had to leave in a hurry, this time for the United States. Garibaldi's hour came in 1859, when he fought with the French and Piedmontese Italians against the Austrians. He was angry and distressed when Cavour ceded Nice and Savoy to

Napoleon III (page 173) as the price of French help, since Nice was his birthplace. Nevertheless, Italy came first, and in 1860 Garibaldi and his small but gallant band of 'Redshirts' invaded and captured Sicily, then proceeded northwards up the Italian mainland, to join King Victor Emmanuel's and Cavour's army moving south. After Italian unity had been won, Garibaldi fought on, notably at the side of the French in the Franco-Prussian War of 1870. He was by then a legendary figure, and especially popular with working people everywhere. When he visited London in 1864 he was given such a welcome that the British government nervously clamped down on his tour in case he should stir up revolution.

GARRICK, David (1717-79)
English actor-manager

David Garrick was an outstanding actor in a wide variety of roles, from those of Shakespeare (page 216) and Jonson (page 135) to the Restoration dramatists closer to his own time. His work as a manager was of even greater importance to the history of the theatre. He made London's Drury Lane theatre one of the main centres of drama and stagecraft in Europe, pioneering new and more natural scenery and the use of concealed lighting to heighten stage effects.

GAUGUIN, Paul (1848-1903)
French artist

Paul Gauguin was a businessman who suddenly gave up money, wife and family in order to paint. He was a restless man, travelling to central America, returning to France, and ending his days on the South Pacific island of Tahiti. He began painting in the manner of the Impressionists, but soon developed a quite distinct style of his own, so becoming classed with other artists of his generation as a Post-Impressionist. Gauguin was attracted to medieval paintings, which lacked perspective; and to sculpture and painting from so-called 'primitive' civilisations, in which effect was more important than technique. In his own paintings, notably those done on Tahiti and other tropical South Seas islands, he used broad, flat areas of strongly contrasted colour, to create an effect of direct and powerful beauty. His work, in which shapes and patterns of colour are so important, helped also to shape ideas about abstract art.

GAUTAMA BUDDHA (about 563-483 BC)
Indian religious teacher

The Sanskrit word 'Buddha' means 'The Enlightened'; and the man who became the Buddha was originally named Siddharta Gautama. He was a prince of Nepal in the north of India, and as a young man had everything he might have wished for; riches, a splendid palace to live in, a lovely wife and family. Yet he was troubled by the problems of poverty, disease and death, and of the suffering that went with them. He gave up his own wealth and rank and sought the answer to the whole problem of suffering. After much deep and sometimes agonised thought, he realised that the basic cause of human suffering was desire in its many guises, such as greed, lust, vanity; and that suffering would cease when desire had been extinguished. A man or woman who achieved this goal was then said to have reached 'nirvana'. This was the state of bliss that would release the soul from the 'wheel of rebirth' – the Hindu belief that the soul must pass from life to life in its progress towards salvation.

Gautama Buddha gathered about him a community of monks called the Sanga, who travelled widely preaching his words of wisdom. He himself wrote down nothing, and when he died his body was cremated in the traditional Hindu manner. So the religion of Buddhism was born. In its pure form, Buddhism is not so much a religion as a way of life aimed at achieving a peaceful and enlightened state of mind and being. It does not even claim the existence of God or any other divine force. However, as it developed, so Buddhism, like all the major religions, took many forms. It has never replaced Hinduism in India itself, but over the centuries it spread to many other parts of Asia, notably to Burma,

Thailand, China and Japan. Today it also has many followers in Europe, the United States and other parts of the Western world.

GENGHIS KHAN (about 1165-1227)
Mongol warrior king

The Mongols were herdsmen who inhabited the vast Mongolian plain and Gobi desert to the north of China. One of their chieftains, Temujin, gathered the various tribes around him, changed his name to Genghis Khan (Mighty King) and set off in search of war and conquest. He and his Mongol warriors were superb horsemen, which made them superior to any other army they encountered. They overran China and Korea, then turned the other way and swept all before them as far as the Black Sea and the Persian Gulf. That gave Genghis Khan an empire stretching for 6500 kilometres across central Asia. He proved that he could rule as well as fight, setting up staging posts for a troop of mounted couriers, who brought him news and conveyed his laws to the ends of his domains. His grandson, Kublai Khan, founded the Mongol or Yuan dynasty in China, and received Marco Polo (page 194) in Peking.

GERSHWIN, George (1898-1937)
American composer

American stage and film musicals were the most glamorous and successful form of entertainment during the 1920s and 1930s. They were originally modelled on the operettas of such European composers as Franz Lehar, but American song writers soon gave them a lively new character. One of these was George Gershwin. His parents were Russian Jewish immigrants to America, who could hardly speak English. George began his career as a pianist in Tin Pan Alley, the old music publishing quarter of New York City. Then, with his brother Ira as lyricist, he wrote many of the finest romantic songs in the English language. George Gershwin's talents did not stop there. He wanted to write music that combined European concert or symphonic styles with American dance music and jazz. His first piece of this kind was *Rhapsody in Blue* for piano and orchestra. Later compositions include the symphonic poem *An American in Paris* for orchestra, and the first all-black American opera, *Porgy and Bess.*

GIOTTO (1266-1337)
Italian artist

Florence is regarded as the city where the Italian Renaissance movement in sculpture, painting and architecture began. Giotto di Bondone – his full name – had much to do with this. Before his time, paintings were often beautiful in their use of colour and form, but seldom were they very life-like. Giotto radically changed this situation, by painting people with individual expressions, and figures that seemed to live and move. This was the new spirit of the Renaissance that Giotto breathed into his work. Though he studied in Florence, he produced two of his finest groups of paintings elsewhere. They are series of frescoes (a type of wall painting), one in the church at Assisi, depicting scenes from the life of St Francis (page 95), the other in a church in Padua. Giotto returned to Florence to design the famous campanile, or bell tower, that stands next to the cathedral.

GLADSTONE, William Ewart (1809-98)
British statesman

William Ewart Gladstone – 'The Grand Old Man' – was Britain's Liberal leader through most of the 19th century. As a young politician he had served in Peel's (page 187) Tory government, but soon changed political sides and became leader of the Liberal Party in 1867. The following year he was Prime Minister, and held that office four times between the years 1868 and 1894, finally retiring at the age of 85. Gladstone introduced many reforms in home affairs, to do with improvements in the law, in education, and in the conduct of elections (including the secret ballot). In foreign affairs he took a truly liberal stand, encouraging international co-operation and speaking out against such events as the Ottoman Turk atrocities in the Balkans. Almost the whole of his career, though, was overshadowed by his desire to bring peace to the troubled country of Ireland, then all part of the United Kingdom. He did what he could to remove some of the centuries-old causes of discontent, in the fields of religion and land-ownership, but his attempts to give the Irish people home rule failed. Gladstone was a sober, serious, deeply religious man and a powerful orator. The parliamentary duels between him and the witty, urbane Disraeli (page 78) are remembered as some of the finest moments in British politics. In his private life Gladstone was a curious man and one of his ways of relaxing was to fell trees at his country estate.

GOETHE, Johann Wolfgang von (1749–1832)
German poet, dramatist, scientist and philosopher

Germany's greatest literary figure stood for the values and ideals of many other German philosophers, writers, artists and composers – a belief that creative work should strive to encompass all human knowledge and experience. Goethe's own largest work is his poetic drama *Faust*, the profoundest version of the old legend about the man who is prepared to sell his soul for knowledge and power. Goethe's treatment of the Faust legend inspired many other writers and composers in the 19th century. Two of his other big literary works are *Egmont*, an historical drama about political resistance in the time of the Spanish Netherlands, and the partly autobiographical *Wilhelm Meister*. Goethe practised what he preached about the need to enlarge experience, by working in as many fields as possible. He studied and wrote about botany and optics, and as a natural historian put forward ideas about the evolution of life well ahead of Charles Darwin (page 71). Because of his work in so many areas of knowledge, Goethe is sometimes spoken of as 'the last Renaissance man'. The Goethe Institute which aims to spread German culture is named after him.

GOGH, Vincent Van (1853–90)
Dutch artist

'I want to say something comforting, as music is comforting,' wrote Vincent Van Gogh. His own life brought him no comfort at all. He tried several jobs before starting to draw and paint. His first subjects were poor farming people in Holland and Belgium. Then he moved to Paris, and down to Arles in the south of France. It was there that he quickly developed his style, capturing the dazzling sunlight, rocky hills and cypress trees of Provence by laying on the paints with thick, sometimes frenzied strokes of his brush. A quarrel with Paul Gauguin (page 102) who had come to stay with him, brought on the breakdown that made him cut off an ear. When he felt better and was painting again, Van Gogh returned to Paris, but soon had another breakdown and shot himself. In three short years he had produced an enormous amount of work. His new and daring use of colour classes him as one of the great Post-Impressionist painters.

GOLDSMITH, Oliver (1728–74)
Irish novelist, poet and dramatist

Oliver Goldsmith spent much of his time working for booksellers and publishers in order to earn some money. He also tried to become a doctor and physician. In spite of these distractions, he produced three famous works of English literature: his novel *The Vicar of Wakefield*; one of the best of all stage comedies, *She Stoops to Conquer*; and his poem *The Deserted Village*.

GOODYEAR, Charles (1800–60)
American inventor

Natural processed rubber goes sticky in hot weather and hard and brittle when it is cold. Charles Goodyear discovered that heating a mixture of rubber and sulphur gives to the rubber the same strong consistency in all weathers and conditions. This vulcanised rubber, as it is called, made possible the manufacture of many new products, from motor tyres to rubber bands, now so much a part of our civilisation. As has been the case with many other scientific and technical discoveries, several people were working on the problem at the same time. One was the Englishman Thomas Hancock, who took out a patent on a similar process shortly before Goodyear. In fact, Goodyear himself made very little money out of his most important work.

GORDON, Charles George (1833–85)
English soldier

General Gordon was a popular British hero at the time when the Empire was at the very peak of its power and extent. He first caught the public imagination when he served as a soldier to the Chinese Manchu government and helped to crush a rebellion. 'Chinese Gordon' as everybody then called him, was later sent to Egypt and the Sudan to deal with a Muslim religious uprising led by a man called the Mahdi (Messiah). Gordon set out to relieve the British garrison at Khartoum, was himself trapped there by the Madhi's warriors, and after a ten-month siege, was killed just before the arrival of another relief force. Because he was so popular at home, Gordon's death caused political trouble for Prime Minister Gladstone (page 105).

GÖRING, Hermann (1893–1946)
German airman and war leader

After Hitler (page 122) himself, the two best-known Nazi leaders were propaganda minister Dr Joseph Goebbels, and Luftwaffe chief, Reichsmarshall Hermann Göring. Göring was ridiculed by the British during the Second World War because he was fat and dressed in fancy uniforms. Twenty-five years earlier, in the First World War, he had been a fighter ace, flying with von Richthofen's (page 205) famous squadron. After the war, he was one of Hitler's earliest supporters, and followed his leader to power. Göring built up the Luftwaffe, the German air force, into the most formidable new fighting force of its time. In the early campaigns of the Second World War, against Poland, Norway, Holland and France, it made a big contribution to German victory. But though Göring's bombers brought great destruction to British towns and cities in 1940 and 1941, his fighters could not defeat the RAF in the Battle of Britain. From that time on, Göring's power and prestige declined. He was put on trial as a war criminal by the Allies and sentenced to death, but committed suicide.

GORKY, Maxim (1868-1936)
Russian novelist and dramatist

Maxim Gorky's life spanned the closing years of the Tsarist regime, the turmoil of the Bolshevik Revolution of 1917, and the foundation of the Soviet Union. He wrote mainly about downtrodden peasants and workers, and expressed revolutionary views, which got him into trouble before the Revolution and made him a hero after it. His most famous work is his play *The Lower Depths*, a comi-tragic portrayal of social outcasts.

GOYA, Francisco (1746-1828)
Spanish artist

Francisco José Goya y Lucientes worked in several quite different styles. Like Velasquez (page 237) before him, he was an artist at the Spanish court, painting portraits of the royal family and their friends. These paintings are remarkable for the way Goya often cruelly exposes character weaknesses in his royal subjects, while still making them look formal and respectable. He lived through the period of the Napoleonic Wars, and the French invasion of Spain (the Peninsular War) moved him to produce many paintings and engravings which portray the brutality and bloodshed of war with a terrible realism. Towards the end of his life, Goya's artistic vision became grimmer still, and he produced paintings, engravings and etchings – called his 'black pictures' – filled with lurid and horrifying images. So Goya progressed from 18th-century Classical court painter to one of the most dramatic and original artists of the 19th-century Romantic movement.

GRANT, Ulysses Simpson (1822–85)
American soldier and statesman

In the American Civil War of 1861–5, General Grant commanded the Federal or Union army, which with a strength of over a million men was one of the largest armies ever assembled up to that time. His dogged strategy was to force the opposing Confederates into battles of attrition which would exhaust their resources and bring them to their knees. His plan was successful, and he received the final surrender of the Confederate General Robert E. Lee (page 145) at Appomattox in April 1865. The second chapter of Grant's career began in 1868 when he was elected President of the United States, and re-elected four years later. Like many another soldier, however, politics was beyond him. He was easily duped, and there was much corruption in his government. Later still, he was swindled by other dishonest businessmen, and had to earn money by writing his war memoirs.

GRIEG, Edvard Hagerup (1843–1907)
Norwegian composer

Grieg's grandfather was a Scotsman who escaped to Norway after the failure of the Jacobite Rebellion of 1745. This side to his family history did not concern Grieg the composer. He was one of the leading nationalist composers of the 19th century, his own music growing out of the folk songs and dances of his Norwegian homeland. Early on he wrote the very popular Piano Concerto in A minor. From then on he found that his refined, often quite delicate musical style was best suited to songs, smaller piano pieces, sets of dances. Some of his loveliest and most atmospheric music is contained in the *Peer Gynt* suite for orchestra, taken from pieces he originally wrote to accompany Ibsen's (page 127) play.

GRIMM, Jacob (1785–1863), and **Wilhelm** (1786–1859)
German scholars and story writers

The Brothers Grimm were philologists – people who study the origins of languages, words and literature. They were most interested in the history of their own German language, and in the course of their studies came across many old German myths, legends and folk tales. It was from this wealth of material that they produced their celebrated collection of *Grimm's Fairy Tales*. The story of *Hansel and Gretel*, the two small children lost in a forest, is one of the best-loved of these – later made into a delightful opera by the German composer Engelbert Humperdinck.

GUSTAVUS ADOLPHUS (1594–1632)
Swedish king

Gustavus Adolphus was a brilliant scholar and administrator, and one of history's greatest military leaders. He organised his soldiers into small regiments that were easy to direct, gave them smart uniforms and a sense of pride, taught them new and better ways of marching and manœuvring, and equipped them with improved firearms. With this brand new army he fought successful wars against Denmark, Russia and Poland, and so made Sweden the strongest power in northern Europe. Gustavus Adolphus then entered the Thirty Years' War on the side of the Protestant German states against the Catholic forces of the Hapsburg Empire. He won a great victory at Breitenfeld in 1631, and the next year led his army to another victory against the Austrian general Albrecht von Wallenstein at the battle of Lutzen, but died from his wounds. Much of the territory he had gained for Sweden was lost within a hundred years to Peter the Great of Russia (page 190).

GUTENBERG, Johannes (1398–1468)
German inventor

Nobody is certain about the origins of printing. There is evidence that in the 8th or 9th centuries AD the Chinese were imprinting images on some kind of paper from hand-carved wooden blocks. The technique of printing whole books of words dates back to the 15th century, and the work of men like Johannes Gutenberg. He worked in his home town of Mainz and in Strasbourg, experimenting with the idea of making small metal casts of the letters of the alphabet that could be assembled into words and sentences, all held securely in a frame. He also experimented with inks to spread over the assembled letters (type), so as to leave their impression on sheets of paper. Others were working on this idea at much the same time. Gutenberg, however, developed the whole new printing technique so well that in 1456 he produced a complete printed edition of the Bible in Latin. It is known as the 42-line Bible, because each page is laid out in two columns of 42 lines each, and it has earned for Gutenberg the title of inventor of printing from movable type. Three copies of this Bible have survived – the most treasured books in the world today.

H

HADRIAN (AD 76–138)
Roman emperor

Like his cousin and guardian, the Roman Emperor Trajan, Hadrian came from the Roman province of Spain, or Hispania. He was probably the most widely travelled man in the world at that time, visiting every corner of the Empire, from Britain, where he had built the fortified wall from the Solway Firth to the river Tyne, to Palestine, Arabia and Egypt. The aim of these great tours of inspection was to tighten up and strengthen the administration of the Empire. To a large extent Hadrian was successful. He created a kind of civil service to carry out his laws, and at the same time endowed Roman civilisation with new libraries, theatres and other fine public buildings. He was one of the Empire's most capable rulers.

HAIG, Douglas, Earl (1861–1928)
British soldier

Field Marshal Haig commanded the British and Commonwealth forces on the Western Front for most of the First World War. He was faced with the problem of how to take the offensive, when millions of soldiers on both sides faced each other in complex lines of trenches. His solution was to put up a tremendous artillery barrage and then send the infantry forward in large enough numbers to overwhelm the enemy positions. Haig's two big offensives of this type were on the Somme in 1916, and the Third Battle of Ypres, known as Passchendaele, in the following year. The cost was nearly a million men killed or wounded. Prime Minister Lloyd George (page 150) wanted Haig dismissed. King George V backed him up, and he stayed in command, to launch the offensive in the summer of 1918 that at last broke through the German lines and ended the war.

HAILE SELASSIE (1892–1975)
Ethiopian emperor

Haile Selassie became a major figure in 20th-century history, mainly because of events forced upon him. He was crowned Emperor of the East African kingdom of Ethiopia in 1930, intent upon reforming his rather backward country. But in 1935 the Italian dictator Mussolini (page 171) invaded and conquered Ethiopia as part of his plan for an African empire. Haile Selassie appealed for help from the League of Nations. The League, however, took no strong action, and Haile Selassie went into exile in London. The episode is seen by historians as an important step in the train of events leading to the Second World War. Soon after the war started, Haile Selassie was restored to his kingdom and remained as emperor until 1974, when he was removed by a military revolt. He has also inspired the Rastafarian religious movement, which regards him as a kind of Messiah. A type of singing and dancing called Reggae, very popular among West Indian people, is also connected with this.

HANDEL, George Frederick (1685–1759)
German-English composer

Handel and J. S. Bach (page 19) were born in the same year, and in neighbouring German towns, but they never met. Bach stayed close to his home. Handel was soon off, first to Italy, and then to London, to seek his fortune as a composer of operas. He settled in London (taking British nationality), and composed many operas in the Italian *opera seria* style of the time. These were usually based on ancient history or mythology and had long and complicated plots, but were very popular. His famous 'Largo' is taken from an aria to his opera *Xerxes*. Handel also composed a number of large-scale religious oratorios, the most celebrated of these being *Messiah*. Two other favourite works are his *Water Music* and *Music for the Royal Fireworks*, written for festive occasions. Handel was a big, florid man, and much of his music has a big and florid sound to it, very typical of the Baroque period of art and music in which he lived.

HANNIBAL (about 247-182 BC)
Carthaginian soldier

Over 2000 years ago the rich and powerful city of Carthage in North Africa (near Tunis) was the only rival to the expanding empire of Rome. This rivalry led to the Punic Wars. The outstanding soldier of those wars was the Carthaginian general Hannibal. At the age of 25 he fought and beat the Romans in Spain, then began a campaign that ranks among the greatest epics in military history. With an army that included elephants, he crossed the Pyrenees, moved across southern France, scaled the Alps, and so advanced on Rome from the north – the most unexpected quarter. For the next 15 years, Hannibal menaced the Romans on their own ground, winning battle after battle, including Cannae (216 BC), where the Romans lost 20,000 men in a day. They finally hit back by sending a new army across the Mediterranean to attack Carthage. Hannibal sailed after them, but his army was weakened after its years of hard campaigning on foreign soil and was beaten by the Roman general Scipio at Zama (202 BC). Hannibal ended his days in exile, finally taking his own life to avoid capture by his enemies.

HARDIE, James Keir (1856-1915)
Scottish politician

James Keir Hardie worked in a coal mine at the age of ten. He had no schooling, but taught himself to read and write, became a trades union leader and then leader of the Scottish Labour Party. In 1892 he was one of three elected to Parliament as Labour MPs, and created a sensation when he made his first appearance in the House of

Commons wearing a workman's cap and tweed suit. This remarkable man was a staunch supporter of the Suffragette movement for women's rights; and he stood up in public places to oppose Britain's entry into the First World War, which was a very brave thing for him to do, when nearly everyone else was waving the flag and shouting for war.

HARDY, Thomas (1840–1928)
English novelist, dramatist and poet

Thomas Hardy came from Dorset, and nearly all his novels are set in and around the region of Wessex, of which Dorset is a part. One important aspect of them is the accurate picture they give of life in 19th-century rural England. They also have very powerful and compelling plots, mostly concerning people who, through some foolish act, bring about their own misery and destruction. *Far from the Madding Crowd, The Mayor of Casterbridge* and *Tess of the D'Urbervilles* are his three most famous novels. Hardy's plays and poetry are not so well known.

HARVEY, William (1578–1657)
English physician and anatomist

A generation before Harvey, the Flemish anatomist Andrea Vesalius had made big advances in knowledge about the human body with his careful dissection of corpses. Harvey, who was physician to Charles I (page 52), made one of the biggest discoveries of all – that the heart does not simply warm the blood but acts as a pump, drawing blood in along the veins and pushing it out again through the arteries. The final details of how the blood circulates through the body in this way had to wait until other anatomists could examine the tiny network of blood vessels under a microscope. But Harvey's basic discovery was very important, because it made physicians and doctors think of the body more as a machine, something that could be examined and put right in a systematic way.

HAYDN, Franz Joseph (1732-1809)
Austrian composer

Joseph Haydn was born at a time when most composers and artists still worked for the Church or for some rich aristocrat. For many years Haydn was musical director at the court of Prince Nikolaus Esterhazy. This was a happy appointment. Haydn served the prince well, composing church masses, operas and other music for the court. He also had time to compose symphonies, string quartets and sonatas, and to perform them with the excellent band of court musicians. In this way Haydn brought to perfection these new Classical forms of music, and became the most famous composer of his time. He visited London twice, for each visit writing a group of symphonies (nos 93-104) that summed up his life's achievement in this field. Several of them have well-known nicknames, such as 'The Surprise', 'The Clock' and 'The Miracle'. One of his finest string quartets has the celebrated nickname of 'Emperor', because it contains the melody known as the 'Emperor's Hymn', which is now the West German national anthem. After his London triumphs, Haydn retired to Vienna. He wrote no more symphonies. He returned to more traditional forms of composition with two big oratorios, *The Seasons* and *The Creation*. These express the same robust, warm-hearted outlook on life that is an outstanding quality of all Haydn's music.

HEMINGWAY, Ernest (1899-1961)
American novelist

As a young newspaper correspondent, Hemingway travelled to Europe to report on the First World War. He became an ambulance driver on the Italian front and was badly wounded. In 1936, like other writers and intellectuals, he joined the International Brigade and fought on the Republican side in the Spanish Civil War. These experiences inspired two of this century's best-known novels, *A Farewell to Arms* and *For Whom the Bell Tolls*. In these and other novels, Hemingway wrote in a terse, straight style about men of action, and of people coming to terms with themselves by facing danger. One of his last books, *The Old Man and the Sea*, has a more poetic side to it, and won him a Nobel Prize. Hemingway had always been proud of his image as a tough, fearless man, but he feared old age and took his own life.

HENRY II (1133-89)
English king

A chronicler described Henry II as 'a man with a reddish, freckled face, and grey eyes that glow fiercely and grow bloodshot in anger'. He was one of England's most dynamic monarchs. In fact, he was much more than king of England. Through inheritance, by his marriage to Eleanor of Aquitaine, and by conquest, he ruled an empire that stretched all the way from Scotland, down through France to the Pyrenees. His reign is noted for such reforms in administration and law as the system of trial by jury. It was also marked by personal strife and sorrow. He had a tragic quarrel with his chief minister and then archbishop, Thomas à Becket (page 25), that led to Becket's murder. He later had to contend with his rebellious sons, and died a sick and broken-hearted man.

HENRY VIII (1491-1547)
English king

When Henry became king at the age of 18, he seemed a fine example of Renaissance man – someone with the broadest interest in life. He was big and athletic, spoke several languages, wrote a book on religion, played and composed music, wrote poetry, excelled at games and the elaborate court dances. From that most promising start he changed into a sick, frustrated tyrant. The root cause of the trouble was his desire for a son and heir. This led him to seek a divorce from his first wife, Catherine of Aragon. When the pope refused to grant him this, he dismissed Cardinal Wolsey (page 250), appointed Thomas Cranmer (page 65) Archbishop of Canterbury and established his own Church of England. With the help of another minister of state, Thomas Cromwell, he closed the monasteries and confiscated their lands. These events changed the whole character of English life. Henry married six times in all, his wives being Catherine of Aragon, Anne Boleyn, Jane Seymour, Anne of Cleeves, Catherine Howard, Catherine Parr. In the end no one was safe with Henry VIII. Among those whom he beheaded were Thomas Cromwell, the great lawyer and scholar Sir Thomas More, and two of his wives, Anne Boleyn and Catherine Howard.

HENRY the Navigator (1394–1460)
Portuguese prince

The life of Henry the Navigator was a true prelude to the great voyages of discovery of the 15th century. Henry established an observatory and school of navigation at Cape St Vincent on the Atlantic coast, to which he invited astronomers, map and instrument makers and leading sea captains. Under his patronage the science of navigation was much improved. He also believed there was a sea route to India and the East round what was still the unknown southern coast of Africa. Henry launched expeditions that charted the islands of Madeira, the Azores and Cape Verde, and the mainland coast of West Africa. Soon after his death, two other Portuguese explorers, Bartholomew Diaz (page 76) and Vasco da Gama (page 237), found the route to India Henry had dreamed of.

HERODOTUS (about 484–424 BC)
Greek historian

By the time Herodotus lived, a great deal of human history had already been made. He wrote mainly about the rise of the Persian Empire when it was under the rules of Cyrus the Great and Darius I (page 70), then the growth of the Greek city-states, and of the ensuing wars between the Greeks and Persians. Modern historians have cast doubt on some of the events and incidents Herodotus recorded, saying that he did not always distinguish between fact and legend. However, he produced a well-organised account of events, and is often called the Father of History.

HERSCHEL, Sir Frederick William (1738-1822)
German-English astronomer

Herschel came to England from Germany to earn his living as an organist and music teacher. He was also a keen amateur astronomer, making his own telescopes to observe the heavens. This led to his discovery of the planet Uranus, to his election as a member of the Royal Society, and recognition as one of the greatest astronomers of his time. Among Herschel's other notable discoveries were white spots on the planet Mars, which he believed to be polar ice or snow caps, and, far out in space beyond the Solar System, the existence of pairs of stars, or double-stars, that revolved around each other. He also tried to assess the distances of other stars from the Sun, so enlarging, quite literally, the picture of our whole galaxy.

HERTZ, Heinrich (1857-94)
German scientist

In 1888 Heinrich Hertz discovered the existence of electro-magnetic waves. These were invisible, but by a series of experiments, Hertz showed that they travelled at the same speed as visible light, and like light waves, could also be focused and reflected. We know them as radio waves. Thus Hertz led the way to the most important means of communication in our modern world. The unit of frequency of various radio waves is named after him.

HILL, Sir Rowland (1795-1879)
English administrator

The dispatch of letters and parcels was a haphazard business until well into the 19th century. Postal rates were complicated, and it was often people who received letters and parcels who had to pay rather than those who sent them. Rowland Hill brought order and efficiency to the situation by introducing postage stamps. They were based on a much simplified postage rate and were a kind of receipt for postage paid, to be stuck onto items of mail. His rate for sending normal letters anywhere in the British Isles was one penny, and the first stamps, issued in 1840, were called 'Penny Blacks'. Hill's system was soon in operation all over the world. It also led to a world-wide interest in philately – collecting postage stamps.

HILLARY, Sir Edmund (born 1919)
New Zealand explorer and mountaineer

There had been seven previous and unsuccessful attempts to scale Mount Everest, the world's highest mountain, when Sir John Hunt led a new British and Commonwealth expedition in 1953. Included in the team were New Zealander Edmund Hillary and the Sherpa Tenzing Norgay. It was these two men who made the final assault on the summit and became the first to stand on the 'roof of the world' – 8848 metres (29,028 feet) above sea level. Hillary later joined an Antarctic expedition, which made the first overland journey to the South Pole since Amundsen (page 10) and Scott (page 215) in 1911 and 1912 respectively.

HINDENBURG, Paul von (1847–1934)
German soldier and statesman

Field Marshal Hindenburg had already retired from active service when the First World War began in August 1914. At the age of 67 he was then recalled to the German high command. Early in the war he was given most credit for the big German victory against the Russians at Tannenberg, and became a hero to the German people. At the end of the war he negotiated the abdication of Kaiser William II (page 248), and in 1925 was elected President of the Weimar

Republic. He was still in office in 1933 when the Nazi Party held the largest number of seats in the Reichstag, or Parliament. Hindenburg then called upon Adolf Hitler (page 122) to form a government. He held Hitler in check until his death the following year.

HIPPOCRATES (about 460–377 BC)
Greek physician

In the ancient world it was widely believed that when somebody fell ill, he or she had angered the gods. The only thing to do was pray for forgiveness. Hippocrates was one of the first to take the problem of sickness and disease out of the realm of superstition and to tackle it in an objective, scientific way. He observed the human body in sickness and in health, compared the symptoms of one case with those of another, and kept extensive notes. His fame spread far and wide, and some time after his death, the Egyptian pharaoh Ptolemy Soter had his writings collected together. Hippocrates's name lives on in the world of medicine, through the Hippocratic Oath, by which doctors and surgeons dedicate themselves to their work of curing the sick.

HITLER, Adolf (1889–1945)
Austrian-German political and military leader

Hitler was born near Linz in Austria, failed to become an architect in Vienna, and was a soldier in the First World War. The defeat of the Central Powers (Germany and Austria-Hungary) in 1918 turned him towards politics. He formed the National Socialist German Workers' Party – or Nazi (short for 'National') Party – and used his gift for oratory to blame the Jews and communists for Germany's defeat and humiliation. He failed to seize power by force (a 'putsch') in 1923 and went to prison, where he wrote his book *Mein Kampf* (My Struggle), setting down his ideas. On his release, Hitler developed his Nazi Party along military lines, with uniformed 'storm troopers' to deal with rival political gangs, and flags and banners bearing the emblem of the swastika. With his by now famous 'toothbrush' moustache and lock of dark hair across his brow, Hitler gained the support of many businessmen who feared a communist revolution at a time of serious political unrest; and he won the votes of working people with promises of fresh jobs in a strong and proud new Germany.

In 1933 the Nazis won enough seats in the German Reichstag (Parliament) for Hitler to become Chancellor, or Prime Minister. He soon swept away all democratic institutions, crushed the opposition, and made himself dictator with the title of 'Führer', or Leader. He did create new jobs. He also started to re-arm the country, and sought to unite all German-speaking people into one great nation, or Reich. By a clever combination of threats, bluff and political daring, he sent troops into the Rhineland, which the Treaty of Versailles of 1919 had made a de-militarised zone, annexed Austria and moved into Czechoslovakia. But when he invaded Poland in 1939, the Allies, Britain and France, declared war, and so began the Second World War.

Hitler and his generals won many early victories, because their armed forces were well prepared. Then he invaded the Soviet Union, hoping to win what he called 'Lebensraum', or 'Living Space' for the German population. Soon after, the United States entered the conflict. In April 1945, with Soviet tanks smashing their way into Berlin, Hitler finally accepted defeat and shot himself. The truth about his terrible extermination camps for Jews and other 'inferior races' was revealed. Germany itself was in ruins. So ended his boasts and dreams of a Thousand Year Reich.

HOLBEIN, Hans, the Younger (1497–1543)
German artist

Holbein was the most eminent portrait painter of his age. He worked for some years in Switzerland, then moved to London where he was employed at the court of Henry VIII (page 118). He painted famous portraits of the king himself and of several of his wives. One of his finest portraits is of two diplomats, called *The*

Ambassadors. A strange feature of this painting is an object in the foreground like an elongated skull, apparently symbolising the fact that however important men may become, death will claim them in the end. Indeed, the subject of death fascinated Holbein as it did many other German Renaissance artists. He produced one set of woodcuts on the old medieval theme of *The Dance of Death*, and another set called *The Alphabet of Death*.

HOMER (7th century BC)
Greek poet

Homer may have been a real person, or his name may have come to stand for a whole group of minstrel poets who wandered about the country composing poetry in their heads and reciting it to the crowds. Whatever the truth about Homer himself, the two epic poems ascribed to him are two of the first and greatest works of world literature. They are *The Iliad* and *The Odyssey*, and they describe events during and after the legendary Trojan Wars between the Greeks and the City of Troy. Helen of Troy, King Priam, Paris, Hector, Achilles, Agamemnon, Odysseus (Ulysses), are some of the characters who feature in them. Their names and deeds have come ringing down the ages, celebrated in countless other poems, novels, paintings, sculptures, plays and operas.

HOOVER, Herbert (1874-1964)
American statesman

Herbert Hoover is a major figure in both American and world history, because he was President of the United States at the time of the Wall Street Crash. Wall Street is the home of the New York stock exchange, and that was where stocks and shares prices suddenly collapsed in 1929. This event, taken with other developments in the American economy, led to a huge financial crisis and to economic Depression in which millions of American people went bankrupt or lost their jobs. Hoover, as a Republican, believed that business and private enterprise would soon restore the nation's fortunes, but many people did not think he did enough to help. In the presidential election of 1932 he was heavily defeated by the Democratic candidate Franklin Roosevelt (page 209), and retired.

HUDSON Henry (about 1550-1611)
English explorer

The Hudson Bay and Hudson river in North America are named after the man who lost his life searching for the North-West Passage from the Atlantic to the Pacific oceans. Henry Hudson's first voyage of discovery was in 1607. In 1609, the Dutch East India company paid for him to search again for the elusive westerly passage to the Far East, during which he discovered Manhattan Island and sailed up the length of the river bearing his name. The very next year he tried again, sailing into the empty, icy waters of the Hudson Bay. His crew mutinied. Hudson, his small son John and seven other members of his crew were cast adrift in an open boat, and were never seen or heard of again.

HUGO, Victor Marie (1802-85)
French novelist, poet and dramatist

Victor Hugo wrote one of the greatest of all historical novels, *Notre Dame de Paris*, featuring the famous hunchback Quasimodo, and one great novel with a strong social theme, *Les Miserables*. He wrote also several powerful historical dramas, including *Cromwell, Le Roi s'amuse* (which inspired Verdi's opera *Rigoletto*) and *Ruy Blas*. With these works he was recognised as France's leading writer of the 19th-century Romantic movement. Hugo's passionate support of liberal and humane causes took him into politics as well. He attacked Napoleon III (page 173) for undemocratic rule, and was exiled to the Channel Islands. When Napoleon's regime ended in 1870, he returned to the French mainland and was elected to the National Assembly. While in exile, Hugo produced a large number of drawings and paintings, mostly of dark and stormy landscapes – one more side to his great talents and powerful imagination.

HUMBOLDT, Baron Alexander von (1769–1859)
German explorer and naturalist

In 1799 Baron Humboldt and the French botanist Aimé Bonpland set out on an expedition to South America that proved to be of immense importance to natural science. They penetrated the steamy jungles round the Amazon and Orinoco rivers, scaled the Andes mountains (attaining what was then a record height of 6297 metres, or 18,893 feet, above sea level), and studied the cold current flowing up the west coast of South America now called the Humboldt current. From all their observations and scientific measurements, Humboldt published his conclusions about the very close connection between altitude and temperature, and between climate, soil, plant and animal life. His work was an inspiration to other 19th-century naturalists, notably Charles Darwin (page 71), and opened the way to our modern study of physical geography and Earth's environment.

I

IBSEN, Henrik (1828-1906)
Norwegian dramatist

The plays of Henrik Ibsen caused an enormous stir when they were first produced. They mostly portrayed stuffy, middle-class people living in small provincial towns, whose lives were riddled with secret guilt and corruption. Some of the issues they raised are not so startling today, but they shocked real-life middle-class theatregoers at the time. The plays, like those of Chekhov (page 53) in Russia, also demanded a new 'naturalistic' style of acting and production that often baffled and perplexed early audiences. *Pillars of Society, A Doll's House, Ghosts, The Wild Duck, Rosmersholm* and *Hedda Garbler* are some of Ibsen's most powerful dramas. *Peer Gynt*, a play in a more Romantic style, had incidental music written for it by Ibsen's fellow-countryman Grieg (page 110).

IGNATIUS LOYOLA (1491-1556)
Spanish religious leader and saint

The Reformation, started by Martin Luther (page 154), was the great religious upheaval that created the new Protestant churches. In response to it, the Roman Catholic Church introduced many new ideas and reforms in the Counter-Reformation. One of the leading figures of this Catholic Counter-Reformation was Ignatius Loyola. He had started out as a soldier knight, was badly wounded in battle, and turned to religion. He then went to Rome, and with the pope's blessing founded the Society of Jesus – the Jesuits – a Catholic organisation devoted to education and missionary work. Some of Ignatius Loyola's early Jesuit teachers travelled about Europe, reasserting the authority of the Church of Rome in the face of Protestant opposition. Others, such as St Francis Xavier, travelled to India, China and other distant parts of the world. Today, there are about 30,000 Jesuit teachers and missionaries working throughout the world.

IRVING, Washington (1783-1859)
American writer

Washington Irving grew up in the newly created United States of America, and his own stories, almost in the style of folk tales, were some of the first pieces of true American literature. Best known are *Rip van Winkle*, the story of the man who slept for 20 years, and *The Legend of Sleepy Hollow*. Both are portrayals of life among the old Dutch settlers of New York state. Irving was not just a writer of charming home-spun tales. He wrote about his travels in Europe, and published an important biography of America's first president, George Washington (page 243).

IVAN IV, The Terrible (1530-84)
Russian tsar

Both Ivan's parents died when he was still a small boy, and he was brought up by the boyars, or Russian nobles – rough, villainous men, most of them, whom he grew to hate. He was crowned emperor, or tsar, at the age of 16 – the first Russian ruler to take that title – and showed strong and intelligent leadership in the early years of his reign. He led his armies against the Tatars and created a Russian empire that stretched southward to the Caspian Sea and east of the Ural mountains into Siberia. He also welcomed the Englishman Richard Chancellor, who had been sent by Sebastian Cabot (page 42) to establish trade links with Russia, and opened up the port of Archangel to shipping. It was the death of his wife and of his favourite son that seem to have aroused in Ivan the brutality he had learnt at the hands of the boyars, and earned him the name of

'Terrible'. In fits of near madness he had the bishop of Moscow strangled to death, put down a suspected conspiracy in the city of Novgorod by slaughtering the entire population, and killed another of his sons with a vicious blow. Another story suggests that even when Ivan was pleased, he could be terrible. This was to do with the building of St Basil's cathedral in Moscow. He liked the building so much, so the story goes, that he had the architects blinded in order that they should not go away and design anything else as good.

J

JACKSON, Thomas 'Stonewall' (1824–1863)
American soldier

General Thomas 'Stonewall' Jackson was the Confederate army's most dashing and successful commander in the American Civil War. He earned his famous nickname by the stubborn defence of his position at the early battle of Bull Run in 1861. The next year he conducted a brilliant campaign in the Shenandoah valley, outmanœuvring his Federal opponents in almost every engagement. His support of General Robert E. Lee (page 145) brought the Confederates two more big victories, at Fredericksburg and Chancellorsville – but at the cost of 'Stonewall' Jackson's own life. He was accidentally shot by one of his own men. His leadership was sorely missed by the Confederates, who needed men of his exceptional calibre to compensate for the Federal or Union superiority in men and guns.

JEFFERSON, Thomas (1743–1826)
American statesman

'We hold these truths to be self-evident, that all men are created equal. . . .' These inspiring words from the Declaration of Independence of 1776 were drafted by Thomas Jefferson. When he was born, the thirteen American colonies were still part of the British Empire. He was one of many Americans who grew increasingly impatient with the way they were being ruled by George III and his government, and by 1776 was a leader among those who wanted complete independence from Britain. When the American War of Independence was won, Jefferson entered Congress, served as ambassador to France, then as Secretary of State, and was President of the new United States of America from 1801 to 1809. His most famous act as president was the Louisiana Purchase – the biggest land deal in history. Louisiana was a huge territory still belonging to France, that stretched from the Mississippi river to the Rocky mountains. Jefferson bought it from Napoleon I (page 172) for 15 million dollars. It immediately doubled the area of the United States. Jefferson, however, was not out to build an old-fashioned empire. He was a rather shy man, a thinker and idealist, who dreamed of the United States as a nation of farmers – free men and women working the land and enjoying 'life, liberty and the pursuit of happiness', to quote again from the Declaration of Independence.

JELLICOE, John Rushworth (1859-1935)
English sailor

In the First World War, Britain and Germany both had large fleets of battleships, cruisers and destroyers, with which they hoped to attack each other's sea routes. Only once in the whole war did these mighty fleets – the British Grand Fleet and the German High Seas Fleet – challenge each other. This was at the battle of Jutland in 1916. The British commander was Admiral John Jellicoe. Before the war, he had been Director of Ordnance, and made big improvements in British naval gunnery. He found at Jutland, however, that the German ships were better protected by armour plating. The result was heavier losses suffered by the British Grand Fleet. Jellicoe made up for this with iron nerve and determination, eventually forcing the German ships to head back across the North Sea for home. Their surface fleet never ventured forth again.

JENNER, Edward (1749-1823)
English physician

Smallpox was once the most widespread disease in Europe. It killed millions, and even those who recovered were left with scarred and pitted faces. Edward Jenner investigated the commonly-held belief that milkmaids and other country people who caught the less dangerous cowpox never seemed to catch the more deadly smallpox. In 1796 he isolated a specimen of cowpox virus and injected it into a boy named James Phipps. The lad caught cowpox but soon recovered. With tremendous faith in his own actions, Jenner then introduced a strain of smallpox into him. James stayed fit and well. The attack of cowpox had made him immune to the more serious disease. Jenner called his amazing new method of preventive medicine 'vaccination', from the Latin word 'vacca', meaning 'cow'. During the 19th century, mass vaccination against smallpox reduced the disease from a common scourge to a rarity.

JESUS CHRIST (about 6 BC–AD 30)
Jewish religious leader and founder of Christianity

Jesus was born at Bethlehem, near Nazareth, in the Roman province of Judea. His mother and father were Mary and Joseph, and he was brought up to be a carpenter. According to the four gospel ('good news') accounts in the New Testament of the Bible, he then began preaching. He often spoke in parables, using a particular story or image to illustrate some broader moral or religious point. He said revolutionary things, about the corruption of wealth and power, and urged compassion and forgiveness in place of the older beliefs in revenge and punishment. From the things Jesus said, and from the reports of miracles he had performed, people began speaking of him as the Messiah – the long-awaited saviour of the Jewish people. At the same time, he upset the priests and other privileged people within the Jewish community, who finally had him arrested and handed over to the local Roman governor Pontius Pilate. He was tried on a charge of blasphemy and sentenced to death by crucifixion – the usual punishment for serious offences. After his death, on a hill called Golgotha just outside Jerusalem, his chosen apostles, and other relatives and friends, believed he had miraculously come alive. The gospels say he appeared among them before ascending to heaven.

'Christ' is the Greek word for Messiah, or 'Annointed One'.

Christianity claims that Jesus was the Son of God, that is, God made Man. The religion began to spread, in the first instance, mainly through the travels and teachings of the apostles Peter (page 189) and Paul (page 186). It was suppressed by the Romans up to the time of the Emperor Constantine (page 62) in the 4th century AD, when it became the official religion of the Roman Empire. Through the Middle Ages and Renaissance periods, Christianity was carried from Europe to many other parts of the world, as well as inspiring most European art and music. It also split into numerous churches or sects. Today it claims more adherents than any other religion.

JOAN OF ARC (1412-31)
French heroine and saint

Joan was 17 when she led a French army to victory against the English outside Orleans and raised the siege of the city. It was a turning point in The Hundred Years' War between the royal houses of England and France. Joan was born in the province of Lorraine. Her father – known as Jacques of Arc – was a ploughman. She was a shepherdess, and said she heard heavenly voices telling her to take up arms like a man and free her land of the English. After the victory at Orleans in 1429 she saw the Dauphin, the heir to the French throne, crowned at Rheims, and went on to win more victories. Then she was captured by the Duke of Burgundy, an ally of the English, and handed over to them. Because of Joan's claim to hear voices from heaven, the English condemned her as a witch and burnt her at the stake.

JOHN (1167-1216)
English king

John, the youngest son of Henry II (page 118), was an unpopular monarch. He showed ability, but somehow managed to upset everybody else of importance, including Pope Innocent III, one of the most authoritative of all church leaders, who excommunicated him for several years. John's greatest quarrel was with his barons. As a result they forced him to agree to the terms of the Magna Carta (Great Charter) at a meeting at Runnymede by the Thames in 1215, by which they would reduce his powers and increase their own. John had no intention of abiding by its terms and conditions for longer than he could help it. Nevertheless, the Magna Carta, with its references to the liberty of life and property, became significant in people's minds in the centuries to come, and is seen as a great landmark in the history of democratic institutions.

JOHN (1st century AD)
Christian apostle and saint

John and his brother James were the sons of a Galileean fisherman named Zebedee. They were both numbered among the twelve original apostles. Jesus (page 132) called them 'Boanerges', meaning 'Sons of Thunder', which may mean that they were rather hot-tempered men. John is supposed to be the author of the last of the four gospels in the New Testament of the Bible, though scholars are not sure about this. He may have written all, or only parts of it. The Gospel of St John is in itself quite different from those of Matthew (page 161), Mark (page 159) and Luke (page 153). While they are fairly straightforward accounts of Christ's life and deeds, John's gospel goes more deeply into philosophy and mysticism.

JOHNSON, Samuel (1709-84)
English lexicographer, novelist and journalist

Dr Samuel Johnson's great work of scholarship was his *Dictionary of the English Language*. It brought him fame after years as a hard-up journalist in London. It is still admired for its very precise definitions, and many quotations to illustrate the various shades of meaning of different words. He published much else besides, including an interesting and rather philosophical novel called *Rasselas*. The image of Dr Johnson as the large, clumsy but brilliant man of literary society comes to us largely from James Boswell's *The Life of Samuel Johnson*. This is the most celebrated biography in the English language. The many anecdotes about Johnson and his marvellous conversation nearly all come from Boswell's account. Beyond his wit and wisdom, Johnson emerges as a kindly and generally broad-minded man – someone standing for the best side of life and society in 18th-century Europe.

JONSON, Ben (about 1572-1637)
English dramatist and poet

Ben Jonson was only a few years younger than Shakespeare (page 216). The two men lived and worked quite closely together for a time, and Shakespeare is known to have performed in some of Jonson's plays. Jonson was probably more successful than Shakespeare in his own day, and was awarded a pension by James I for the many masques, or court entertainments, that he wrote. He was a scholarly man, with a good knowledge of Greek and Roman literature, which influenced his own work. He was also a believer in the idea of 'humours', or temperaments, which make each of us the kind of person we are. *Every Man in his Humour* was one of his first successes, for which he wrote the sequel, *Every Man out of his Humour. Volpone, The Alchemist* and *Bartholomew Fair* are his other most famous plays.

JOYCE, James (1882-1941)
Irish novelist

James Joyce left his home town of Dublin as a young man, and lived for the rest of his life in Switzerland, Italy and France. Yet nearly everything he wrote was about Dublin and Ireland. *Dubliners* and *Portrait of the Artist as a Young Man* are recollections of his Irish boyhood and youth. *Ulysses*, despite its title taken from Greek mythology, is also about Dublin. Beyond that, it is one of the most original books ever written. In it Joyce used an entirely new style of writing, called the 'stream of consciousness' style. He wanted to convey the impression of how all our minds move restlessly from one thought and feeling to the next, like a kind of mental kaleidoscope. He also considered the sound of words, even their shape and appearance on the page, as ways of re-creating this kaleidoscopic effect of the mind. Joyce went on to write *Finnegan's Wake*, which carries his 'stream of consciousness' style to even greater lengths. Both books have had an overwhelming effect on 20th-century writing and thought.

JUSTINIAN (AD 483-565)
Roman-Byzantine emperor

In the 5th century AD, the Huns, Vandals, Goths and other barbarian races swept across Central and Western Europe, destroying large parts of the Roman Empire. The eastern part of the empire, however, remained largely intact. This became the Byzantine Empire, with its capital of Constantinople, founded on the site of the ancient city of Byzantium. One of the Byzantine Empire's most illustrious rulers was Justinian. With two fine generals, Belisarius and Narses, he won back territories that had been overrun by the barbarians. He drew up a code of laws that later became the basis of law in many European countries. And he promoted a magnificent style of art and architecture. The massive domed church of Santa Sofia in Constantinople (now Istanbul) was built during his reign. Both Justinian and his gifted wife Theodora are also commemorated by mosaic portraits in a church in Ravenna. This Italian town was another important centre of the Byzantine Empire, and mosaic work was one of the chief glories of Byzantine art.

KANT, Immanuel (1724–1804)
German philosopher

The main theme of Kant's philosophy was to do with the limits of human knowledge and experience; what we can hope to experience and understand, and what may be beyond the realms of thought and experience. His great work on the subject was *Critique of Pure Reason.* Kant hardly ever left his home town of Königsberg in East Prussia (now Kaliningrad), but his philosophical speculations made him so famous and respected that people came from all over the world to seek his advice on politics and many other subjects.

KELVIN, Lord William Thomson (1824–1907)
Scottish scientist

Lord Kelvin was active in many scientific fields. He invented equipment that made possible submarine cable communication, and pointed the way to the discovery of radio waves by Heinrich Hertz (page 120). Kelvin's investigations into thermodynamics – the science of heat and energy – led him to create a new temperature scale. This scale, named after him, is based on the concept of Absolute Zero – the coldest anything can get. It is recorded as 0 degrees Kelvin, which is equal to −273·15 degrees Centigrade.

KENNEDY, John Fitzgerald (1917–63)
American statesman

'Fellow Americans, ask not what your country can do for you – ask what you can do for your country,' said Democrat John F. Kennedy when he took office as President of the United States in 1961. At 44 he was the youngest man to be elected president, and he gave new hope to millions. He was also the first Roman Catholic president. At home, Kennedy introduced an important civil rights bill, but could not get Congress to agree to other reforms. Abroad he had to deal with a grave international crisis over missile sites in communist Cuba, and stepped up American aid to Vietnam, which was the prelude to a long and terrible war. All this, his successes and failures, was overshadowed by his assassination in Dallas, Texas in 1963. Lee Harvey Oswald was charged with the crime, then he was shot by a man named Jack Ruby. According to the Constitution, the Vice-President, Lyndon Baines Johnson, had meanwhile taken over as president. Kennedy's death was a shock to the whole world. It was a personal tragedy that his family had to live through again in 1968, when John's younger brother Robert was also shot dead while campaigning for the office of president.

KEPLER, Johannes (1571-1630)
German astronomer

The idea that the Earth was not the centre of the universe, and that perhaps it and the other planets moved round the Sun, can be traced back to ancient times. It was revived in the 16th century by Nicolaus Copernicus (page 64), and confirmed by Johannes Kepler. Kepler was an assistant to the Danish astronomer Tycho Brahe, and could study the most accurate observations of the stars and planets available at that time. He concluded that the Earth and other known planets did indeed move round the Sun. Furthermore, he proposed that their orbits were not circular, but slightly oval, or elliptical, and that they also moved faster as they approached the position on their orbits nearest to the Sun. Kepler based his Laws of Planetary Motion on his belief in a mystic rule of numbers that accounted for the structure and operation of the whole universe. Many other scientists, writers and musicians believed in this mysterious 'Harmony of the Spheres' as well.

KING, Martin Luther (1929–68)
Black American social reformer

During the 18th and 19th centuries, millions of African Black people were shipped across the Atlantic ocean to work as slaves on America's cotton plantations. President Lincoln (page 147) freed them from slavery in 1863, but they were still very under-privileged people. Martin Luther King, a Baptist minister from Atlanta, Georgia, was a great leader in their long struggle for equality in law and society. He did not believe in violence, although often imprisoned and sometimes beaten up himself, and finally won the open support of President Kennedy (page 138) in his campaign for civil rights. He organised long marches for Black people, and made moving speeches that carried his name and message far beyond America's own shores. Legislation was passed, to give Black American people their rightful status. King himself was awarded the Nobel Peace prize. In 1968, while leading a Poor People's March in Memphis, Tennessee, he was shot dead. There followed a wave of Black revenge and violence that would have broken King's heart.

KIPLING, Rudyard (1865–1936)
English novelist and poet

Rudyard Kipling wrote mainly about India, when it was Britain's proudest imperial possession. In his *Barrack Room Ballads* he wrote poems about the ordinary British soldier of those days, underlining the sad or bitter feelings that often lay behind all the pomp and ceremony of Empire. He wrote many stories about India and the East that are full of vivid description, and in the *Jungle Books* for children created characters based on the animal life of India.

KITCHENER, Lord Horatio Herbert (1850–1916)
British soldier

The most famous recruiting poster ever produced in Britain showed a man with a big moustache staring straight out of the poster and pointing a finger at the viewer. The caption said, 'Your Country Needs YOU!' The man was Field-Marshal Kitchener. He commanded the British and Egyptian army at the battle of Omdurman in 1898, and became commander-in-chief of the British army in the Boer War of 1899 to 1902, during which he set up concentration camps to help break the resistance of the Boer people. At the outbreak of the First World War in 1914 he was made Minister of War. His recruiting campaign, with its very effective poster, was a great success, and the millions who went off to fight were known as 'Kitchener's Army'. He was drowned when the ship taking him to a war conference in Russia, HMS *Hampshire*, was sunk by a mine.

KNOX, John (about 1500–1572)
Scottish religious leader

Scotland was a dangerous place for Protestants when John Knox was converted to the faith in about 1544. It was ruled by the French Catholic Mary of Guise, widow of James V, on behalf of her infant daughter Mary Queen of Scots (page 159); and Knox's own Protestant teacher, George Wishart, was burnt at the stake. Knox himself was arrested and served time as a French galley slave. Later he went to Geneva in Switzerland to meet the French Protestant leader John Calvin (page 42), then in 1559 returned home for good. He gained so many converts to Calvinism that in the end he had Mary of Guise and her court expelled. Soon after, the Catholic Mary Queen of Scots returned to Scotland from France, where she had been brought up. By then, however, the stern and fiery Knox was very influential in Scotland's affairs, and had turned it into a mainly Protestant country.

KOCH, Robert (1843–1910)
German scientist

Robert Koch was a bacteriologist, studying the minute organisms called bacteria that cause disease. Following research into the subject already begun by Louis Pasteur (page 185), he started cultivating bacteria under laboratory conditions. He identified the bacteria responsible for tuberculosis, cholera and other deadly diseases, and produced a form of inoculation against anthrax. He was awarded a Nobel prize.

KRUSHCHEV, Nikita (1894–1971)
Soviet Russian statesman

Nikita Krushchev, the son of a miner, was a life-long member of the Soviet Communist Party. He fought with the newly created Red Army in the Civil War of 1920, and fought a guerrilla war against the Germans in the Second World War. When Stalin (page 220) died in 1953, he was elected First Secretary of the Communist Party and took over as leader of the Soviet Union. Three years later, he made a dramatic speech, criticising Stalin's long years of rule. He spoke of what was called the 'cult of personality', meaning the dangers of hero-worship and abuse of power, which he associated with Stalin. At the same time, Krushchev made moves to ease the situation of the 'Cold War' – the dangerous antagonism between the Soviet Union and the United States, and their allies. He visited the United States and other Western countries. There were bad setbacks, notably at the time of the Cuban Missile Crisis of 1962. But Krushchev's image, as a man who spoke his mind, genuinely trying to do his best for the Soviet Union and for peace, did bring a period of relaxation in world affairs.

L

LAFAYETTE, Marie-Joseph, Marquis de (1757–1834)
French soldier

Lafayette was an aristocrat, but also a great champion of liberty, and took part in three revolutions. The first was the American War of Independence of 1775 to 1781, during which he recruited French aid for the American rebels and fought with them at the decisive battle of Yorktown in 1781. With the outbreak of the French Revolution in 1789, Lafayette was active again, taking command of the National Guard, which gave protection to the new National Assembly. He was against the execution of Louis XVI (page 151), however, fled from France and was held prisoner by the Austrians. After the Napoleonic Wars he paid another visit to the United States, where he was welcomed as a hero, and was back in France to assist in the Revolution of 1830. Lafayette remains a hero to Frenchmen and Americans alike. When General Pershing (page 189) arrived in France with the first contingent of American troops at one of the gravest moments of the First World War, he recalled his own nation's debt to Lafayette when he declared: 'Lafayette, nous sommes ici!' – 'Lafayette, we are here!'

LA SALLE, René, Cavelier de (1643–87)
French explorer

After Cartier (page 46) and Champlain (page 50), René de La Salle was the third great French pioneer of North America. He first travelled round the region of the Great Lakes, and recorded a vivid description of the Niagara Falls. He then set off southward, along the Illinois river, and eventually down the whole length of the

Mississippi river to the Gulf of Mexico. The vast lands to the west of the Mississippi he claimed on behalf of Louis XIV of France (page 151), calling them Louisiana. La Salle went back to his homeland, whereupon Louis made him governor of the Louisiana territory. From that time on, things went from bad to worse for La Salle. He was furnished with a new expedition, but the commander of the small fleet of ships landed at the wrong place, then abandoned him. La Salle struggled on, but was killed when others mutinied.

LAVOISIER, Antoine (1743-94)
French scientist

Lavoisier was a chemist who discovered that combustion does not take place on account of a mysterious substance called phlogiston (which nearly everybody then believed in), but is due to oxygen in the air. This discovery made scientists think again about the whole nature of chemical changes. Lavoisier also worked out a new system for naming compounds, which formed the basis for modern chemical classification. Unfortunately, he did not confine himself to chemistry. He had been a tax inspector for the French King Louis XVI, and for that he was guillotined during the Revolution.

LAWRENCE, David Herbert (1855-1930)
English novelist

D. H. Lawrence was brought up in a mining town near Nottingham, and the strong, sometimes violent family atmosphere he experienced influenced nearly all his work. His major novels, *Sons and Lovers, The Rainbow, Women in Love, Lady Chatterley's Lover*, are all very powerful and very sensitive accounts of the relations between men and women and between themselves and society as a whole. Some of Lawrence's work was at first considered obscene, and one of the most famous law cases of this century was to do with the publication of the first complete version of *Lady Chatterley's Lover* in 1960. The publishers won their case.

LAWRENCE, Thomas Edward (1888–1935)
British soldier and writer

'Lawrence of Arabia' was one of the heroes of the First World War. He first went to the Middle East as an archaeologist, learned Arabic and came to love the Arab way of life. When Turkey joined Germany's side in the First World War, he led the Arabs in a guerrilla war against Turkish garrisons and communications in Palestine and Arabia. After the war he became depressed because he thought the Allies had betrayed the Arabs with false promises of independence. He was also upset by all the publicity that came his way. So this strange and complex man tried to find obscurity by enlisting in the RAF and the army under the assumed names of Ross and Shaw. T. E. Lawrence was killed in a road accident, leaving behind him one remarkable book, *The Seven Pillars of Wisdom*, being his account of his wartime exploits.

LE CORBUSIER (1887–1965)
Swiss-French architect

Many of this century's leading architects have made creative use of the new materials of the age – concrete, steel, plate glass and plastics. They have believed that to go on building in traditional ways, with bricks and tiles and timber frames, was timid and dull. One architect who thought this way was the German Walter Gropius, who established a famous school of design called the Bauhaus. Another was Le Corbusier, whose real name was Charles Jeanneret. He defined a house as a 'machine for living in', meaning a place as comfortable and convenient as modern technology could make it. Le Corbusier believed in using steel and concrete to make buildings that looked clean and strong, like the materials themselves. He also had new ideas about town planning and community living. One of his projects was a building in Marseilles called 'Unité d'Habitation', a combination of apartments, shops, recreation centres, planned as a whole community centre. Another major scheme he worked on was the United Nations headquarters in New York City. Some of the most exciting and original buildings and town developments in the world today owe much to Le Corbusier's thinking and methods.

LEE, Robert E. (1807-70)
American soldier

In the American Civil War of 1861-5, the Federal or Union Army of the north had the most men, guns and equipment. The Confederate south partly made up for this by having two of the war's finest commanders in General 'Stonewall' Jackson (page 130) and General Robert E. Lee. Lee was no great enthusiast for slavery or for a separate confederacy, but he remained loyal to his home state of Virginia and so gave his services to the Confederate cause. In the early years of the war, Lee won many victories, notably at Fredericksburg and Chancellorsville; but when his army advanced into Pennsylvania in 1863 it got drawn into the bloody and costly battle of Gettysburg. From that time on, he was forced to fight a war of attrition that he could not hope to win. He finally surrendered to General Grant (page 110) at Appomattox in April 1865. It was a sad moment for both men, who had fought as comrades in arms in the earlier Mexican War of 1846.

LEEUWENHOEK, Anton van (1632-1723)
Dutch scientist

Anton van Leeuwenhoek was a cloth merchant, whose interest in early microscopes revealed a whole new world to science and medicine. He made his own microscopes with great care and ingenuity, and astonished himself with the things he saw through them. Leeuwenhoek was the first man to describe red blood cells, and to observe the tiny living organisms called bacteria, though the significance of these was not fully understood for another 200 years. The science of microbiology that Leeuwenhoek founded corrected many old notions as well, including the one about 'spontaneous generation' – that fleas, for example, were formed out of sand.

LENIN, Vladimir Ilyich (1870–1924)
Russian revolutionary and Soviet leader

In October 1917 a train pulled into the Finland Station in Petrograd (formerly St Petersburg). A stocky, bearded little man in plain suit and cap stepped onto the platform. He was not sure of the reception he would get. Suddenly he was grasped, lifted shoulder high and carried through cheering crowds out into the streets. The man was Lenin. Earlier in the year Tsar Nicholas II (page 178) had abdicated. A government led by Alexander Kerensky was trying to continue the war against Germany. There were mutinies in the army, strikes in the factories. Lenin's hour had come. 'Comrades! Soldiers! Workers!' he cried. 'Long live the world socialist revolution!'

Vladimir Ilyich Ulyanov (Lenin's real name) became a revolutionary in his youth, after his brother was executed for a plot against the tsar. In 1895 Lenin himself was arrested and sent to Siberia. Upon his release he escaped abroad, to Brussels, Paris and London. He returned to Russia for the uprising of 1905, and when this failed was forced once more into exile. Lenin was in Switzerland at the time of the First World War. The Germans cunningly helped him to return home, hoping he might lead a revolution that would take Russia out of the war. Their hopes were fulfilled. Lenin, as head of the Bolshevik (or Majority) Communist Party, and with the support of Workers' Councils, or Soviets, quickly overthrew Kerensky and formed a new government. Just as quickly he made peace with Germany, then took measures to bring the whole of the nation's wealth and economy under state control. He also had to deal with a ruinous civil war, when royalists, with foreign help, tried to topple the new Soviet state. In 1923 he was wounded in an attempt on his life, and died the following year.

Lenin based his life's work on the idea of world revolution, as predicted by Karl Marx (page 160). He did not achieve this, but he did transform the old Russian Empire into the Union of Soviet Socialist Republics, soon destined to become one of the world's super powers. In his honour, the old imperial Russian capital of St Petersburg was renamed Leningrad, and thousands still queue every day to pay homage to his embalmed body in Moscow's Red Square.

LEONARDO DA VINCI (1452-1519)
Italian artist, scientist and engineer

Painter, sculptor, inventor, engineer, anatomist, philosopher – Leonardo da Vinci was a true 'Renaissance Man', someone skilled and learned in all the arts and sciences of his day. He was born near Florence, and as a youth was apprenticed to the artist Verrochio, learning how to paint, to carve in stone, and cast metal figures. He was soon producing fine paintings of his own, but because of his inquiring mind was constantly turning his attention to other matters. For the Duke of Milan he prepared drawings of remarkable new war machines, including 'covered chariots' (the first real notion of a tank) and bridges that could be transported on rollers. Later, he became absorbed in civil engineering, with plans for canals, locks and roads; then fascinated with anatomy, producing hundreds of superb drawings of different parts of the human body. He had other remarkable ideas about flying machines, which he described as being like 'great birds on which man can ride'. He also wrote essays on such scientific subjects as force and motion, the action of gears and levers, and magnification. Yet another example of his astonishing mind and ingenuity was a private kind of writing-in-reverse, or mirror-writing, which he devised.

Many of Leonardo's schemes and inventions were never put into practice, simply because they were too far in advance of the technology of his age. But they express perfectly the spirit of Renaissance times, when men were increasingly interested in why and how things worked, and in knowledge and ideas for their own sake. Leonardo is, however, thought of first and foremost as an artist because of such famous paintings as his wall fresco *The Last Supper* and his portrait known as the *Mona Lisa* – probably the world's most celebrated painting.

LINCOLN, Abraham (1809-65)
American statesman

As a young man, Abraham Lincoln saw a group of Black slaves, shackled together, on their way to market, to be bought and sold like cattle. The scene affected him deeply, and drove him on to become one of America's greatest presidents. Lincoln was born in a log cabin that did not even have proper windows. He had hardly any schooling, but taught himself to read and write and eventually to become a lawyer. From the law he moved to politics, and in 1847 was elected a congressman for his home state of Illinois. In 1860 the Republican Party nominated him as their presidential candidate, and he won the election. His anti-slavery views were well known, and seven southern states – where the majority of Black slaves worked on the cotton plantations – broke away from the United States to form their own Confederacy. Lincoln was determined to hold the United States together, although this led to a Civil War that lasted from 1861 to 1865. The war went badly for the Union at first, but Lincoln stood fast until he found the right generals to turn the tide of battle. It was just after one of the bloodiest battles, at Gettysburg in 1863, that he delivered his famous Address, with the resolve that 'government of the people, by the people and for the people, shall not perish from this earth'. That same year he formally abolished slavery.

With the war almost won, and the Union saved, Lincoln planned to heal his nation's wounds – 'with malice towards none, with charity to all'. He did not have the chance. He was shot dead in his seat at a theatre by a political fanatic named John Wilkes Booth; and the nation's wounds, especially in the devastated southern states, took a very long time to heal.

LINDBERGH, Charles (1902–74)
American aviator

The years between the two world wars were exciting ones for aviation. Alcock and Brown (page 8) first flew non-stop across the Atlantic in 1919. In May 1927 the American Charles Lindbergh made the first solo flight across the same ocean. His aircraft was a single-engined monoplane named *The Spirit of St Louis*, and his flight, from America to an aerodrome near Paris, took just over 33 hours. The English woman Amy Johnson was another glamorous figure of the same period, with her solo flight from England to Australia. Lindbergh made the headlines again a few years later, when his infant son was kidnapped, then tragically killed.

LINNAEUS, Carolus (1707-78)
Swedish scientist

In the 18th century, after the great voyages of discovery had opened up the word, new kinds of plant and animal were being identified all the time. Linnaeus started the enormous task of classifying these thousands of species. The system he used was binomial: he used two Latin names for each plant or animal, one for its genus (or general category), and one for its particular species. This is the form of classification still used in zoology and botany today. While he was such a pioneer in this respect, Linnaeus did not accept any of the new ideas about evolution among plants and animals. He believed that nothing had changed since the creation of the world.

LISTER, Lord Joseph (1827-1912)
English surgeon

By the middle of the last century, serious diseases like smallpox and cholera were beginning to be controlled. Surgery was still a dangerous business, because of the risk of infection from open wounds. Joseph Lister, a surgeon working in Glasgow, learnt of Louis Pasteur's (page 185) research into the causes of putrefaction and decay. This made him realise that germs and bacteria on surgical instruments, on a surgeon's own hands, and in the air itself, could easily set up infection in an exposed wound and perhaps cause the patient's death. His answer was to make hospitals in general, and operating theatres in particular, as clean and germ-free as possible. He also started using carbolic acid on surgical dressings in order to kill harmful germs. Lister was thus a pioneer in the use of antiseptics – agents against septic infection.

LIVINGSTONE, David (1813-73)
Scottish explorer and missionary

Africa in the 19th century was the 'Dark Continent', for the most part still unexplored, mysterious and fascinating. David Livingstone first went there as a doctor and missionary, but was soon drawn to the challenge and thrill of exploration. He made three major expeditions into central and east Africa, discovering such great natural features as Lake Victoria and the Victoria Falls (both named after the British queen), Lake Nyasa and the Zambesi river. He also saw how Black Africans were captured and enslaved by Arab traders, and his reports on the matter helped to stop the slave trade. On his third expedition, Livingstone fell ill, and a newspaper reporter named Henry Morton Stanley went in search of him. The moment of their encounter – the only two White men in hundreds of kilometres of uninhabited jungle – is immortalised by what were reported as Stanley's first words: 'Dr Livingstone, I presume'. Livingstone died in Africa, searching for the source of the river Nile. His native bearers reverently carried his body all the way back to the coast, where it was shipped to England. Stanley became a great explorer of Africa in his own right.

LLOYD GEORGE, David (1863-1945)
British statesman

David Lloyd George did more than anyone else to lay the foundations of the British welfare state. The 'Welsh Wizard', as he was called, trained as a solicitor, then entered Parliament as Liberal MP for Caernarvon in north Wales, the constituency he represented all his life. A Liberal government came to power in 1905 and three years later he was Chancellor of the Exchequer. He introduced old age pensions and the National Insurance Act that provided benefits for the unemployed and the sick. To pay for these reforms and to reduce the power of the very rich, Lloyd George also introduced the 'People's Budget' that put a new super tax on high incomes and a tax on property and land values. The House of Lords, then made up almost entirely of members with inherited titles and wealth, rejected this budget. Consequently the Liberals brought in the Parliament Act to curtail their powers.

When the First World War broke out in 1914, Lloyd George became Minister of Munitions, and in 1916 replaced Herbert Asquith as Prime Minister of a coalition government with the Conservatives. He kept up morale during some of the darkest days of the war; and in the face of opposition, he introduced the convoy system for merchant ships when it looked as though German U-boat sinkings might starve Britain into surrender. With victory won, he represented Britain at the Paris Peace Conference that produced the Treaty of Versailles. In 1922 Lloyd George resigned as prime minister after arguments within his coalition government. He was still an energetic man, a splendid orator, and looked every inch a statesman with his fine head of silver hair. But the 'Welsh Wizard' was never in government again.

LONGFELLOW, Henry Wadsworth (1807–82)
American poet and scholar

Longfellow was one of the most respected and admired literary figures of the 19th century. He was a professor of modern languages at Harvard University, and he wrote poetry that described romantic scenes and events in a straightforward but vivid style that was extremely popular both in his own country and in Victorian Britain. *The Village Blacksmith*, *The Wreck of the Hesperus* and *Hiawatha*, a long, lyrical piece about Red Indian life and culture, were three of the poems that brought him such fame.

LOUIS XIV (1638–1715)
French king

Louis XIV was called 'Le Roi Soleil' – 'The Sun King'. As a young man, fond of dancing, he appeared in a costume representing the sun. In a broader sense this title stood for the splendour of his exceptionally long reign of 72 years – the longest of any European monarch. Louis came to the throne at the age of five, and began to rule personally aged 18. Cardinals Richelieu (page 204) and Mazarin (page 161) had already concentrated power and authority into the hands of the monarch, and Louis used this to become the most illustrious monarchy of his time. He pushed France's frontiers northwards and eastwards to the natural barrier of the river Rhine, and waged war against the rival Hapsburg Empire of Austria and Spain. He was, however, checked in the War of the Spanish Succession of 1702–13 by the Duke of Marlborough (page 55), whose victories over the French helped to maintain the European balance of power.

At home Louis XIV focused attention upon himself with the magnificent Baroque palace he had built at Versailles, near Paris. Part of his intention was to draw France's nobility into such a round of pomp and ceremony that they would have no chance to exercise any authority of their own. Not only the nobility, but the nation's finest artists and architects, and great dramatists like Jean Racine and Molière (page 166), did indeed revolve around Louis at Versailles like planets round the sun. The price for all this glory was a high one. France was made bankrupt, and the almost absolute power of the monarchy left little room for reform. Both these factors led, just over 70 years after Louis XIV's death, to the upheaval and bloodshed of the French Revolution.

LOUIS XVI (1754-93)
French king

Louis XVI was to a large extent the victim of circumstances. His two previous namesakes, Louis XIV and Louis XV, had led extravagant lives, and made the monarchy very unpopular with the mass of the French people. Louis XVI hoped to improve matters. He gave support to the Americans in their War of Independence against Britain, which was sound policy for France. He also wanted to introduce much-needed reforms at home. Unfortunately, he was married to the Austrian princess Marie Antoinette, whose own thoughtless extravagance created even more bitterness and resentment among the French people. In 1789 came the Revolution. Louis and Marie Antoinette were taken from their palace at Versailles and held virtual prisoners in Paris. They made an ill-advised attempt to escape, were caught, and went to the guillotine. There were later attempts to restore the monarchy to France, but none lasted for long.

LUKE (1st century AD)
Christian apostle and saint

Luke was born in a province of what is now a part of Turkey, and accompanied the apostle Paul (page 186) on one of his missionary journeys. He wrote the third of the four gospel accounts of Jesus's (page 132) life in the New Testament of the Bible; also the very substantial Acts of the Apostles. By tradition, Luke is thought to have been a physician, and is the patron saint of doctors and surgeons.

LUTHER, Martin (1483-1546)
German religious leader

Martin Luther was a priest and monk, and a scholar at Wittenberg University in Germany. On a visit to Rome he was depressed by what he saw as the corruption and decadence of religious life there. The sale of indulgences – pardons or remissions for sin – as a way of making money particularly upset him. In 1517, back in Wittenberg, Luther drew up a list of his religious grievances which he defiantly nailed to the door of the castle church. News of this event spread quickly. Luther was commanded by his fellow churchmen to withdraw his complaints. He refused, and was excommunicated by Pope Leo X. Some of the German states supported his action, others remained loyal to the pope. Luther, in danger of his life, was given protection by the Elector, or Prince, of Saxony.

Luther's demands for church reform were the start of the great religious movement called the Reformation. Those who joined him in his protests against the Church of Rome were called Protestants. Luther himself went on to translate the Bible into German, so that ordinary people could hear readings from the scriptures in their own language, instead of scholarly Latin. He also composed hymns, or chorales, with strong but simple tunes, for church congregations to sing together. One other thing he did, in defiance of the Roman Church, was to marry. Luther ended his life quite peacefully, but for the next 200 years the conflict between Protestants and Catholics brought turmoil to large parts of Europe, and a great deal of hatred and violence.

MACARTHUR, Douglas (1880–1964)
American soldier

'I shall return!' declared General MacArthur after the Japanese had swept the Americans from the Philippine Islands in 1942. As senior army commander in the Pacific battle zone during the Second World War, his strategy from then on was to recapture key islands, sea and airports that would disrupt Japanese communications and isolate large pockets of their forces. This 'island hopping' campaign carried him back to the Philippines and on to the final Japanese surrender, which he personally received on board the battleship USS *Missouri* in September 1945. As Supreme Commander of the American occupying forces, MacArthur also became Japan's virtual ruler, removing from the position of Emperor or Mikado the ancient claim to divinity, and setting up modern democratic institutions. In 1950 he returned to the wars, as commander of the United Nations forces in Korea. When Communist China joined in the fighting, he quarrelled with President Truman (page 231) on the issue of bombing mainland China. MacArthur was a glamorous figure and a national hero, but he had finally taken too much upon himself, and Truman dismissed him from his post.

MACHIAVELLI, Niccolo (1469–1527)
Italian writer and statesman

Niccolo Machiavelli lived in Renaissance Italy. It was the time when Leonardo da Vinci (page 147), Michelangelo (page 164) and others were creating some of the world's greatest works of art. It was also the place where men like Cesare Borgia – son of the unscrupulous

Pope Alexander VI – schemed and killed in pursuit of power. This was the side of Italian Renaissance life that appealed to Machiavelli, and he wrote all about the ways and means of gaining and holding power, as he observed them for himself, in a book called *The Prince*. This had a big influence on the actions of many other rulers and power-seekers of the time, and it is still a fascinating document for people interested in political history. Its author has given us the word 'machiavellian' to describe any plan or event noted for its ruthlessness and cunning.

MAGELLAN, Ferdinand (1480–1521)
Portuguese navigator

In September 1519, under the auspices of Charles V of Spain (page 52), Ferdinand Magellan set sail with a small fleet of five ships. The object of the expedition was to find a new route to the Far East by going in a westerly direction. The ships sailed across the Atlantic and down the coast of South America. There was a mutiny, and only three ships entered the cold and stormy waters of what is now the Magellan Strait. After 38 days they emerged into the calmer waters of a great ocean, which Magellan named the Pacific (Peaceful) ocean. With hardly any food or water left, they proceeded westward again across the ocean to the Philippines, where Magellan got involved in a local war and was killed. One more ship then deserted, another was wrecked. The last of the five ships, the *Vittoria*, commanded by Sebastian del Cano, finally got back to Spain in September 1522. It was the first to circumnavigate the globe, so proving beyond all doubt that the world was round.

MANET, Edouard (1832–83)
French artist

Manet started painting in Paris at a time when the city's artistic life was largely in the hands of business men and society ladies who liked paintings of historical scenes and other 'respectable' subjects.

His painting *Déjeuner sur l'herbe* (Lunch on the Grass) was one of those that scandalised Parisian society because of its unconventional subject, showing people having a good time in the open air. With paintings like these, Manet broke away from the stuffy academic world of the art galleries and dealers, and prepared the way for the great period of the Impressionists.

MAO, Tse-tung (1893–1976)
Chinese revolutionary leader and statesman

In 1934 Mao Tse-tung led his followers in an epic march across China. They were communists who had fought a grim civil war with Chiang Kai-shek's (page 54) nationalist army in the south Chinese province of Kiangsi. After three years of fighting Chiang's forces threatened them with annihilation. So with Mao at their head, they set off on a 13,000-kilometre trek across mountain, swamp and desert. They were pursued by the nationalists. Thousands of them perished. But Mao and the survivors reached Shensi province in the country's north-west corner, where they had time to rest and re-group. This heroic Long March was the turning point in the long struggle for control of China between Mao's communists and Chiang's nationalists. Two years later the Japanese invaded China, and from then until the end of the Second World War, Mao and Chiang entered into an uneasy truce. In 1946 they resumed their struggle. Now Mao had the great mass of the peasants behind him, and in 1949 emerged victorious as chairman and leader of the Chinese People's Republic.

Mao faced the gigantic task of trying to bring order and efficiency to the world's most populous nation. He launched what was called the Cultural Revolution, to spread political education among China's teeming millions of peasants. There were internal arguments over policy, also threats from the United States, which still backed Chiang on the island of Taiwan, and quarrels with the Soviet Union, which shared a common frontier with China for thousands of kilometres. Mao gradually retired into the background, becoming almost a cult figure with his celebrated 'Sayings of Chairman

Mao'. Like Stalin (page 220) in the Soviet Union, his leadership then began to be criticised by his own people. But going back to the days of the legendary Long March, it was he who forged China's communist revolution.

MARAT, Jean Paul (1743–93)
French revolutionary leader and journalist

In the French Revolution Marat was a member of the radical Jacobin Party and a colleague of Danton (page 70) and Robespierre (page 206). He published a newspaper called *L'Ami du Peuple* (The People's Friend), calling for a republican dictatorship and death to aristocrats and royalists. He suffered from a bad skin infection and spent much of his time in a medical bath. It was there that he was stabbed to death by a fanatical royalist lady named Charlotte Corday. This incident was commemorated in a famous painting, *The Dead Marat*, by Jacques-Louis David, who was official artist for the revolutionary government and later to Napoleon I (page 172).

MARCONI, Guglielmo (1874–1937)
Italian inventor

When he was just 20 years old, Marconi built the world's first 'wireless' transmitter and receiver – equipment that changed sounds into radio wave signals, picked up the signals and changed them back into sounds. Two years later, in 1896, he was able to transmit and receive wireless radio signals over a distance of three kilometres. Because he could get no backing for his amazing invention in his own country, Marconi went to London, where the British Post Office gave him money to experiment further. By 1898, Marconi was sending and receiving radio signals across the Channel, and in 1901 he had his greatest triumph, when a signal was transmitted and received between Newfoundland in Canada and Cornwall in England. Just after the First World War, he set up the world's first broadcasting company in Chelmsford, England. Marconi was awarded a Nobel Prize for his great pioneer work on today's most widespread means of communication.

MARIA THERESA (1717-80)
Austro-Hungarian empress

Early in Maria Theresa's reign, Frederick the Great of Prussia (page 97) captured from Austria-Hungary the province of Silesia. Her attempts to recover this territory dragged most of the other European nations into two costly wars to do with politics and power: the War of the Austrian Succession and the Seven Years' War. She never did win back Silesia, though she did gain land from Poland by joining in one of the frequent partitions of that country. Maria Theresa was unlucky to have as her opponent such a brilliant military leader as Frederick. This did not diminish her as a ruler. She was a truly regal figure, greatly respected throughout Europe. Her daughter was Marie Antoinette, married to Louis XVI of France (page 152) in order to cement an alliance between France and Austria.

MARK (1st century AD)
Christian apostle and saint

Mark was born in Cyprus, and joined the apostle Paul (page 186) on his first missionary journey. Mark's gospel account of the life and death of Jesus (page 132) is placed second among the four gospels of the New Testament of the Bible; but it was the first to be written.

MARLBOROUGH, Duke of *see* **CHURCHILL, John**

MARY QUEEN OF SCOTS (1542-87)
Scottish queen

Mary Queen of Scots was a tragic figure. She was the Catholic daughter of James V of Scotland and Mary of Guise, and was brought up in France. By the time she returned to Scotland as queen, the country was largely in the hands of the Protestant John Knox (page 140), and there was little she could do about it. Already a stranger in her own land, she married her cousin Lord Darnley, who turned out to be a rake and villain, and who, in a fit of drunken jealousy, strangled her own secretary before her very eyes. Darnley was mysteriously killed in an explosion. Mary then married the Earl of Bothwell, who was then almost immediately suspected of Darnley's own death. In despair, Mary gave up the throne and fled to England, hoping that Elizabeth I (page 88) might befriend her. Elizabeth, though, saw her as a threat. For 18 years the hapless Mary Queen of Scots was kept in prison, the focus of English Catholic plots to put her on the English throne. In the end she herself was charged with plotting treason, and after another agonising delay she finally went to the block after Queen Elizabeth eventually signed her death warrant.

MARX, Karl (1818–83)
German political philosopher and revolutionary

'Workers of the world unite! You have nothing to lose but your chains!' This famous slogan comes from *The Communist Manifesto*, written by Karl Marx and his friend Friedrich Engels. They issued it in 1848, 'The Year of Revolutions', when it looked as though there might really be revolution throughout Europe. This did not happen, but Marx was not dismayed. He moved to London and began to work on *Das Kapital*, his book of political philosophy, in which he argued that the whole of history was a struggle between those who created wealth (the workers) and those who used and exploited it (the capitalists). This situation, he believed, must inevitably lead to world revolution. The first part of *Das Kapital* appeared in 1867, and two more volumes, edited by Engels, were published after Marx's death. His thinking and beliefs – Marxism – became the basis for international communism. They inspired the Russian Bolshevik Revolution of 1917 and still have great influence in the world.

MATTHEW (1st century AD)
Christian apostle and saint

Not much is known for certain about Matthew. He was a tax collector, one of the original 12 apostles of Jesus (page 132), and may have been martyred about 15 years after Jesus's own death. Scholars are not even sure whether he is the author of the whole, or only part of the gospel which is placed first among the four gospel accounts in the New Testament of the Bible. Whatever the truth of the matter, Matthew's Gospel is the most popular and most often quoted of the four, because it, in turn, quotes most extensively from Jesus's own sayings and parables.

MAUPASSANT, Guy de (1850-93)
French novelist

Guy de Maupassant wrote several full-length novels, but is best remembered as the author of over 300 short stories or 'contes' (tales). One of these, *Boule de Suif*, made him famous, and many others are regarded as masterpieces of the short-story form. They are, for the most part, realistic, unsentimental stories, often set in Maupassant's own region of Normandy. Towards the end of his life, Maupassant fell ill. He began to suffer from hallucinations, and some of his last stories are filled with strange and macabre images and ideas.

MAZARIN, Jules (1602-61)
French statesman

Mazarin was Italian by birth. He went to France as a diplomat of the pope, and entered the service of Cardinal Richelieu (page 204). He modelled his own career almost exactly on that of Richelieu (page 204), becoming a cardinal and then French chief minister of state. Mazarin served Louis XIV (page 151), and continued Richelieu's policy of concentrating power and authority in the person and office of the sovereign. Louis XIV became the most powerful and illustrious of monarchs, and Mazarin had much to do with it. Mazarin was a skilled negotiator and was responsible for gaining France much new territory at the Peace of Westphalia at the end of the Thirty Years War.

McADAM, John Loudon (1756–1836)
Scottish engineer

Two thousand years ago the Romans built good roads of rock and stone throughout their empire. But when their empire broke up, their roads broke up too. Right up to the end of the 18th century, most roads in Europe and America were little better than tracks, turned either to mud or dust and full of bumps and pot holes. John McAdam was one of the first to improve the situation. He started to repair roads with a foundation of large stones, then a layer of stone chippings which would be crushed into an ever more strong and compact mass by the passage of cart and coach wheels. He also took into account a curve or camber across the surface, to allow for drainage. By the end of the 19th century, many roads in Europe and America were built to his specifications. Modern road construction still uses such terms as 'macadamise' and 'tar macadam'.

MELVILLE, Herman (1819–91)
American novelist

Herman Melville wrote two outstanding novels about the sea and ships, based on his own experiences as a sailor. *Moby Dick* is the story of a whaler captain's obsession with the hunt for a huge white whale – Moby Dick. The book vividly describes what whaling was like in the days of sail, and is also full of strange and mystical thoughts about man and the elements. Melville's other famous novel, *Billy Budd*, is a grim but gripping story about the British navy in Nelson's time, which Benjamin Britten (page 37) turned into one of his finest operas.

MENDELSSOHN, Felix (1809–47)
German composer and conductor

His full name was Felix Mendelssohn-Bartholdy, and he was just as amazing a child prodigy as Mozart (page 170). He had far more success than Mozart when he grew up, moving in the highest social circles and counting Queen Victoria (page 239) and Prince Albert among his admirers. Mendelssohn composed symphonies, concertos, and many piano pieces called *Songs Without Words*, all in a tuneful, tasteful style that pleased his society audiences. He also wrote, at the age of 17, an overture to Shakespeare's play *A Midsummer Night's Dream* that is one of the loveliest pieces of Romantic descriptive music; and the equally descriptive *Hebrides* or 'Fingal's Cave' overture, inspired by a visit to the Western Isles of Scotland. Mendelssohn's work as a conductor – one of the first true conductors in the modern sense of the word – helped to spread his fame. He, in turn, brought to people's attention some of the long-forgotten music of J. S. Bach (page 19).

METTERNICH, Clemens (1773–1859)
Austrian statesman

In 1815, after the final defeat of Napoleon I (page 172) at the battle of Waterloo, ministers and emperors of the leading nations of Europe met at the Congress of Vienna. Their object was to re-shape the political map of their continent, parcelling out the territories in a way that satisfied them all. The dominating figure at the Congress was Austria's foreign minister Clemens Metternich. His rather reactionary policy was to keep government in the hands of Europe's monarchs and their advisers, and convene other conferences when desired, to adjust frontiers and maintain an acceptable balance of power and influence among them. Metternich was driven from office by the rising tide of social and industrial unrest that led to the uprisings of 1848 – 'The Year of Revolutions'. But his basic plan for diplomacy did keep the peace among the leading European states for the rest of the 19th century.

MICHELANGELO, Buonarroti (1475-1564)
Italian artist and architect

Like so many great artists of the Renaissance, Michelangelo grew up in Florence. He considered himself first and foremost as a sculptor. One of his early masterpieces is his six-metre high statue of David, carved from a single, very difficult lump of rock. Another is his *Pietà*, a representation of Mary holding the dead body of Christ. He also designed, with all its sculpted figures, a chapel for the Medici family of Florence – the most celebrated of all patrons of the arts in Renaissance Italy. Then for 40 years, on and off, he worked on the design for a monumental tomb for Pope Julius II, though this project was never completed. His seated figure of Moses is one of the pieces of sculpture intended for it. Julius, meanwhile, had asked Michelangelo to paint the ceiling of the Sistine Chapel in the Vatican, Rome. Scaffolding was erected, and the artist lay uncomfortably on his back over a period of four years, while he painted a series of scenes from the Book of Genesis in the Old Testament of the Bible, depicting with tremendous power the Creation, the Fall of Man and the Flood. Many years later, he was commissioned to paint the Chapel's altar wall, which he filled with a stupendous vision of the Last Judgment, with the damned being cast into hell. Still in Rome, Michelangelo took over the planning and building of the new basilica of St Peter's, which had been started by the architect Donato Bramante. Michelangelo's crowning achievement was the huge dome, one of the most ambitious and brilliant conceptions in the whole of architecture.

MILTON, John (1608-74)
English poet

John Milton was a scholar of Greek, Latin and Hebrew, and a Puritan who supported Oliver Cromwell (page 66) and Parliament in the Civil War and afterwards. When the monarchy was restored in 1660 Milton was in disgrace and retired from public life. He also went blind, but continued dictating poetry to his faithful daughters.

This poetry is some of the noblest in the English language. Milton had a wonderful feeling for the rhythm and flow of words, giving his poetry a lofty and majestic sound. He was mostly inspired by grand and lofty subjects as well, notably in his two long epics about Man's relationship with God, *Paradise Lost* and *Paradise Regained*. Some of his shorter poems, such as *L'Allegro* and *Il Penseroso*, despite their learned foreign titles, are lighter in style and spirit. He also wrote the Classical drama *Samson Agonostes* and prose pamphlets on censorship.

MOHAMMED (about AD 570-632)
Arabian religious leader

Mohammed founded the religion of Islam. He was born in the Arabian city of Mecca, became a merchant, and married. Then he began to ponder upon religious matters and came to believe that instead of many gods there was only one divine force in the universe, one God, whom he called Allah. He claimed also that he was visited by the angel Gabriel, who commanded him to be Allah's prophet on earth, warning of damnation for those who would not believe, and promising salvation for Muslims – 'Submissive Ones' who accepted the word of Allah through his Prophet Mohammed. Arabia was a barren, hard and brutal land, and Mohammed needed courage to start preaching his new faith. He and his early followers were frequently stoned and beaten, and in AD 622 Mohammed had to flee from Mecca to the neighbouring town of Medina – an event called the 'Hegira', which marks the beginning of the Islamic era. Gradually, though, Mohammed's message was accepted, and his sayings recorded in a holy book called the Koran.

By the time of Mohammed's death, the tribes of Arabia were united in the new faith of Islam. In the centuries to come the Islamic faith itself and the civilisation that grew up with it – rich in both the arts and sciences – spread from Spain and North Africa right across the Middle East to India, and into a large part of eastern Europe. Today there are about 500 million Muslims in various parts of the world.

MOLIÈRE (1622-73)
French dramatist

Molière was the pen name of Jean-Baptiste Poquelin, and he wrote some of the finest comedies in the French language. They are mostly satires, poking fun at hypocrites and people who pretend to be what they are not. *Tartuffe, Le Misanthrope, Le Bourgeois Gentilhomme, L'Avare* (The Miser) and *Le Malade Imaginaire* are his best-loved plays. They got him into a good deal of trouble from the people and institutions he satirised, including the Church, and some of them were banned at the time. Molière was, nevertheless, a most successful man, and received a royal pension from Louis XIV (page 151). Like Shakespeare (page 216), he was an actor as well as playwright, and the company he performed with later became the world-famous *Comédie Française*. He died while playing the title role in *Le Malade Imaginaire* (The Hypochondriac).

MONET, Claude (1840-1926)
French artist

In 1874 Monet exhibited a painting entitled *Impression: Sunrise*. He thus came to give a name to the whole Impressionist movement in painting – though 'Impressionism' was at first used as a term of abuse by those who disliked such paintings. Monet himself developed the Impressionist style more than any other artist. He worked almost entirely out of doors, and was concerned with analysing and capturing the subtlest effects of colour, light and shade as they changed with the weather, or the time of day – he painted the same scene of Rouen cathedral at different hours to illustrate this point. Monet was especially fascinated by effects of mist and vapour. He painted several pictures of London and the river Thames wrapped in fog, and another of the St Lazare railway station in Paris filled with smoke and steam. Towards the end of his life Monet began to go blind, but by then he could almost sense colours as abstract patterns, as he did in a marvellous series of paintings of water lilies in a pond.

MONTEVERDI, Claudio (1567-1643)
Italian composer

Monteverdi was for many years director of music at St Mark's basilica in Venice. The building was noted for its special sound qualities, and Monteverdi wrote music to be performed by groups of voices that answered each other across its lofty, dark interior in a very dramatic way. The technical word for this kind of music is 'antiphonal', meaning 'sounding across'. Monteverdi wrote equally dramatic and arresting music for the theatre. He was the first important composer of operas, transforming opera from a fairly slight entertainment among Italian noblemen and scholars into a tremendously exciting new art form. Apart from the music he wrote for the actual singers, he used instruments to add 'colour' and drama in a way that nobody had dreamed of before. With his own strong, passionate music, Monteverdi forged the link between the Renaissance and Baroque periods in music. His most famous operas are *L'Orfeo. Il Ballo del Ingrate* and *L'Incoronazione di Poppeo* which are still performed today.

MONTFORT, Simon de (about 1208-65)
French soldier and ruler

Though he carried the title of Earl of Leicester, Simon de Montfort was a Norman French knight. He first served the English King Henry III, then led the English barons in a revolt against him. Simon won a big victory at Lewes in 1264, and in the following year tried to establish himself as ruler by summoning a form of parliament (the word comes from the French meaning 'to speak' or 'debate'), with representatives from the English towns and shires. Simon de Montfort's parliament is seen as a landmark in the long history of parliamentary democracy. It did not, however, succeed very long for him. Henry's son Edward raised a new army which defeated Simon at the battle of Evesham. He was killed in the fighting and his body was hacked to pieces and distributed round the kingdom as a warning against any further trouble.

MONTGOMERY, Bernard Law, Viscount (1887-1976)
British soldier

Field-Marshal Montgomery was Britain's most successful army commander of the Second World War. In October 1942 he launched a well-prepared attack against the German and Italian armies at El Alamein in Egypt, which smashed through their lines and forced them into a retreat all the way back to Tunisia. El Alamein was the first decisive British victory of the war, and it made 'Monty' into a hero. In 1944 he commanded the British and Commonwealth forces that landed on the Normandy coast of France (D-Day). He took the main weight of the German counter-attacks close to the beaches, allowing the Americans to advance rapidly inland, then led the left-hand flank of the Allied advance across France and into Belgium. Montgomery had an argument with the Supreme Allied Commander General Eisenhower (page 86) about strategy. Montgomery wanted to concentrate all the Allied forces for a single thrust into north Germany. Eisenhower stuck to his plan for a broad advance on all fronts. Late in 1944 there were Allied setbacks, when the British airborne attack on Arnhem in Holland failed, and when the Germans launched a surprise winter attack through the Ardennes ('The Battle of the Bulge'). But in May 1945 it was Montgomery who received the final surrender of the bulk of the German armed forces in the West.

MORRIS, William (1834-96)
English artist

William Morris belonged to an interesting British movement of the 19th century called the Pre-Raphaelite Brotherhood. They reacted against what they saw as the soul-destroying ugliness of the Industrial Revolution, and in poetry and painting tried to create an ideal world of beauty based on the chivalry and art of the Middle Ages. Morris held strong political beliefs as well, seeing capitalism as the evil thing that made people crowd together in factories and smoky towns and cities. He wanted people to go back to the land

and make the best use of their own labours and skills, and set an example with his own work in the fields of arts and crafts. Morris's dream of a better world never came about, but his designs of such things as furniture and fabrics were brilliant, and they have continued to influence domestic design right up to the present day.

MORSE, Samuel (1791-1872)
American inventor

Samuel Morse started out as a successful artist and portrait painter. He then became interested in electricity and magnetism, and devised a very early form of electric telegraph. Morse's unique contribution to telegraphy was his invention of a signal code consisting of combinations of short and long impulses – dots and dashes – for each letter of the alphabet and for numbers. In 1844 he sent his first coded message from Baltimore to Washington, and his Morse Code was soon being used all over the world. Its most famous signal is the international distress call SOS, made up of three dots, three dashes, three dots. Another Morse Code signal, made famous in the Second World War, is the V for Victory call of three dots and a dash.

MOSES (13th century BC)
Hebrew leader

When Moses was born the Hebrews or Israelites were held captive in Egypt. The Book of Exodus in the Old Testament of the Bible tells how the infant Moses was hidden among bullrushes, found by pharaoh's daugher and brought up by her. In about 1280 BC, he led the Israelites out of captivity. According to the Bible, he parted the waters of the Red Sea for himself and his people, which then closed in again upon the pursuing Egyptians. The most significant part of Moses's life was to do with the Ten Commandments. The Bible says he received these from God on Mount Sinai. They formed the basis of Hebrew law and were taken over by Christianity. Their force and influence is still felt throughout the world.

MOZART, Wolfgang Amadeus (1756-91)
Austrian composer

Wolfgang Amadeus Mozart was the most famous child prodigy in music. As a little boy of six years he was writing simple pieces, and was shown off to kings and queens all over Europe, including London, by his father Leopold. When he grew up he was employed by the archbishop in his home town of Salzburg, and after a quarrel with his employer went with his wife Constanza to seek his fortune in Vienna. He did find work, and some of his operas were a big success. Haydn (page 117), who was already famous, praised Mozart highly. But neither he nor Constanza could manage their affairs, things went wrong for him, and when he died his body was thrown into a pauper's grave.

Mozart composed music in every form and style of his time: masses and other choral and vocal pieces for the Church; serenades and sets of dances for fashionable events; symphonies, concertos and sonatas in the new Classical style for special concerts. Above all, he was a composer of operas. He worked well with a librettist named Lorenzo da Ponte, and the music he wrote for their operas *The Marriage of Figaro* and *Don Giovanni* was far more dramatic and expressive than any previously heard. These were composed in the Italian 'opera buffa' or 'comic opera' style of the period. Another of his operas, *The Magic Flute*, was composed in the quite different, German-Viennese style of 'Singspiel', which was a kind of pantomime with music. The drama and deeply expressive beauty of the music in these operas found their way into the finest of Mozart's symphonies, piano concertos, string quartets and other instrumental works. Among these are the last three symphonies, nos 39, 40 and 41 (nicknamed 'Jupiter'). The way he combined in them music that is both perfect in form and style and so rich and passionate in sound, makes him one of the very greatest composers. Mozart's compositions are often quoted with their 'K' number, after Ludwig Köchel, a scholar who listed them in their probable order of composition. The last work listed is the unfinished Requiem Mass, K626. His works were catalogued by Ludwig Köchel, which is why the numbers are prefixed with a K- for Köchel.

MUSSOLINI, Benito (1883–1945)
Italian political and military leader

Mussolini was the son of a blacksmith; a tough, stocky man with a large head and chin that he liked to thrust out in an attitude of pride and defiance. He was first a teacher, then the editor of a socialist newspaper. When Italy entered the First World War on the Allied side, he joined the army and was wounded. Soon after, he changed his politics. He formed a new party called the Fascists, taking its name from the Old Imperial Roman symbol of authority – an axe surrounded by a bundle of sticks, or 'fascis'. He saw himself as a new kind of caesar, destined to restore to Italy past glories. Mussolini was backed by many businessmen, who were frightened by the wave of strikes and the riots then rocking the country, and by the threat of a communist take-over. In 1922 he and his uniformed 'Blackshirts' organised a so-called March on Rome. The existing government collapsed, and Mussolini came to power. He kept the monarchy, but stamped out political opposition, called himself 'Il Duce' (The Leader) and became dictator.

'Mussolini is always right' was one of his propaganda slogans, and he did make some improvements at home with slum clearance and public building programmes. With parades and bombastic speeches he also persuaded the people they needed a strong army and an empire. In 1935 he conquered the almost defenceless African kingdom of Ethiopia (Abyssinia). Soon after he joined Hitler (page 122) in sending arms to support the right-wing General Franco (page 96) in the Spanish Civil War, and formed an alliance with the German dictator known as the Pact of Steel, or the Axis. Still hoping for easy victories, in 1940 Mussolini brought Italy into the Second World War on Germany's side. He had made a fatal mistake. His armies were beaten by the British in North Africa, and by the Greeks, and he had to call on German aid. In 1943 the Allies invaded Sicily and Mussolini, once so proud and boastful, was deposed. Hitler arranged for him to be rescued from internment and set him up as head of a puppet regime called the Salò Republic. But Mussolini was doomed. Early in 1945 he and his mistress Clara Petacci were captured by communist partisans and shot.

N

NANSEN, Fridtjof (1861-1930)
Norwegian explorer

Nansen was the first man to cross the icy wastes of Greenland, then conceived a most original and daring plan for reaching the North Pole. His idea was deliberately to sail into the pack ice of the polar seas and be carried along by its natural flow closer and closer to the pole. To this end Nansen built a specially constructed ship called the *Fram*, and in 1893 sailed back into the frozen north. For 16 months Nansen and his brave crew drifted with the ice, until they were only 420 kilometres from their objective. Nansen tried to cover the final stretch by dog sledge, but had to give up. It was, nonetheless, a brilliant and courageous venture. Later in life, Nansen turned to public affairs. He organised food supplies to famine-stricken Russia at the time of the civil war, and worked for the League of Nations. For these deeds he was awarded the Nobel Peace Prize.

NAPOLEON I (1769-1821)
French soldier and emperor

The image of Napoleon as a fat little man with a chubby face, holding one hand inside his waistcoat, is one of the most popular in history. As a young man, though, he was quite thin, with sharp features and a swarthy complexion. He was born in Corsica, and the family name of Bonaparte is more Italian than French – a reminder that the island belonged to Italy for most of its past. Napoleon Bonaparte went to military school, and at 16 years was already an officer. He rose to fame in the years following the Revolution, when France was under attack. One of his first successes was to break a

British naval blockade of Toulon. Soon he was commanding victorious French armies in Italy and Egypt. Admiral Nelson (page 176) destroyed his fleet at Aboukir Bay near Alexandria, but back in France he quickly strengthened his position, becoming First Consul in a new form of government. In 1804 he proclaimed himself Emperor of the French.

Napoleon's domestic reforms – the 'Code Napoleon' – made France the best governed country in the world. Abroad, he extended French control over much of continental Europe, with sweeping victories at Marengo, Ulm, Austerlitz, Jena, Friedland and Wagram. Only at sea, where Nelson won other victories, and in Spain, where Wellington (page 245) harassed his army (the Peninsular War) was he denied complete success. Then in 1812, Napoleon invaded Russia on the grounds that Tsar Alexander had broken an earlier treaty. He won the bloody battle of Borodino, but arrived in Moscow to find the city deserted and in flames. He withdrew his 'Grande Armée'), which then suffered dreadfully in the winter retreat. An allied army then defeated him at Leipzig (the Battle of the Nations), after which he was exiled to the Mediterranean island of Elba.

Napoleon was not finished yet. In 1815 he returned to France and began the period known as The Hundred Days. He quickly gathered support, formed a new army and advanced to meet Wellington's forces at Waterloo near Brussels. This stupendous clash of arms hung in the balance for many hours before Napoleon finally accepted defeat. He died in exile but now lies in state in Paris.

NAPOLEON III (1808-73)
French emperor

Louis Napoleon Bonaparte was a nephew of Napoleon I, and dreamed of becoming as powerful as his uncle. He was involved in various plots to gain power, which had him exiled from France. When he tried to return, to stir up revolution, he fell into the sea at Boulogne and was promptly re-arrested, which made him something of a laughing-stock. Nevertheless, he was a determined man, and his chance came in 1848–'The Year of Revolutions' – with the downfall of the French King Louis Philippe. A new republic was proclaimed, Louis Napoleon stood in the election for president and won. Three years later he carried out a successful 'coup d'état', or seizure of power, and, had himself made Emperor of France.

Napoleon III brought fresh power and prestige to France with the way he handled his country's part in the Crimean War, and for the support he gave to Cavour (page 48) in Italy. At home, new industries made France prosperous, while Paris gained many splendid new buildings and boulevards. This was the period known as the Second Empire. It came to an abrupt end in 1870 when Bismarck (page 28), as part of his strategy for uniting Germany, provoked the Franco-Prussian War. The French were badly beaten at Sedan and Napoleon himself was taken prisoner, leaving behind a grim siege of Paris and another revolution. He ended his days in exile in England.

NASSER, Gamal Abdul (1918–70)
Egyptian soldier and statesman

Gamal Abdul Nasser worked to make his country independent after years of foreign interference, and became a key figure in world affairs. He first claimed attention as one of the group of army officers who deposed King Farouk in 1952. The leader of the group, General Mohammed Neguib, became prime minister of the new Egyptian Republic, but two years later Nasser succeeded him, first as prime minister and then as president. Nasser created the United Arab Republic, as a hoped-for move towards full Arab unity in the Middle East, and started such ambitious schemes as the Aswan dam across the river Nile to give Egypt more agriculture and industry. In 1956 he nationalised the Suez Canal, which provoked an attack on Egypt by Britain and France. Both the United States and the Soviet Union condemned the action, and the British and French forces were soon withdrawn. Thus in a few years Nasser had made Egypt a focal point in world politics. As a result of the Suez Crisis he had also brought about the downfall of the British prime minister, Anthony Eden. In 1967 Israel defeated Egypt, Syria and Jordan in the so-called Six-Day War, and took territory from Egypt. Nasser resigned soon after. He is, nevertheless remembered as an outstanding leader of the Arab World.

NEBUCHADNEZZAR II (about 605-562 BC)
Babylonian king

Babylonia in the Middle East was one of the mightiest nations of the ancient world, and King Nebuchadnezzar was its most famous ruler. He was a conqueror, and in about 587 BC captured the city of Jerusalem, destroyed the Temple and took the Jews into captivity. This event is described in the Old Testament of the Bible, where Nebuchadnezzar is portrayed as a tyrant. He was, at the same time, a great builder. He gave the city of Babylon by the river Euphrates a magnificent palace, which included a terraced garden overflowing with trees and flowers – the Hanging Gardens of Babylon one of the Seven Wonders of the Ancient World.

NEHRU, Pandit Jawalharlal (1889-1964)
Indian statesman

Pandit Nehru was educated in England, but was an early opponent of British rule in India. He joined Mahatma Gandhi's (page 101) non-violent campaign for Indian independence, and was president of the Indian National Congress, which was like an Indian government in the making. Like Gandhi he went to prison for his activities. During the Second World War, though, Nehru supported Britain, and soon afterwards worked closely with Lord Louis Mountbatten, whose job as Viceroy of India was to arrange the country's long-awaited independence. One of the tasks they tackled together was the division of old British India into the separate states of India and Pakistan. From 1947 until his death, Nehru was India's prime minister, facing the problem of bringing more industry and more efficient agriculture to a country of hundreds of millions of poor peasants. He kept India in the British Commonwealth, but became a leader of the so-called Third World nations that took a neutral stand in international affairs. His daughter, Mrs Indira Gandhi, became prime minister in 1966.

NELSON, Horatio, Lord (1758-1805)
English sailor

Admiral Horatio Nelson was a slight and quite delicate man. Yet he went to sea at the age of 12, at a time when life in the British navy was tough and brutal, lost an eye and most of his right arm in battle, and became his country's greatest naval hero. He also had a love affair with Emma, Lady Hamilton, which caused a scandal, since both of them were married already.

Nelson fought four major battles during the Napoleonic Wars. The first, in 1797, was the battle of Cape St Vincent off the coast of Portugal, where his own ship engaged six Spanish ships, one after the other. The following year he pursued a French fleet to Egypt and sunk most of it at anchor in a night attack at Aboukir Bay near the mouth of the river Nile. In 1801 he joined in the attack that sunk a large Danish fleet at Copenhagen that was preparing to take reinforcements to France. Finally, on 21 October 1805, in his flagship *Victory*, Nelson engaged and put to flight the combined French and Spanish fleets off Cape Trafalgar near Cadiz. His celebrated signal to his fleet before the battle was 'England expects that every man will do his duty.' Early in the fighting he was mortally wounded and died below decks, where his last words were reported to be, 'Thank God, I have done my duty'. Nelson's great victories could not prevent any of Napoleon's (page 172) conquests in Europe, but they kept control of the seas firmly in British hands, which hampered Napoleon and helped to defeat him in the end.

NERO (AD 37-68)
Roman emperor

Popular legend says that Nero fiddled while Rome burned. He did play the lyre and liked acting, and during his reign there was a disastrous fire in the Imperial capital. The importance of this fire was that Nero blamed it on the Christians, and to a large extent started the long period of Christian persecution within the Roman Empire. He also raised heavy taxes to pay for the damage. These taxes, plus the fact that he was already hated as a cruel and callous tyrant who had murdered both his mother and his wife, provoked uprisings in many parts of the empire. The Roman senate passed the death sentence upon him, but he fled from Rome and committed suicide.

NEWCOMEN, Thomas (1663-1729)
English engineer

Thomas Newcomen went into partnership with Thomas Savery to build large water pumps driven by steam. Savery had already made steam engines to pump water out of flooded mines. Newcomen's design, dating from 1712, was far more powerful. It was an 'atmospheric' engine. Steam raised the piston in a cylinder. The steam was then condensed, so creating a partial vacuum, which drew the piston down again. Newcomen's engine was large and cumbersome, but several of them were built, and went on working for a hundred years or more. Meanwhile, no real improvement in steam engine design took place until the time of James Watt (page 244) over 50 years later.

NEWTON, Sir Isaac (1642-1727)
English scientist and mathematician

In 1687 Isaac Newton published his book *Philosophiae Naturalis Principia Mathematica*. It has been called 'the greatest single work of science in the world', and it presented ideas and calculations that Newton had been working on since he was a student at Cambridge university. Much of his most important thinking, in fact, was done when he was 23, staying at home during an outbreak of plague.

Newton's most celebrated and far-reaching work was in connection with his laws of motion and gravity. With these he was able to explain the movement of the planets and other heavenly bodies already observed by Galileo (page 100), Kepler (page 138), and others; and he corresponded with the first British Astronomer Royal John Flamsteed on the subject. His laws on gravitation also enabled him to explain such phenomena as the Moon's effect on the tides. Newton was equally interested in optics – the science of light and its properties. He built the first reflecting telescope, which was a big advance on any telescope made up to that time; and with the aid of prisms he demonstrated that sunlight is composed of a whole spectrum of colours, as seen in a rainbow. The mathematical 'language' that Newton needed to express his thoughts and discoveries led him to develop the two forms of calculus, called the differential and the integral calculus. Whether he actually invented this branch of mathematics is not certain. His close contemporary, the German philosopher and mathematician Gottfried Leibnitz also claimed the distinction, and the two men argued about it.

NICHOLAS II (1868–1918)
Russian tsar

Nicholas II, a cousin cousin of the British King George V, was the last of the tsars. The Russian Empire he inherited lagged far behind most other European nations in its government and administration, industry and agriculture. Nicholas resisted any real changes, despite the fact that a disastrous war against Japan in 1904 showed what a poor state the country was in. He survived an uprising in 1905, and in 1914 led Russia into the First World War. The Tsarina Alexandra, meanwhile, had fallen under the influence of a very sinister and corrupt priest named Rasputin, which made a bad situation worse. With defeats and mutinies in the army and navy, and with strikes and riots in the cities, Nicholas abdicated in 1917. In October of that year came the Bolshevik Revolution. Nicholas and his family were arrested, kept under guard for several months, then shot although a few historians believe that one of his daughters escaped.

NIETZSCHE, Friedrich (1844–1900)
German philosopher

Nietzsche held strong opinions about the way people should look at themselves and act. He believed that the most valuable life-force in men and women was the will towards personal power and self-fulfilment – a force which he called 'Übermensch', meaning 'Overman' or 'Superman'. The greatest need and duty of the individual was to 'sublimate' his passions and urges; that is, channel them towards the highest purposes. Nietzsche attacked Christianity and other religions because he said they excused weakness and failure. His most famous work, *Also Sprach Zarathustra* (Thus Spoke Zarathustra), has been praised as a great piece of literature as well as philosophy; and his ideas have had a deep influence on many 20th-century writers and thinkers. Hitler (page 122) exploited some of Nietzsche's ideas to try and justify his own policies.

NIGHTINGALE, Florence (1820–1910)
English reformer

Florence Nightingale came from a wealthy family, who strongly opposed her wish to take up nursing, which at that time was regarded as a very humble, almost disreputable job. She became a nurse, nonetheless, and during the Crimean War (1854–56) went with a small group of other nurses to tend the wounded. On arrival, Florence soon realised that as many men were dying from infection and disease as from their actual wounds, because of the insanitary conditions. Consequently she set up a hospital at Scutari by the Bosporus which was well organised and clean. It was there that her tireless supervision and inspections of the wards earned her the name of 'The Lady with the Lamp'. She herself almost died of a fever, but returned to England a heroine, and spent the rest of her life founding nursing schools and making nursing one of the most important and respected of professions. Among the training establishments she founded was the nurses training unit at St Thomas's Hospital in London.

NKRUMAH, Kwame (1909–72)
Black African statesman

Kwame Nkrumah led the way among Black African leaders who took over from British colonial rule after the Second World War. His homeland was the old territory of the Gold Coast in West Africa. He founded the Convention People's Party, which campaigned for independence, went to prison for his political activities, then in 1957 was elected prime minister of the newly created state of Ghana. Three years later he became his country's president. Nkrumah was one of the most respected of the first generation of Black African leaders, until people began to accuse him of personal extravagance and to criticise his lavish public spending. In 1966 he went on a visit to China. He was deposed in his absence and not allowed to return home. He accepted refuge in the nearby West African state of Guinea, where he died.

NOBEL, Alfred (1833–96)
Swedish inventor and philanthropist

Alfred Nobel was an explosives expert. He invented dynamite, which was a much safer form of the highly dangerous nitroglycerine, and cordite. Nobel made a fortune from these inventions, and with his money set up a foundation to award prizes to men and women working in the fields of chemistry, physics, medicine and literature, and working also for the cause of world peace. The first Nobel prizes were given in 1901, and they are now among the most coveted honours in the world.

O

OFFENBACH, Jacques (1819-80)
German composer

Offenbach was born in Germany (his real name was Jakob Wiener), but he spent nearly the whole of his life in Paris. He specialised in writing light operas, or operettas – a type of stage entertainment that helped to shape the American stage and film musical of the 20th century. Offenbach's operettas were high-spirited and full of sparkling music, while also satirising Parisian society. Most famous of them is *Orpheus in the Underworld*. This includes the celebrated can-can dance that became almost a signature tune for what people thought of as the 'naughty' night life of Paris in the 1880s and 1890s – or the 'naughty nineties' as they were called. Despite his enormous popularity, Offenbach had a hard time during the Franco-Prussian War of 1870-1, because he was German by birth. For many years he also wanted to write a more serious opera, and died desperately trying to finish *The Tales of Hoffmann*.

OHM, Georg (1789-1854)
German scientist

Around the year 1800 Hans Christian Oersted in Denmark, André Marie Ampère in France, Volta (page 240) in Italy and Georg Ohm in Germany all made important discoveries about electricity. Ohm investigated the conditions and effects of an electric current flowing through a wire, and formulated the law relating electrical pressure (volts) and strength (amps) to resistance. Ohm's Law is one of the foundations of electrical science. The unit for measuring resistance is also named after him.

O'NEILL, Eugene (1888–1953)
American dramatist

Eugene O'Neill did a great deal to create an American style or type of drama. He wrote with a down-to-earth realism, mainly about American family problems and situations. *Desire under the Elms, Mourning Becomes Electra, The Iceman Cometh* and *A Long Day's Journey into Night* are four of his best-known plays. O'Neill also gave much practical help to American theatre, by working closely with theatrical companies.

OWEN, Robert (1771–1858)
British social reformer

Robert Owen from Wales has been called 'the father of British socialism'. After proving his success as a factory manager in Manchester, in 1799 he took over the running of a group of mills at New Lanark in Scotland. Owen was humane as well as a good businessman. He was distressed by factory conditions in those early days of the Industrial Revolution, and also reckoned that decently treated workers would do better work. He cut the working day in his mills from 14 or 15 hours to around ten, built pleasant homes for his employees, shops where they could buy food and clothing at fair prices, and a school for their children. Owen's new model industrial community at New Lanark attracted much attention. He also wrote a book, *A New View of Society*, started a trades union and a profit-sharing co-operative movement, and by his example helped to get industrial reforms made law. Among his admirers was the English political philosopher Jeremy Bentham, who argued that the aim of society should be to create the greatest good for greatest number.

P

PADEREWSKI, Ignacy (1860–1941)
Polish pianist and statesman

With Franz Liszt of Hungary as their model, a whole succession of pianists in the late 19th and early 20th centuries became the super stars of the musical world. In the days before radio and television they were legendary figures, whom people flocked to see wherever they were billed to appear. Most sensational of all was Paderewski. With his great mop of hair and pounding fingers, he was treated like an idol. Songs were written about him, cartoons drawn of him; everybody talked about Paderewski. Indeed, so internationally famous did he become that his fellow countrymen chose him to be their prime minister when the modern Polish state was created in 1919. He did not remain prime minister for long, but right at the end of his life he returned briefly to politics as speaker of the exiled Polish parliament after the German attack on Poland in 1939.

PAINE, Thomas (1737–1809)
English revolutionary politician

Thomas Paine is regarded by some people as a traitor, and by others as a hero. He emigrated to the American colonies just before the War of Independence started in 1775, fought with the American rebels in the war and was afterwards a member of their Continental Congress. He then returned to England, just before the outbreak of the French Revolution in 1789; wrote a famous treatise called *The Rights of Man*, in which he proposed the abolition of the British monarchy and a republican form of government; and went to France to fight for the Revolution. Outlawed by his own country, he finally went back to the new United States of America to live out his days.

PANKHURST, Emmeline (1858–1928)
English social and political reformer

'Votes for women!' was the passionate cry of the Suffragettes – the name given to the movement campaigning for women's suffrage, or the right to vote. Its leader was Mrs Emmeline Pankhurst. She started her long campaign with her husband's support in 1889. When he died, Mrs Pankhurst and her two daughters, Sylvia and Christabel, carried on. In 1903 they founded the Women's Social and Political Union, and when peaceful activities got them nowhere, they and their followers took to more desperate measures, smashing windows, chaining themselves to public buildings, in order to attract attention to their cause. One of them, Emily Davison, threw herself under the king's horse at a race meeting and was killed. The Suffragettes were manhandled, sent to prison, and forcibly fed by brutal means when they went on strike. During the First World War Mrs Pankhurst called off the campaign, while thousands of women went to work in factories, or on trains and buses. It was their war work that really changed things in their favour, and in 1918 women over 30 years got the vote. Mrs Pankhurst was not satisfied, and went on campaigning for women to have the vote at 21. This was granted in 1928.

PARNELL, Charles Stuart (1846–91)
British social and political reformer

In the long, troubled history of Ireland one of the biggest names was that of Charles Stuart Parnell. He was not an Irishman, but his English father owned land in Ireland. Parnell was soon convinced that the only salvation for Ireland was home rule. He became an MP and spoke up for home rule in parliament. He also founded the Irish Land League, encouraging Irish peasants to boycott, or refuse to work for English landowners – the word 'boycott' comes from a Captain Boycott who was one of these detested landlords. Parnell became a hero to the Irish, and finally won the support of prime minister Gladstone (page 105) for home rule and other reforms. Alas, he was involved in a much publicised divorce case. It wrecked Parnell's career and the troubles and tragedies of Ireland went on.

PASCAL, Blaise (1623-62)
French scientist, mathematician and philosopher

Pascal did important work in the field of hydrodynamics (the study of the physical behaviour and properties of water and other fluids) and investigated atmospheric pressures. As a mathematician he thought out the theory of probability, and invented a type of calculating machine. Pascal was also a deeply religious man, and it was this side of his life and thought that inspired his best-known work, the collection of essays published shortly after his death under the title of *Les Pensées* (Thoughts).

PASTEUR, Louis (1822-95)
French scientist

With Robert Koch (page 141) in Germany, Louis Pasteur was a founding figure in the science of bacteriology. His researches into the processes of fermentation in wine and beer led to the most valuable discovery that heating foodstuffs to a critical temperature destroys harmful bacteria and prevents food from going bad. This method of 'pasteurisation' was soon being widely used to preserve foods, particularly milk. Another problem Pasteur investigated was silkworm disease – a serious matter in 19th century France, where silkworm cultivation was an important industry. This led him to inquire into the whole subject of germ bacteria and disease. Like Koch, he studied ways of combating anthrax, a deadly disease among cattle and sheep, by inoculation – infecting the animals with a mild (attenuated) form of germ bacteria to build up the body's resistance to the real thing. Cholera and rabies were two other diseases that Pasteur began to conquer. A famous research institute in Paris was dedicated to him, and today there are over 50 other branches of the Pasteur Institute across the world.

PATRICK (about AD 385–461)
British Christian missionary and saint

Patrick was born somewhere near the river Severn towards the end of the Roman occupation of Britain. He was captured by pirates and taken to Ireland as a slave. He escaped, went to Gaul (France) to study for the priesthood, was made a bishop and sent back to Ireland by the pope to convert the people to Christianity. Patrick and his missionary band of priests built churches and monasteries throughout the country, which in the early Middle Ages formed one of the most important centres of learning in Europe. He wrote a book about his work called *Confession* – the only complete British document to survive from his times.

PAUL (1st century AD)
Christian apostle and saint

He was originally named Saul, the son of a wealthy Jewish family from Tarsus in southern Turkey. He persecuted the first Christians; then, according to the Acts of the Apostles in the New Testament of the Bible, he was converted to Christianity by a miraculous flash of light on the road to Damascus. He was baptised in the new faith, changed his name to Paul, and became the Church's greatest missionary teacher. The Acts of the Apostles, written by his companion Luke (page 153), describes his travels about the eastern Roman Empire; how he was often stoned and beaten, smuggled in and out of towns, shipwrecked on the island of Malta, thrown into prison. He ended up in Rome, where he was probably executed during the reign of the emperor Nero (page 176). Paul's many letters, or epistles, form an important part of the New Testament.

PEARY, Robert Edwin (1856-1920)
American explorer

Robert Peary was a naval officer and arctic explorer. He made several expeditions to the north polar regions, on one of them passing round the northern end of Greenland and so proving it to be a huge, frozen island. He achieved his final goal when he made a dramatic dash with his Black servant Matthew Henson and a small team of dogs and sledges across the ice-bound Arctic ocean, to raise the American flag over the North Pole on 6 April 1909. There was an upsetting time for Peary when Frederick Cook, a surgeon who had accompanied him on previous expeditions, claimed to have reached the pole quite independently the year before. But after investigating the matter, the American government recognised Peary as the first man to stand on the North Pole.

PEEL, Sir Robert (1788-1850)
English statesman

Sir Robert Peel is best remembered as the man who in 1829 created London's Metropolitan Police, the first modern police force in Britain. Its constables were known as 'Peelers' or 'Bobbies'. As home secretary he also introduced many changes in criminal law, reducing the number of offences carrying the death penalty from 200 to 12. Peel was later at the centre of one of the biggest political issues in 19th-century Britain. He was a member of the old, land-owning Tory Party, and was expected to support the Corn Laws, which protected British farmers from foreign competition and kept the price of corn high. But as Tory prime minister he came to regard the Corn Laws as unfair to many people, especially the poor. In 1846, therefore, he repealed them. This split the Tory Party, and Peel was forced to resign. Nevertheless, by his actions Peel started to change the character of the old Tory Party into the more moderate and progressive Conservative Party – a process continued by Benjamin Disraeli (page 78). Peel died in a hunting accident four years after he resigned.

PENN, William (1644-1718)
English religious reformer and pioneer

William Penn was a Quaker – a member of the religious puritan sect called the Society of Friends. Through family connections he was also owed a large sum of money by the king, Charles II. In payment of this debt, he was granted a large area of land in the new American colonies, and went there with a small band of fellow Quakers to found a religious settlement free from the persecution they had often suffered in England. This new settlement was named after him Pennsylvania, with its capital at Philadelphia, a name taken from the Greek words meaning 'Brotherly Love'. Penn was a true man of peace. He made friends with the local Indians, and established a model new community in Pennsylvania. When he went back to England on business, quarrels broke out and the community broke up. Nevertheless, the idealism of Penn and his original settlers was not forgotten. The Declaration of Independence of 1776 – one of the most significant documents in the history of social democracy – owed a good deal to it, and Philadelphia was where it was adopted.

PEPYS, Samuel (1633-1703)
English diarist and administrator

Samuel Pepys wrote his celebrated Diary over a period of nine years, starting in 1660, the year that Charles II was restored to the English throne. His entries were often quite long and detailed, recording such dramatic events as an outbreak of the plague and the Great Fire of London (1666), and the attack of the Dutch fleet up the Medway in 1667. He made note also of many events in his own life, such as visits to the threatre, and of gossip and scandal in court society, so producing an immensely valuable record of life in 17th-century London. Apart from the Diary, Pepys held an important post in the Admiralty, and helped to make the navy into a truly professional fighting force. A scoundrel named Titus Oates spread word of an alleged Catholic plot to kill Charles II. In the scare that followed Pepys was implicated and imprisoned but later released.

PERÓN, Juan Domingo (1895–1974)
Argentinian statesman

Juan Perón joined a group of army officers who seized power in Argentina in 1943. He was given a job in their government, and in 1946 was elected president. Perón himself brought in some social reforms, and his popularity was much increased by his glamorous wife Eva, who also helped the country's poor people. Together, Juan and Eva Perón were the biggest names in Latin America. But when Eva died in 1952, President Perón's position weakened, and he was deposed in 1955. He was not forgotten by many people and in 1973 returned from exile to become president again, but died within the year.

PERSHING, John Joseph (1860–1948)
American soldier

'Black Jack' was the nickname earned by General Pershing on account of his toughness and discipline. He commanded the American forces in Europe during the First World War. He and his first units arrived in France in the summer of 1917, when the British and French armies were exhausted by nearly four years of war. Their commanders wanted to fill the gaps in their own ranks with the new arrivals. Pershing refused this piecemeal use of his own men and insisted on building up his American Expeditionary Force. Through 1918 this force more than proved its worth, first helping to stem the last big German offensive, then going over to the offensive itself, notably at the battle of the Argonne Forest. By the time of the Armistice of November 1918 Pershing had a great army of two million men under his command.

PETER (about AD 10–68)
Christian apostle and saint

Peter was one of the 12 apostles of Jesus (page 132). His original name was Simon, and he was a Galileean fisherman when he first met Jesus. According to the Gospel of St Matthew (page 161), Jesus changed his name to Peter, meaning 'rock', with the words, 'On this rock I will build my church'. Also according to the gospels, at the time of Jesus's arrest, Peter denied knowing him three times, as Jesus himself had predicted. After the events told in the gospels, Peter went to Rome and by tradition became the first bishop of Rome, or pope. He was probably crucified upside down during the Emperor Nero's (page 176) persecution of the Christians, and the basilica of St Peter's is built on what is thought to have been his burial place.

PETER I, 'The Great' (1672-1725)
Russian tsar

Leningrad, with its broad avenues, great squares and palaces, was built on a half frozen swamp, at enormous cost in money, labour and lives, by the will of one man – Peter the Great. He wanted a naval base and port that would give Russia access to the Baltic sea. Being tsar, with absolute authority, he built the city formerly called St Petersburg and the capital of Imperial Russia for nearly 200 years.

Tsar Peter was a giant of a man, also a brute who was quite capable of strangling with his own hands anybody was argued with him. The Russia he inherited was a vast land of forest and steppe, with few roads to connect the scattered towns and villages, hardly any schools, no industry, no proper government. Peter went to Holland, England and elsewhere in Europe to see for himself what other nations were doing, then returned home determined that Russia should follow their example. He opened schools, started industries, published Russia's first newspaper. With fanatical zeal, he even made Russian men cut off their traditionally long beards as a mark of change. Peter also wanted Russia to become a major European power. He achieved this mainly through war with Sweden, which under Charles XII had one of the best armies in Europe. Peter tempted the Swedish army to advance deep into Russia, then surrounded and defeated it at the battle of Poltava

(1709). As a result he acquired new lands on the Baltic sea. With these gains, and with St Petersburg as a base for the new Russian navy, Tsar Peter gave Russia what was called its 'window on the west'. So this ferocious but amazing man made Russia a new force in world affairs.

PHILIP II (1527-98)
Spanish king

The man who sent the Armada against England in 1588 was Philip II of Spain. He inherited Spain itself, its possessions in Italy and the Netherlands, its growing empire in the Americas, from his father, the Emperor Charles V (page 52). Philip was a strong and capable ruler. His ships helped to defeat the Ottoman Turks at the great sea battle of Lepanto in 1571, and he annexed Portugal. He also wanted to restore the Catholic faith to Europe after the upset of the Reformation. He married Mary I of England (Bloody Mary), who was an equally ardent Catholic, but she died in 1558. Her successor, Elizabeth I (page 88), proved to be an enemy and not a friend. From then on things did not go well for Philip. He had to contend with a long and bitter rebellion among the protestants in the Netherlands. The great Armada of ships sent against Elizabeth's England met with catastrophe. He fought a costly war against the French Huguenot King Henry IV (Henry of Navarre). Philip died in his great and gloomy palace of the Escorial in the mountains near Madrid, having well-nigh exhausted his country's power. Spain's decline in world affairs dates from that time.

PICASSO, Pablo (1881-1973)
Spanish artist

Though Spanish by birth, Picasso went to Paris in 1900 and remained in France for almost the whole of his life. Like his near contemporary, the composer Stravinsky (page 222), Picasso kept changing his ideas and styles. His early paintings belong to what are called his 'blue' and 'pink' periods, because those were the two predominant colours of his paintings at that time. These works are still representational – they portray quite clearly and directly figures and scenes. With a painting called *Les Demoiselles d'Avignon*, Picasso dramatically changed his style, showing his interest in cubism. This was a style that Cezanne (page 49) had already begun to develop. Picasso and the French artist Georges Braque took cubism – the analysis of shapes and colours in terms of a kind of geometry – much further, often painting pictures of people showing two or three sides of their face and figure in the same plane. Another of his greatest paintings is called *Guernica*. It is named after a town that was badly bombed in the Spanish Civil War, and expresses the artist's sense of outrage against the horrors of war. Picasso went on changing and developing, astonishing some people, perplexing and infuriating many more. He was amazingly versatile, painting, sculpting, making ceramics and lithographs with equal ease and skill, and has long been considered one of the greatest artists of our age.

PITT, William, the Elder (1708–78), **the Younger** (1759–1806)
British statesmen

William Pitt, the Elder and the Younger, were a brilliant team of father and son. George II disliked William Pitt the Elder, but eventually appointed him secretary of state at a time when Britain and France were struggling against each other to create overseas empires. Their rivalry led to the Seven Years' War of 1756–63, and the chief territories involved were India and Canada. Pitt the Elder planned Britain's war strategy and picked the military leaders to carry it out. Within a space of two years, Britain had won decisive victories under General Clive (page 59) in India and General Wolfe (page 250) in Canada. George III, who became king in 1760, wanted the war to end, and Pitt resigned. He was honoured with the title of Earl of Chatham. He returned to office briefly as prime minister, but his greatest days were over.

In contrast to his father's slow rise to power, William Pitt the Younger became the youngest-ever prime minister at the age of 24.

His first interest was in finance, and by new systems of taxation greatly improved the country's economy. He also developed the modern form of government by prime minister and a cabinet of other senior ministers. However, he too got drawn into war with France, this time against Napoleon Bonaparte (page 172). As his father had Clive and Wolfe to fight on land, so Pitt the Younger had Admiral Nelson (page 176) to defeat the French at sea. But on land it was a different story. He died with Napoleon still victorious everywhere. 'Oh my country! How I leave my country!' were supposed to have been his last words. In fact, he left it better governed and in a far stronger position than he found it, as events would prove.

Despite his interest in finance, his own affairs were badly organized and when he died a fund was launched to pay off his substantial debts.

PLATO (about 427-347 BC)

Greek philosopher and teacher

Plato was a pupil or disciple of Socrates (page 218), and in many of his writings, or 'Dialogues', used his master's technique of asking and answering questions as a means of discussion. Plato also wrote a book called *Republic* – one of the first works of political philosophy – in which he discussed such matters as systems of justice and the relationship between citizen and state. Plato's third achievement was the founding of his Academy in Athens, not a school in the modern sense, but a place where people could debate philosophy and politics, mathematics, science and astronomy. Plato's life and work were based on the Classical Greek ideal of the well-balanced human being as the person who engaged in both thought and athletics so that health of mind and of body should go hand in hand. He lived in a society where slaves or humble artisans did all the heavy work, leaving those of rank and wealth to cultivate their talents and form an 'élite' in government, philosophy, science and the arts. That being said, Plato's work and ideas are regarded as one of the foundations of European or Western civilisation.

PLINY the Elder (AD 23–79), **and the Younger** (AD 62–113)
Roman writers and historians

Pliny the Elder wrote a very large work on natural history, which is now a most interesting document about the way the Romans studied such matters as rocks and soil, plants and animal life. What makes his own life and that of his nephew, Pliny the Younger, really fascinating is that both of them witnessed one of the greatest natural disasters in human history – the eruption of Mount Vesuvius in AD 79 that destroyed Pompeii and other Roman townships. Pliny the Younger wrote a most graphic account of the eruption and its aftermath, describing the huge mushroom cloud rising high above Vesuvius until it blotted out the sun, and recording the terror and confusion among the population. His uncle got too close to the eruption and was suffocated to death by sulphur fumes.

PLUTARCH (about AD 46–120)
Greek historian and biographer

'Plutarch's Lives' is probably the best biographical account we have of many of the greatest figures of the ancient world. The full title of his work is *Forty-six Parallel Lives of Illustrious Greeks and Romans*. In it he compares such men as Alexander the Great (page 8) and Julius Caesar (page 42), which today's historians still find fascinating to read.

POLO, Marco (about 1254–1324)
Italian merchant and explorer

Over a century before Columbus (page 61) made his great voyage of discovery by sea, Marco Polo made what was in some ways an even more remarkable voyage of discovery by land. His father and uncle were Venetian merchants who had already visited China on a trading mission. Marco, aged 17, went with them on their second journey to the orient. They took a ship from Venice to Palestine, and then travelled through Persia, along the northern edge of the Himalaya mountains and across the trackless wastes of Mongolia to Peking. This was the court of Kublai Khan, grandson of Genghis Khan (page 104) and founder of the Yuan dynasty. The Polos were welcomed at the court, and Marco was employed by Kublai Khan, who sent him on other missions to places as far afield as India and Burma. The three of them were finally asked to escort a Mongol princess by sea all the way back to Persia, and they got back to Venice after an absence of 24 years. Marco Polo was captured soon after in a sea battle with the rival Italian city-state of Genoa. While in prison he wrote of his travels in the fabled orient, describing the strange and exotic things he had seen, including such wonders as burning stones (the Chinese already used coal). When others first read his account they laughed at him. It was a long time before people realised he was telling the truth.

POMPEY, the Great (106–48 BC)
Roman soldier and statesman

Pompey the Great, or Pompeius Magnus, was winning victories for the Roman Empire in the east, while Julius Caesar (page 42) was campaigning in the west. In 66 BC he defeated and put to flight King Mithridates of Asia Minor, who had been opposing the Romans for years. He then pushed the empire's frontiers as far east as the Caspian sea and the Euphrates river. Pompey returned to Rome in triumph, but soon clashed with Caesar for political power. Pompey was the loser. He was forced to flee from Rome, saw his army beaten at Pharsalus in Greece and fled again to Egypt, where he was killed.

POPE, Alexander (1688–1744)
English poet

'The proper study of mankind is man,' said Alexander Pope, who lived at a time when new ideas, and the manners and attitudes of fashionable society, were more than enough to fill anyone's life. Pope was a leading member of London's literary scene, which then included Jonathan Swift (page 225), Joseph Addison and Richard Steele; and one of the cleverest, wittiest, most polished writers of any age. His best-known work, *The Rape of the Lock*, is both a parody of a Classical Greek or Roman epic poem, and a satirical commentary upon the follies and foibles of mankind.

PRIESTLEY, Joseph (1733-1804)
English scientist

The Swedish chemist Karl Scheele may have discovered oxygen a few years earlier, but in 1774 Joseph Priestley was the first scientist to publish an account of the new wonder gas that made flames burn brighter and supported life. In fact, he called it 'dephlogisticated air', in accord with a widely held belief that air contained a mysterious gas called phlogiston. Nevertheless, the discovery had been made, and Priestley went on to isolate nine other new gases, including ammonia. He also found out how to make soda water by passing carbon dioxide through ordinary water. A mob burnt Priestley's house and laboratory because he was in favour of the French Revolution. On the other side of the Channel, the French chemist Antoine Lavoisier (page 143), who had also experimented with oxygen, was executed by the Revolutionaries.

PROKOFIEV, Sergei (1891-1953)
Soviet Russian composer and pianist

Prokofiev spent some years in Paris, where he wrote music that was generally considered very advanced and difficult for its time. Then he returned to the Soviet Union, where communist doctrine said that creative artists should produce music, paintings and other works of art that inspired or entertained the mass of the people. Prokofiev complied with music to the ballet *Romeo and Juliet*, to such famous films as *Alexander Nevsky*, and for the musical folk tale

Peter and the Wolf. His 'Classical' Symphony – a light-hearted parody of an 18th-century symphony – is another concert favourite. Prokofiev wrote other more substantial symphonies, also much very fine music for the piano, mostly in the form of concertos or sonatas. He also wrote operas, including *Love For Three Oranges*.

PROUST, Marcel (1871-1922)
French novelist

Marcel Proust spent most of his life working on one very long and complex work in several volumes called *Remembrance of Things Past* (French title *A la Recherche du Temps Perdu*). The basic inspiration for it was Proust's own experience of total recall, of being carried back most sharply and vividly to some past time by a particular sensation. He explored this idea of recapturing the past in a moment of the present in tremendous depth and detail, and his work has made a big impression on many other writers and artists of our time. The last three volumes were not published until after his death.

PTOLEMY, Claudius (about AD 90-168)
Greek astronomer

Claudius Ptolemy of Alexandria – a different man from the kings of that name who had earlier ruled Egypt – presented an idea of the universe that was not seriously questioned for over 1000 years. Ptolemy believed that the Earth was at the centre of a number of hollow, revolving, concentric spheres, to which the Sun, Moon, planets and stars were attached. Beyond the outermost of these spheres was the 'primum mobile', or 'prime mover' that gave the universe its energy and motion. This picture of the cosmos became official Church doctrine, because it was assumed that God must indeed have placed the Earth and mankind at the centre of things. When other astronomers, notably Copernicus (page 64) and Galileo (page 100) first began to cast doubt on these notions, they found themselves in trouble.

PUCCINI, Giacomo (1858–1924)
Italian composer

Puccini was the successor to Verdi (page 238) in the field of Italian opera. Like Verdi and all other Italian operatic composers before him, Puccini knew how to write melodies that drew the best from the singers' voices; and some of his soaring vocal arias are among the all-time favourites with opera and concert audiences. At the same time, Puccini could write the most subtle and often delicate 'impressionistic' music for the orchestra, creating just the right mood for a scene. *La Bohème, Tosca, Madame Butterfly* and *Turandot* (not quite finished when he died) are his best-loved operas. In some of his other works, Puccini was influenced by an operatic style or movement called 'verismo', meaning real or true to the darker, seamier side of life.

PURCELL, Henry (1659–95)
English composer

Purcell was born at the time of the Restoration to the throne of Charles II. The king brought back to England from his exile on the continent a taste for the new kind of instrumental music then being written in Italy and France, such as dance suites and early forms of sonata (from the Italian word 'suonare', meaning 'to sound'). Purcell wrote music of this type, also anthems and odes for choirs, and many songs. Some of his finest music was composed for the stage, including *Dido and Aeneas*, his only opera and the first true opera written by an Englishman. The famous Trumpet Voluntary, long thought to have been by him, was in fact composed by his colleague Jeremiah Clarke.

PUSHKIN, Alexander (1799–1837)
Russian dramatist, novelist and poet

In the 18th and 19th centuries, educated Russians often spoke French or German among themselves, regarding their own language as fit only for peasants. Pushkin helped to make Russian a literary language with a strong character of its own, and prepared the ground for such giants of literature as Tolstoy (page 229) and Dostoevsky (page 79). As a point of interest, it was Russian composers who were most inspired by Pushkin's work, and his plays, poems and stories were nearly all made into operas by Modest Mussorgsky, Tchaikovsky (page 226), Rimsky-Korsakov (page 205), and others. These include his dramas *Eugene Onegin* and *Boris Godunov*, his short story *The Queen of Spades*, and his poem *The Golden Cockerel*.

PYTHAGORAS (about 582-500 BC)
Greek philosopher and mathematician

Pythagoras founded a school that was like a monastic order in the way its members obeyed strict rules and followed a moral way of life. They were dedicated to a widely-held belief of the ancient world that the whole universe was controlled by a wonderful system of mathematics – of numbers combined in special proportions to create a 'Harmony of the Spheres'. Pythagoras's geometry, including his famous theorem about the sides of a right-angled triangle, were all tied in with this; so was his fascinating research into the frequencies (speed or rate of vibrations) of musical sounds. The design and proportion of much Classical Greek architecture was another reflection of this mystical belief that mathematics and numbers were the key to all the secrets of the universe and of life itself.

R

RABELAIS, François (about 1494–1553)
French writer, priest and physician

'Rabelaisian' is the word we now use to describe a person or situation of boisterous, bawdy humour. François Rabelais wrote in just such a manner, mocking what he saw as the stupidities of his age. At the same time, he was a great scholar, so that behind all the bawdy, sometimes quite coarse joviality, there is much knowledge and erudition. He also loved playing with words and phrases for their own sake, and published much of his work under the anagram of Alcofribas Nasier – the letters of his true name placed in a different order. His big satirical book in several volumes is *Gargantua and Pantagruel*. These were the names of two giants, and one of them has added another word to our vocabulary – 'Gargantuan', describing someone or something of giant size.

RACHMANINOV, Sergei (1873–1943)
Russian composer and pianist

Among a generation of such great virtuoso pianists as Paderewski (page 183), Rachmaninov was considered to be the finest. He left his homeland in 1917 at the time of the Bolshevik Revolution and settled in America; but all his music has a rich but melancholy sound to it that is very Russian in character. Rachmaninov composed in a fairly traditional, conservative style, mostly for his favourite instrument, including four piano concertos and the *Rhapsody on a Theme of Paganini*. But he also wrote three symphonies and a very atmospheric orchestral piece inspired by a strange painting called *The Isle of the Dead*.

RALEIGH, Sir Walter (1552-1618)
English explorer, soldier and poet

Sir Walter Raleigh was one of Elizabeth I's (page 88) favourite courtiers; and from the American colony he named Virginia – in honour of her title of 'The Virgin Queen' – he brought back to Europe tobacco and potatoes. Beyond that, his ventures were not very successful, and finally ended in tragedy. Raleigh's greatest dream was to find El Dorado, a fabulous city of wealth and gold, which he believed existed somewhere up the Orinoco river in South America. In 1595 he set sail, but returned empty-handed. When Elizabeth died in 1603 and James I succeeded her, Raleigh was suspected of treason and sent to the Tower of London. He was released so that he might try again to find El Dorado, and bring back its treasures for the king. On the way he had a fight with some Spaniards, just at the moment when James I was trying to arrange a marriage between his son and a Spanish princess. Raleigh's own son was killed in the fight. He returned home broken-hearted, and in blackest disgrace, and was beheaded.

RAPHAEL, Sanzio (1483-1520)
Italian artist

Sanzio Raphael, or Raffaello Santi, lived at the same time as Leonardo da Vinci (page 147) and Michelangelo (page 164), and belonged to what is called the High, or late Renaissance period. The main starting point for the whole of the Renaissance was a rediscovery of Classical Greek and Roman art, thought and literature. Raphael's admiration for the order and proportion of Greek art and architecture is clear in all his own paintings. In the most famous of them he added his admiration for Greek philosophy and science as well. This is a very large wall painting, or fresco, in the Vatican palace, Rome, called *The School of Athens*. Plato (page 192) and Aristotle (page 13) stand surrounded by other great thinkers of their time, all forming a beautifully proportioned and harmonious group of figures.

RAVEL, Maurice (1875–1937)
French composer

Maurice Ravel was interested in many different aspects of music: in the new kind of musical impression created by his fellow countryman Debussy (page 73); in old styles of music, like 18th-century court dances and the waltz; in writing for such Classical forms as the string quartet and sonata; and in jazz and dance music. Ravel's own style was very clear and refined, and he could write with wonderful tenderness or with steely brilliance for piano or orchestra alike. In fact, he often composed music first for the piano and orchestrated it later, so that many of his pieces exist in two equally attractive versions. Examples of the work of this many-sided composer are: *Jeux d'eau* (Fountains) and *Gaspard de la Nuit* (Night Phantoms) for piano; the ballet *Daphnis et Chloé* and *Bolero* for orchestra; the opera *L'Enfant et les Sortilèges* (The Spell-bound Child); a string quartet, piano concerto in G, and concerto for the left hand.

REMBRANDT HARMENSZ VAN RIJN (1606–69)
Dutch artist

Rembrandt was the greatest Dutch artist of the Baroque period. His career started brilliantly. He married well, was an excellent portrait painter, much in demand by the wealthy merchants of Amsterdam, and lived in high style. Two things changed all that. His wife died, leaving him to try and manage on his own, and he produced a painting called *The Night Watch*. This was a group portrait, but in the interests of the painting itself, Rembrandt left some of the figures in shadow, which upset the people who had posed for the portrait, because they could not properly be seen. His popularity quickly declined, and he lost most of his money. It was, in fact, Rembrandt's increasing interest in contrasts of light and shade – known technically by the Italian term 'chiaroscuro' – that raised his paintings to the level of genius. He was a religious man, though not in a sober Dutch puritan way, and painted scenes from the Bible, or other dramatic scenes from ancient times, that glow with radiance against a deep dark background in a way that no other artist has achieved. He also developed a penetrating insight into human character as revealed in the face, and through his life painted a series of most moving self-portraits, showing himself growing older, sadder and wiser. In addition to his paintings, Rembrandt produced hundreds of black and white etchings.

RENOIR, Pierre Auguste (1841-1919)
French artist

The Impressionist movement in painting had three big figures: Camille Pissaro who held the whole movement together, Monet (page 166) who gave the movement its name, and Renoir. The principal aim of the Impressionists was to analyse and paint effects of light. Renoir had an especially keen eye for colour, and some of his most famous paintings, of groups of people out in the open on fine summer days, are drenched in light and colour. Renoir ws also interested in building up a sense of volume or depth, and of form, in his paintings by the use of colour alone. His son, Jean Renoir, was a great film director, similarly concerned with effects of light and of people set in outdoor scenes, though many of his films were in black and white.

RICHARD I (1157-99)
English king

Richard I was called 'Coeur de Lion', or 'Lionheart', because of his prowess as a knight and warrior. He was the son of Henry II (page 118), and inherited both the throne of England and the large French province of Aquitaine. In 1190 he joined the Third Crusade to try and win back Palestine, the Holy Land, from Muslim occupation. On his journey home he was captured and held to ransom by the Archduke of Austria. When the ransom was paid and he was released, Richard was soon involved in a war against King Philip Augustus of France. England was little more than a source of money to him, and he spent less than a year actually in the country. He died fighting in France, whereupon his brother John (page 134), who had earlier tried to usurp the English crown, officially became king.

RICHARD III (1452–85)
English king

The Wars of the Roses in the 15th century were a struggle for power between the two English royal houses of Lancaster (whose emblem was a red rose) and York (a white rose). Richard was a member of the house of York. He gave loyal support to his brother, Edward IV. When Edward died, Richard became regent (substitute ruler) on behalf of his nephew, the boy king Edward V. He housed the lad and his little brother in the Tower of London, may have had them murdered, and took the crown for himself. He was defeated and killed at the battle of Bosworth by Henry Tudor, who then became Henry VII. This ended the Wars of the Roses. Richard III lives on, largely through Shakespeare's (page 216) portrayal of him as a hunchbacked villain. But some people point out that Shakespeare wrote his play when the Tudors were in power and that it paid him to turn Richard into a scheming murderer. They claim that the real man was not nearly as black as he has since been painted.

RICHELIEU, Duc de (1585–1642)
French churchman and statesman

Richelieu was a cardinal of the Roman Catholic Church, and nearly always portrayed in his scarlet robes of office. He also became Louis XIII's chief minister of state, and was the real power behind the throne. Within France, Cardinal Richelieu took political power and privilege away from the nobility and concentrated it on the person of the king – in effect upon himself. He also directed what amounted to a civil war against the French protestants, the Huguenots, bringing about their defeat with the capture of their stronghold at the port of La Rochelle. Abroad he waged war against the rival

Hapsburg kings of Spain and Austria, this time seeking support from protestant armies in Germany and Sweden. As a result, France gained territory and influence at the expense of both Spain and Austria. Richelieu gave France a strong administration, and made it a powerful nation. But the almost absolute power he gave to the monarchy sowed the seeds for future trouble, leading eventually to the Revolution.

RICHTHOFEN, Manfred von (1882-1918)
German airman

In the First World War aircraft were originally used for reconnaissance over the Western front, to observe the other side's troop movements and trench positions, and the effect of their own side's artillery. As the war continued, Allied and German aircraft often encountered each other, and they began to fight their own air battles. The most glamorous figure in this new aerial warfare was Manfred von Richthofen. He was known as the 'Red Baron' because he flew in a bright red combat plane, and he led a squadron called the 'Flying Circus'. He was the leading fighter ace of the whole war, with 80 victories against Allied pilots to his credit; but was finally shot down and killed in April 1918.

RIMSKY-KORSAKOV, Nikolai (1844-1908)
Russian composer

'The Five' were a group of Russian composers who created between them a national school or style of music. Nikolai became a leader among them. He had been a naval officer before turning to music – none of 'The Five' started life as a professional musician – but soon showed a splendid gift for orchestration. He loved to write for the orchestra as an artist might fill his canvasses with strong, rich colours, choosing exotic fables and stories to turn into music. One of the most popular of all pieces of concert music is his *Scheherazade*, inspired by the 'Tales from the Arabian Nights'. Another of his most vivid works is his opera *The Golden Cockerel*, based on a play by Pushkin (page 198). Rimsky-Korsakov became a noted teacher at the St Petersburg Conservatory, and often corrected what he considered to be faults of weaknesses in the work of his colleagues. For example, he produced an entire revised edition of Mussorgsky's opera *Boris Godunov*.

ROBERT BRUCE (1274-1329)
Scottish king

Robert Bruce continued the struggle for Scottish independence from England begun by William Wallace. In 1306 he defiantly had himself crowned King of Scotland at Scone. For several years after that he and his supporters had to fight a guerrilla war against the occupying English army. But under Robert's leadership they grew in strength and courage, capturing the big Scottish castles from the English, one by one. By 1314 only Stirling castle remained in English hands, and that fell to the Scots after their great victory at Bannockburn of the same year. The war continued for several more years before England's Edward III was forced to recognise Robert Bruce as Scotland's rightful king.

ROBESPIERRE, Maximilien de (1758-94)
French revolutionary leader

Maximilien de Robespierre was the kind of fanatic who often gets to the top in times of grave national crisis. In his case it was the French Revolution. He was a member of the radical Jacobin Party; then headed the Committee of Public Safety, set up to deal with internal security after the execution of Louis XVI (page 151) and the invasion of France. Robespierre, who saw himself as a true patriot and friend of the common people, arrested and executed thousands of royalists and others whom he considered enemies of the state. This was the so-called Reign of Terror that lasted for about a year through 1793-4. Dr Joseph Guillotine's new instrument of execution, invented as a relatively humane way of beheading people, played a big part in it. Guillotines were installed in many French towns and cities, to deal with Robespierre's victims. In fact, Robespierre never wielded complete power, and when other revolutionary leaders thought he had gone too far, they had him arrested. He tried to take his own life, then went to the guillotine himself. The Reign of Terror was over.

RODIN, Auguste (1840–1917)
French artist

Rodin was the most celebrated sculptor of modern times. When he started working, most sculpture showed figures in elegant poses, often dressed in Greek or Roman garments in the fashionable artistic style of the time. Such sculpture was often beautifully executed but usually looked quite lifeless. Rodin made his figures look like real people, and showed the human body as it really is, tough and rugged, or weak and failing. His portrait of the writer Balzac (page 22) has the figure thrusting upwards like the trunk of a tree. His group of figures called *The Burghers of Calais*, based on an event in medieval history, shows men bowed and broken in defeat. Two more of Rodin's famous pieces are *The Kiss* and *The Thinker*. Michelangelo (page 164) had sculpted a figure called *The Thinker* ('Il Pensiero') 300 years before. Rodin also followed Michelangelo's example in some of his later pieces, by showing figures as though they were half-finished and struggling to get free of the surrounding stone.

ROLLS, Charles (1877–1910), **and ROYCE, Frederick** (1863–1933)
English industrialists

Rolls-Royce is probably the most famous manufacturing name in the history of the automobile. Charles Rolls was a clever businessman and salesman, Frederick Royce a brilliant engineer. Together they produced and marketed motor cars of the highest mechanical quality and comfort. Their first major design was called the 'Silver Ghost', which was in production from 1906 to 1925, and right up to the present day their vehicles stand for luxury in motoring. Today their name is equally famous in the aviation industry, where many jet airliners are powered by Rolls-Royce aero-engines.

ROMMEL, Erwin (1891–1944)
German soldier

Field-Marshal Erwin Rommel was Germany's best-known military commander of the Second World War. In 1940 he showed himself a master of the new mobilised tank warfare, when he commanded a 'panzer' division in the attack on France. Rommel's greatest days followed his appointment in 1941 as commander of the German Afrika Korps, fighting the British 8th Army in Libya and Egypt. Friends and foes alike called him the 'Desert Fox' as a tribute to his cunning, speed and surprise in attack, and for a time he seemed unbeatable. But when the British 8th Army had been reinforced, General Montgomery (page 168) was able to defeat him at El Alamein in October 1942. In 1944 Rommel was given charge of the coastal defences in northern France. He put new vim and vigour into the construction of gun sites and underwater obstacles, but could not stop the Allied landings of June 1944. Soon after, he was hurt when his staff car was machine-gunned by Allied aircraft; then he was suspected of having been involved in the bomb plot that nearly killed Hitler (page 122) in July 1944. He was forced to commit suicide.

RÖNTGEN, Wilhelm (1845–1923)
German scientist

Towards the end of the last century, one big area of scientific research was concerned with the effects of passing an electrical charge through a vacuum or through various gases contained in a tube. Through his own experiments in this field, Wilhelm Röntgen discovered that a special kind of radiation was being produced. It penetrated the glass walls of the tubes he was using, affected photographic plates, and could produce fluorescence in some other chemicals. Röntgen was at first quite mystified by these new rays, which for want of a better name, he called X-rays. Their value in medical science was soon realised. They could reveal certain internal parts of the body on a special kind of photographic plate, and though they could damage bodily tissue, they could also attack cancers and other malignant growths. X-rays now have many other uses, in industry where they can detect weaknesses in metal structures, and in chemical analysis. Röntgen was one of the first people to receive a Nobel prize for his great discovery.

ROOSEVELT, Franklin Delano (1882-1945)
American statesman

Franklin D. Roosevelt achieved the unique distinction of being elected president four successive times. He was distantly related to President Theodore Roosevelt (see below), and after training as a lawyer entered politics himself, as a member of the Democratic Party. He had already served in President Wilson's (page 251) administration when he contracted polio, which left him paralysed from the waist down. He did not let this handicap stand in his way, and in 1932 was elected president for the first time.

Following the Wall Street 'crash' of 1929, millions of Americans were out of work. Roosevelt in his election campaign had offered them a 'New Deal'. This he swiftly put into effect. 'We have nothing to fear but fear itself,' he declared, and through a series of acts which gave him greater powers embarked upon a big public spending programme to create new jobs. Not everyone approved of the way he controlled private business while stepping up government spending; but 'FDR' had given millions new hope and confidence, and in 1936 he won a second great presidential victory. He was elected yet again in 1940, by which time there was war in Europe. Many Americans did not want to be involved in European affairs. Roosevelt maintained his country's neutrality, while supplying food and arms to Britain through a scheme which was called Lease-Lend.

The surprise attack by the Japanese on the American naval base at Pearl Harbor in December 1941 immediately changed public opinion, and Roosevelt brought America into the war on the Allied side. He conferred frequently with the other Allied leaders, especially with Churchill (page 56). Their war aims were by no means the same. Churchill wished to preserve the British Empire. Roosevelt did not approve of the old-style colonial rule of Britain and France. Nevertheless, their meetings helped to decide war strategy. With victory in sight, the American people once more voted FDR president. But within months of this triumph he was dead.

ROOSEVELT, Theodore (1858-1919)
American statesman

Theodore Roosevelt was descended from a family of Dutch settlers. He was a cattle rancher, police commissioner, and in the Spanish-American war of 1899 formed a cavalry force known as 'Roosevelt's Rough Riders'. He was then nominated by the Republican Party to run as vice-president in partnership with William McKinley. They won, and when President McKinley was assassinated in 1901, Roosevelt stepped into his shoes. He used the slogan 'speak softly and carry a big stick' to clean up politics and break the power of big business trusts and monopolies. In foreign affairs, he extended United States' influence across the American continent, one of his acts being to help finance the building of the Panama Canal. Re-elected president in 1904, he helped to settle the Russo-Japanese War, for which he was awarded a Nobel Peace prize. A great lover of the outdoor life, 'Teddy' Roosevelt then quit politics and went big game hunting in Africa and exploring in South America. This energetic, successful and popular president has one more claim to fame – he gave his name to the world's best-loved toy, the Teddy Bear!

ROSSINI, Gioacchino (1792–1868)
Italian composer

In the 19th century there was a type of Italian opera called 'bel canto', or 'beautiful singing', for which composers wrote arias that gave the singers special opportunities to show off the qualities of their voices. Vincenzo Bellini and Gaetano Donizetti were masters of this style. Rossini also wrote in the 'bel canto' style, and wrote a lot more music that tested the singers' technique and agility to the utmost. He was also known as 'Signor Crescendo' because of the special way he had of making the music become louder and more exciting bar by bar. For 19 years Rossini turned out opera after opera, his last being *William Tell*, which he composed for the Paris Opera. By then he was worn out, and stayed in Paris to lead a life of ease, though he did not stop composing altogether. Rossini wrote some of the liveliest music of any composer. The overtures to many of his operas, such as those to *The Thieving Magpie, The Silken Ladder, The Barber of Seville*, not to mention the thrilling overture to *William Tell*, are favourite concert pieces.

RUBENS, Peter Paul (1577–1640)
Flemish artist

Peter Paul Rubens was an immensely successful man. Early on, he was court painter to the important Duke of Mantua in Italy, where the work of the painter Caravaggio (page 44) greatly impressed him. Then he returned to his home town of Antwerp, to become court painter to the Spanish governor of the Netherlands. Demand for his talents increased all the time, to paint portraits, altarpieces for churches, to plan and execute designs for entire rooms and halls. Consequently, Rubens set up a large workshop in Antwerp, where many assistants worked under his general direction. Among his greatest commissions were those to decorate rooms in the Luxembourg Palace in Paris and the Banqueting House in Whitehall, London. In addition, to all this, Rubens was employed as a diplomat, travelling widely on political and trading missions. His paintings, of religious subjects or of scenes taken from Greek and Roman mythology, overflow with exuberant colour and life.

RUTHERFORD, Ernest, Lord (1871-1937)
New Zealand scientist

Ernest Rutherford was a key figure in the history of atomic physics. He began by investigating the radiations given off by radium and uranium already discovered by Henri Becquerel and Madame Curie (page 66) in France. This led to his own discovery of 'alpha' and 'beta' rays – named by him after the first two letters of the Greek alphabet – for which he was awarded a Nobel prize. Rutherford inquired further into radioactivity, and the 'decay' or disintegration of one element into another. This 'decay', by which an element lost a part of itself, made him then realise that the individual atoms could not themselves be indestructible particles of matter, but must hve a central nucleus, surrounded by electrically charged particles, or electrons. One of his assistants, Niels Bohr (page 31), developed this picture of the atom, linking it with the German scientist Max Planck's equally important quantum theory about radiation and energy. These were all vital steps along the road to nuclear physics and power.

RUYTER, Michel de (1607-76)
Dutch sailor

The Dutch Wars of the 17th century between England and Holland were caused by rivalry over shipping and trade. They were a series of naval engagements. Both sides had magnificent commanders. England had Admiral Blake (page 29). The Dutch had Admirals Tromp (page 231) and Ruyter. In the second of these wars, fought between 1664-7, Ruyter defeated an English squadron off Dunkirk. Soon after he commanded one of the most audacious raids in naval history, when he sailed right up the Medway estuary and pounded English men-of-war as they lay helpless at their moorings.

S

SALADIN (about 1138–93)
Muslim soldier and statesman

'This land is holy to us as well as to you. It was ours to begin with, and you invaded it.' So wrote Saladin to Richard I of England (page 203). He was referring to Palestine, the Holy Land to both Christians and Muslims, and which both fought over during the long period of the Crusades. Saladin was Turkish by birth and Sultan of Egypt. He was a devout Muslim, and a man of learning, at a time when the arts and sciences were far more advanced in the Arab world than in Christian Europe. He was also a great military leader, who took Jerusalem from the Christian Crusader knights in 1187 and held it against the onslaught of a new Crusade led by Richard I. Saladin finally signed a truce with Richard, by which he allowed Christian pilgrims to visit Jerusalem. He is remembered by both Christians and Muslims as a man of honour and decency.

SARTRE, Jean-Paul (1905–80)
French philosopher, novelist and dramatist

Jean-Paul Sartre was the leading member of a philosophical school of thought called Existentialism. Based on the work of the Danish philosopher Soren Kierkegaard, it argued that life has no meaning or purpose beyond that which the individual might choose to give it; that our fate is entirely in our own hands, for good or ill. Sartre's best-known work is his play *Huis Clos* (translated as 'No Exit' or 'Vicious Circle'), about a small group of people forever confined to a room and to each other's company. 'Hell is other people' is the message of the play, and expresses one side to Existential thinking.

Sartre was offered a Nobel prize, but rejected it on the grounds that it would prejudice his work in the minds of his readers.

SCHUBERT, Franz Peter (1797-1828)
Austrian composer

Haydn (page 117), Mozart (page 170), Beethoven (page 24) and Brahms (page 35) all moved to Vienna to work. Franz Schubert was born there. He wrote symphonies, string quartets, piano sonatas and other works in the Classical style. Many of these have lovely melodies – the Symphony no 8, called the 'Unfinished Symphony' because it has only two movements instead of the usual four, has one very well-loved tune. Above all, Schubert was a song writer. He composed over 600 songs, or 'Lied' to give them their special German name. Some are simple; some are complex and dramatic; some of the finest are contained in two big groups, or song-cycles, called *Die Schöne Müllerin* (The Fair Maid of the Mill) and *Die Winterreise* (The Winter Journey). In nearly all of them, Schubert gave expression to feelings of love, despair, hope, fear, in a way that heralded the whole Romantic movement in music. At the same time he founded a great tradition of German 'Lieder' that was enriched by Robert Schumann, Mendelssohn (page 163), Brahms, Hugo Wolf, and others. Schubert himself died at the age of 31 – within a year of Beethoven's own funeral – with much of his music still unpublished and unheard.

SCHWEITZER, Albert (1875-1965)
German scholar, musician and missionary

Albert Schweitzer was a brilliant scholar, and a great musician whose performances as an organist won the highest praise. He gave all this up, trained as a doctor and in 1913 went to a place called Lambaréné in French Equatorial Africa (now Gabon) to set up a missionary hospital. There he stayed for almost the rest of his life, treating people suffering from leprosy and other diseases, and preaching Christianity. In 1952 he was awarded the Nobel Peace prize, and used the money to improve his hospital.

SCOTT, Robert Falcon (1868-1912)
English explorer

Captain Scott was a naval officer who wanted to be the first man to reach the South Pole – a much colder place than the North Pole because it is land rather than water. He commanded an expedition to the continent of Antarctica in 1901-4 in his ship the *Discovery*; then set off again in 1911 in a new ship, the *Terra Nova*, to try and reach his goal. He and a small party did get to the South Pole, on 18 January 1912, only to find the Norwegian flag planted on the spot a few weeks earlier by Roald Amundsen (page 10). Bitterly disappointed, sick, exhausted, short of food, Scott and his companions started back on the long journey to base. They were trapped by blizzards and perished, one by one. Their bodies and diaries were recovered later.

SCOTT, Sir Walter (1771-1832)
Scottish novelist and poet

Sir Walter Scott was a major figure in the Romantic period of literature, with his liking for full-blooded adventure and vivid descriptions of places and events. He was a lawyer and businessman for a number of years, combining these activities with the writing of such pieces as the long poem called *The Lay of the Last Minstrel*. Then he started work on the series of novels, based on Scottish history and legend, that made him world-famous. These 'Waverley Novels' include *Ivanhoe, Kenilworth, The Heart of Midlothian* and *Rob Roy*; and they largely set the tone and style for the historical novel as a special form of literature. Scott wrote some of them to pay off debts he had incurred over the building of a large house and through business failures. In addition to this heavy output, he contributed regularly to literary journals and translated books from German.

SHAKESPEARE

SHAKESPEARE, William (1564-1616)
English dramatist and poet

The plays of William Shakespeare belong to the Renaissance period, when artists, scientists and writers were broadening the whole field of knowledge and experience. Shakespeare's own plays take the broadest view of human thought and feeling. They are performed around the world more often than any other stage works, and are quoted more often than any other group of plays or books. They have also inspired countless other writers, artists and composers. The author of these marvellous works is something of a mystery. He was born in Stratford-upon-Avon, married Anne Hathaway, and spent much of his working life with a company of actors at the Globe theatre in London. All classes of people in Elizabethan London loved going to the playhouse, and Shakespeare, as playwright and actor, appears to have been popular with them. Consequently he was able to retire again to Stratford, quite comfortably off. Apart from that outline of his life, very little is known about him for certain. It is thought by some scholars that parts of some of his plays were written by others, since he must have been a very busy man. A few people even suggest that he did not write the plays at all, though they cannot say who did.

Whatever the truth of the matter, the record says that Shakespeare wrote 37 plays. Some are not often performed. The famous ones are generally divided into three or four groups. There are the historical plays, dealing with the lives of previous English kings, notably *Richard II, Richard III, Henry IV* (parts 1 and 2), and *Henry V*; also the small group based on Roman history, *Coriolanus, Anthony and Cleopatra, Julius Caesar.* There are the comedies, *As You Like It, Twelfth Night* and *Midsummer Night's Dream.* There are the great tragedies, *Hamlet, Macbeth, Othello, King Lear.* There are a few more famous plays that do not fit so easily into one of the above categories or groups, such as *Romeo and Juliet, The Merchant of Venice* and *The Tempest.* In addition to this stupendous output of poetic drama, Shakespeare wrote several long poems, and the famous group of 154 sonnets. More mystery surrounds these sonnets. They are probably addressed to one particular person, but nobody knows whom.

SHAW, George Bernard (1856-1950)
Irish dramatist and journalist

George Bernard Shaw was a lifelong socialist and pacifist, and his ideas about class-consciousness, capitalism and other social and political issues run through his plays. He was, at the same time, a very clever and witty writer, so that while most of his plays carry a serious moral or political message, they are also highly entertaining. Among his lasting successes are *Arms and the Man, The Devil's Disciple, Man and Superman, Major Barbara* and *St Joan*. Another of them, *Pygmalion*, was made into a fine film and into an even more successful stage and screen musical, *My Fair Lady*. Shaw wrote Prefaces to his plays, which some people consider as important as the plays themselves, and he was also an eminent music critic. He was awarded a Nobel prize for literature. 'Shavian' is the adjective often used to describe his work, or the kind of sharp wit that is thought typical of him. He lived to the ripe old age of 94.

SHELLEY, Percy Bysshe (1792-1822)
English poet

Percy Bysshe Shelley was a friend of Byron (page 41) and John Keats. Like them he travelled and died abroad – in his case, he was drowned in a storm off the coast of Italy. All three were leading figures of the Romantic period of literature, when freedom of expression and a love of the natural world were the things that poets and writers most cared about. Shelley expressed his belief in personal freedom in his own unconventional way of life, while his poetry is filled with images of earth, sea, wind, sky, and all the other wonders of nature. He wrote several long poems, but is best remembered for his two fairly short odes, *To a Skylark* and *To the West Wind*. His wife, Mary Shelley, wrote the classic 'gothic' horror story *Frankenstein*.

Shelley drowned when the boat he was sailing in Italy capsized. Ironically, when he died he was working on a poem called *Triumph of Life*.

SHOSTAKOVICH, Dmitri (1906-75)
Soviet Russian composer

In the Soviet Union and other communist countries, writers, artists and composers work for the state and are expected to produce books, paintings, compositions that will inspire or please the majority of their fellow citizens. Shostakovich tried to do this all his life, though there was a famous occasion when Stalin (page 220) disliked one of his works, and then he was in trouble. He wrote 15 symphonies, one of them, known as the 'Leningrad' Symphony, during the terrible siege of that city in the Second World War. They are mostly big, serious works, but popular with audiences everywhere. Shostakovich also wrote string quartets and other compositions in fairly conventional forms, but always in his own distinctive style. A very personal touch to several of his works was the way he used the notes corresponding to the initials of his name.

SMITH, Adam (1723-90)
Scottish economist

Adam Smith was one of the first people to treat economics as an important subject in its own right, and to make it a specialist study. He did this in a large, multi-volume work called *The Wealth of Nations*. This deals with capital and investment, the cost and use of labour, and the way to increase wealth by increasing production and free trade. *The Wealth of Nations*, published in 1776, has a very important place in history because of its influence on the course of the Industrial Revolution which, in turn, changed the economy of the whole world during the 19th century.

SOCRATES (about 470-399 BC)
Greek philosopher and teacher

Socrates was one of the first and greatest teachers. He believed he could lead men from ignorance to wisdom, not by telling them a lot of facts and ideas, but by asking them questions which he encouraged them to answer for themselves. More specifically, he developed the method of inquiry using a hypothesis, or proposed statement of a fact or idea, and then testing it out by question and answer. It was a method followed not just by other teachers and thinkers, but by all the great men of science. Socrates was such a brilliant teacher among the young men of Athens, that the city's leaders began to worry in case he grew too influential and threatened their own position. They had him arrested on a charge of treason and condemned to death by taking poison. The Death of Socrates has inspired many works of art, poems and plays. He wrote no books himself, but many of his 'Dialogues' were recorded by his friend and pupil Plato (page 193).

SOLOMON (about 980-20 BC)
Hebrew king

Solomon was a son of David (page 71), and king of Israel. He reigned for about 40 years, making allies of Tyre and Egypt, trading with all the countries of the eastern Mediterranean and the Middle East, and giving the kingdom of Israel its greatest period of peace and prosperity. Solomon himself lived in luxury, and he built a magnificent new temple in Jerusalem. He was also noted for his wisdom, and the Queen of Sheba was among those who came to consult him. His story is told in the two books of Chronicles in the Old Testament of the Bible, and he is credited with writing the books of Proverbs, Ecclesiastes and the Song of Solomon.

STALIN, Joseph (1879-1953)
Soviet Russian military leader and statesman

Joseph Vissarionovich Djugashvili was the son of a poor village cobbler in Georgia, a province in the Caucasus mountains. He studied for the priesthood, but soon joined a revolutionary group plotting against the tsar. Twice he was arrested, sent to a Siberian prison camp and escaped, the second time to join in the real Revolution of 1917. By now he had adopted the name of Stalin (Man of Steel), and worked closely with Lenin (page 146) to establish a Soviet Communist Union of states. After Lenin's death in 1924, Stalin emerged as undisputed leader. He was determined to turn the Soviet Union from a backward agricultural nation into a strong industrial one. In a country so vast in size and with a largely peasant population, this was an immense task. From a small, bleak office in the Moscow Kremlin, he directed millions to work, either on large, state-run collective farms or on big industrial projects. He retained absolute power by 'purging', through arrests and executions, those whom he suspected of being class enemies.

Abroad, Stalin faced world-wide hostility towards the Soviet Union. Above all, he feared Hitler (page 122), the declared enemy of communism. To the amazement of the whole world, Stalin made a non-aggression pact with the German dictator. This pact seemed to be working well for Stalin, when Germany attacked France and Britain. But in June 1941 a massive German invasion of the Soviet Union took Stalin by surprise. He commanded the Soviet war effort, and thanks to the bitter resistance of the Russian people, finally turned defeat into victory. By 1945, Soviet forces occupied most of eastern and central Europe. Stalin used their presence to help other communist leaders gain power in Poland, Hungary, Czechoslovakia and East Germany. Churchill (page 56) said that Europe was then divided by an 'Iron Curtain', and relations between Stalin and his other wartime allies soon became very strained. This 'Cold War' lasted up to his death in 1953, and the results of it are with us still. A few years after his death, Stalin began to be criticised in his own country, and his embalmed body was removed from its honoured place next to Lenin's in Moscow's Red Square.

STENDHAL (1783–1842)
French novelist

Stendhal was the pen name of Marie Henri Beyle. He was an army officer who took part in Napoleon's (page 172) Russian campaign of

1812. Once out of the army, Stendhal led a life of comparative ease, but also wrote two of the most influential novels of the 19th century, *Le Rouge et le Noir* and *La Chartreuse de Parme*. In them he cultivated a very clear, exact, unemotional style, using it with the precision almost of a surgeon to probe into the minds and feelings of his characters.

STEPHENSON, George (1781-1848), **and Robert** (1803-59)
English engineers

The Stephensons, father and son, did much to create the railways of Britain. George Stephenson came from a poor family of miners. He began working at a colliery near Newcastle, where he learnt how to operate the steam engine used for pumping water out of the coal pits. Soon he had ideas for a travelling engine, or steam locomotive, and with financial backing built his first locomotive, the *Blücher* (named after the Prussian general who fought with Wellington at Waterloo). George Stephenson was then asked to build two more locomotives for the Stockton and Darlington railway, the world's first commercial railway, opened in 1825. His greatest triumph was his locomotive the *Rocket*, built in 1829, and by far the best steam locomotive to date. It could travel at up to 48 kph, and won a famous competition called the Rainhill Trials, held in connection with the building of the Liverpool and Manchester railway. Robert Stephenson had a big hand in the design and construction of the *Rocket*. He went on to build locomotives of his own, and to plan some of the other early railway lines of Britain. Like Brunel (page 38), he was also a great bridge builder. The Britannia bridge over the Menai Straits was his finest achievement in this field.

STEVENSON, Robert Louis (1850-94)
Scottish novelist

Robert Louis Stevenson developed one of the most accomplished and readable styles of any writer. He also produced two of the world's finest adventure stories. The first was originally called *The Sea Cook*, and then re-titled *Treasure Island*. It made him famous, and the book's chief villain, Long John Silver, is one of literature's best-loved characters. Stevenson's second great adventure story was *Kidnapped*, set in Scotland at the time of the 1745 Jacobite Rebellion. Stevenson turned his beautiful writing style to a wide range of other books, from *Travels with a Donkey*, an account of his journey across rural France, to *Dr Jekyll and Mr Hyde*, the classic story of a scientist who releases the evil side of his own nature with terrible consequences. Because of ill health, Stevenson moved with his family to the Pacific island of Samoa, where he died.

STRAUSS, Richard (1864–1949)
German composer

Richard Strauss was a musical wizard. He started composing at the end of the 19th century, when the symphony orchestra had grown in size to 100 or more players, and other composers, notably Wagner (page 242), had shown what amazing sounds could be drawn from it. Young Strauss wrote a series of symphonic poems – pieces describing in music a particular story or scene – in which he made the orchestra depict such events as the German folk hero Till Eulenspiegel being hung on the gallows, Don Quixote charging at a flock of sheep and, in *Ein Heldenleben* (A Hero's Life), the composer himself having an argument with his critics. These orchestral works caused a sensation. For the rest of his very long creative life Strauss wrote mainly operas, always with a rich-sounding orchestral score. He was not related to the Johann Strausses of Vienna, who wrote all the famous waltzes.

STRAVINSKY, Igor (1882–1971)
Russian/American composer

Igor Stravinsky was Russian by birth, lived for many years in France and finally settled in America. Like his close contemporary, the artist Pablo Picasso (page 191), he went through several creative styles or periods, and for over 50 years was a central figure in 20th century music. He first made an impact on the musical world with the three ballet scores he wrote for Diaghilev's (page 75) Russian ballet company in Paris: *The Firebird, Petrushka* and *The Rite of Spring*. The last of these was so overwhelming in sound and force that it caused a riot at the first performance in 1913. The First World War put an end to such elaborate productions, and Stravinsky himself realised there was nothing else he could write that would add to the orchestral power and complexity of *The Rite of Spring*. So he started composing much more modest stage pieces, and quite restrained instrumental works, like the Octet for Wind Instruments. Then he wrote some bigger works again, including the opera-oratorio *Oedipus Rex*, the Symphony of Psalms and the Symphony in Three Movements; and towards the end of his life he started using Schönberg's '12-tone' methods of composition.

STUART, Charles Edward (1720–88)
Scottish prince and soldier

Charles Edward Stuart – 'Bonnie Prince Charlie', or the 'Young Pretender' – was both a romantic and a tragic figure. In 1688 the British Catholic King James II lost his crown to William of Orange (page 248), but there were still people who supported him, called Jacobites. In 1715 they tried and failed to restore to the throne James Edward Stuart, James II's son, known as the 'Old Pretender'. In 1745 the Jacobites tried again with his grandson, Charles Edward. The handsome and dashing young prince landed in Scotland from exile in France, gathered the clans and beat a government army at Prestonpans near Edinburgh. He and his supporters moved into England, with the intention of overthrowing the Hanoverian George II. They got as far as Derby, hesitated and turned back. A new government army, commanded by the Duke of Cumberland, pursued them all the way into the Highlands and in 1746 routed them at the battle of Culloden Moor, near Inverness. This was the last pitched battle fought on British soil. Cumberland mercilessly hunted down the Highlanders, but Charles Edward was protected by Flora Macdonald and other loyal Jacobites and escaped back to France, and thence to Italy, where he died.

SULEIMAN I, 'The Magnificent' (about 1495-1566)
Ottoman sultan

The Ottoman Empire was created by the Turks and was a part of the Islamic or Muslim civilisation. It was founded about 1300, and in 1453 the Ottoman Turks captured the Christian city of Constantinople, making it their capital. The Empire reached its greatest extent during the rule of the Sultan or Emperor Suleiman I. His armies advanced into south-eastern Europe and conquered an area corresponding to the present-day nations of Greece, Bulgaria, Romania, Yugoslavia and Hungary. They almost took Vienna. To the east they pushed the Ottoman boundaries as far as the Caucasus mountains and Caspian sea. Suleiman commanded a great fleet of ships as well, with which he controlled the whole of the Mediterranean sea. He himself lived up to his title of 'The Magnificent', bringing to Constantinople the finest artists and architects of the Islamic world and building four beautiful mosques. After his death the Ottoman Empire began to decline, though it did not actually come to an end until Turkey's defeat in the First World War.

SUN, Yat-sen (1866-1925)
Chinese revolutionary leader and statesman

Sun Yat-sen received a European education, which opened his eyes to the old-fashioned and corrupt way of life in his own country under the rule of the Manchu emperors. He started working for revolution, and when the Manchu government was overthrown in 1911 he became president of the new Chinese republic. He resigned in favour of a much tougher man named Yuan Shih-k'ai, but his period of dictatorship brought anarchy to the country, and Sun was recalled as president in 1923. He then formed the Kuomintang, or

National Party, on what he called the three principles of nationalism, democracy and socialism. Upon his death two years later China was a unified nation, but more years of conflict lay ahead, and invasion by Japan, before the modern People's Republic of China was established under Mao Tse-tung (page 157).

SWIFT, Jonathan (1667-1745)
Irish novelist and journalist

Jonathan Swift wrote *Gulliver's Travels*. This has long been regarded as a children's book, because of the fanciful adventures of Lemuel Gulliver in the land of Lilliput, where he appears as a giant among a race of midgets. In the complete book, Gulliver visits other strange lands, including Brobdingnag, where the scale of life is reversed and he is the midget among giants; and the whole work was intended by Swift as a quite savage satire on 18th-century society. He openly attacked what he saw as the failings and abuses of his time in many other political essays, and edited a political journal. He also took holy orders and became Dean of St Patrick's cathedral in Dublin, where he continued to criticise government and society.

T

TASMAN, Abel Janszoon (1603–59)
Dutch navigator and explorer

In 1642 the governor-general of the Dutch East India Company, Van Diemen, sent Tasman on a voyage of discovery into the southern ocean. One of his objectives was to look for the rumoured continent of 'Terra Australis'. Tasman sailed south and west from the Dutch East Indies, then turned almost due east until he came to a large island which he named Van Diemen's Land, and is now called Tasmania in his own honour. From there he sailed north-eastwards, discovering a part of New Zealand and the Tonga and Fiji islands, before returning to base. In the course of his travels, Tasman did not discover Australia, but without realising it at the time, he was the first man to sail right round the continent.

TCHAIKOVSKY, Peter Ilyich (1840–93)
Russian composer

Peter Tchaikovsky belonged to the Late Romantic period of music, when most composers combined a good deal of feeling and emotion with writing for a large orchestra. Tchaikovsky showed how brilliantly he could compose in this style in his early work, the fantasy-overture *Romeo and Juliet.* Thereafter his other big concert works, his symphonies and concertos, blazed with sound, drama and passion. The First Piano Concerto in B Flat minor, and the Sixth Symphony, called 'Pathétique', are especially loved for these qualities. Tchaikovsky also wrote many fine stage works: the operas *Eugene Onegin* and *The Queen of Spades*, and the beautifully orchestrated ballet scores for *Swan Lake, The Sleeping Beauty* and

The Nutcracker. Early on he received valuable financial help from a lady named Nadezhda von Meck, whom he never actually met. Later he became rich and famous. Tchaikovsky was, though, a very shy, unhappy man, and probably took his own life by drinking unboiled water during a cholera epidemic in St Petersburg.

TELFORD, Thomas (1757-1834)
Scottish engineer

Thomas Telford stands with I. K. Brunel (page 38) and Robert Stephenson (page 221) as one of the great architects of the Industrial Revolution. He was the son of a crofter-shepherd and was apprenticed to a stonemason before going to London to study engineering. Telford returned to Scotland to construct nearly 2000 kilometres of roadway, and the Caledonian canal. In other parts of the British Isles he built more canals, roads and bridges, and planned part of the London docks. One of his finest works was the road suspension bridge across the Menai Strait, as part of his project for the London to Holyhead trunk road. Telford's fame spread abroad, and he also planned the Gotha canal in Sweden, which linked up with other rivers and lakes to form a waterway between the North and Baltic seas.

TENNYSON, Alfred, Lord (1809-92)
English poet

Alfred, Lord Tennyson was one of the best poets to hold the honorary post of Poet Laureate. He had a very fine sense of the rhythm and flow of language, and shared with other writers of the Romantic period of literature a strong feeling for mood and atmosphere. One of his largest works is *Idylls of the King*, inspired by the long-lost world and deeds of King Arthur (page 14). In his own day, Tennyson won wide popularity for such dramatic pieces as 'The Charge of the Light Brigade', recalling the famous cavalry charge at Balaclava during the Crimean War.

THACKERAY, William Makepeace (1811–63)
English novelist and essayist

For many years Thackeray was both a painter and a writer. He finally settled for a writing career, mainly in journalism, when he needed to earn some quick money. For the rest of his life Thackeray wrote essays and articles, and also became a popular lecturer on English history and literature. Today he is remembered as one of the most distinguished novelists of the Victorian period. The best-known of his novels is *Vanity Fair*, a well-mannered but quite biting satire upon social life in his own Victorian age. Thackeray took the title from another famous work of English literature – John Bunyan's (page 39) *Pilgrim's Progress*. Thackeray's other novels include *Pendennis, Henry Esmond* and *The Newcomers*.

TITIAN (about 1487–1576)
Italian artist

The two main centres of art in Renaissance Italy were Florence and Venice. Titian, or Tiziano Vecellio, was the most celebrated of the Venetian school of painters. He studied with the artist Giorgione and learnt from him how to fill his paintings with soft, rich colours – the special glory of Venetian painting. Though the exact dates of his life are not certain, Titian lived until at least his 90th year, and produced an enormous quantity of work. Many of his early paintings, such as the famous *Triumph of Bacchus and Ariadne*, are inspired by scenes from Greek and Roman mythology. His career was subsequently influenced by political events. When the Hapsburg Emperor Charles V (page 52) invaded Italy, Titian became his court artist. His fame as a portrait painter spread throughout Europe, so that kings, popes, ambassadors, and their ladies, were all represented by Titian in the same rich, glowing colours. In some of his last pictures, which are mainly of religious subjects, he also created dramatic effects of space and movement that looked forward, like some of the work of Michelangelo (page 164), to the Baroque period of art.

TITO, Marshal (1892-1980)
Yugoslav soldier and statesman

Josip Broz, to give him his real name, joined the Bolshevik Revolution in Russia in 1917, then returned home to work for the cause of communism. For this he went to prison for several years. Tito's moment came with the Second World War. He led communist partisans in a guerrilla war against the Germans with such success that he became his country's virtual leader. In 1945 he was elected prime minister, and in 1953 became President of the Yugoslav Republic. Marshal Tito's great political skill as a leader was shown in the way he established socialism in his own country, while maintaining a neutral and independent position in world affairs. A big, impressive looking man, he welded the different races within Yugoslavia into a true nation. He was a hero to his own people, and widely admired abroad.

TOLSTOY, Count Leo (1828-1910)
Russian novelist

Count Leo Tolstoy's own life was as full of passion and conflict as the lives of any of the characters he created in his books. He was born into a rich, landowning family. As a young man he enjoyed himself in St Petersburg and Moscow, then joined the army and went off to fight in the Crimean War against the British and French. Soon afterwards he experienced a kind of religious conversion, and started to lead a very simple life, working in the fields alongside the peasant labourers on his own estates. At the same time, the deep feelings within himself brought intolerable strains to his marriage, and in the last months of his life he finally left home, fell ill and died on a lonely railway station. Tolstoy wrote two of the greatest, grandest of all novels. *War and Peace* is an immense epic about Russia at the time of Napoleon's (page 172) invasion of 1812. Tolstoy discusses the military campaign itself, the state of Russian society at the time, his ideas on the progress and purpose of history, and on religion. All this is combined with a story involving over 500 characters. How he managed to hold all these themes and thoughts in his head and forge them into one immense novel is one of the truly great feats of the human mind. Tolstoy's second famous novel is *Anna Karenina*, the story of a woman whose own moral and religious problems and conflicts are like a more personal expression of his own tortured inner life.

TOULOUSE-LAUTREC, Henri de (1864–1901)
French artist

Toulouse-Lautrec lived at the same time as the French Impressionist painters, but worked in a quite different way from them. Like Degas (page 74), whose own work did influence him, Toulouse-Lautrec was far more interested in people and indoor scenes than in landscapes and natural effects of light. He spent nearly the whole of his creative life in and around the cafés and dance halls of the Montmartre district of Paris. With his on-the-spot sketches and paintings, and his superbly designed theatre and café posters of such famous places as the 'Moulin Rouge', he perfectly captured the rather lurid atmosphere of what was called the 'demi-monde' or 'half-world' of Parisian night life. Toulouse-Lautrec himself came from an aristocratic French family and was crippled in a youthful riding accident.

TREVITHICK, Richard (1771–1833)
English engineer

Thomas Newcomen (page 177) built the first successful stationary steam engine in 1712. Nearly a century went by before Richard Trevithick from Cornwall found a way of using steam power to propel a vehicle, when he built his steam carriage in 1801. Three years later he made a second big advance in steam traction when he designed a proper steam locomotive to haul heavy loads at an iron works near Merthyr Tydfil in South Wales. The significance of this locomotive was that it ran on rails, which proved a more efficient method of transportation than bumping along on a road. In 1808 Trevithick built a small circular track in London, near the site of the present Euston station, to demonstrate another of his locomotives called *Catch-Me-Who-Can*. These events are now regarded as real milestones in the history of steam power and the railways. They did not make Trevithick's fortune. He travelled to such distant lands as Peru in South America, showing what his steam locomotives could do, but died a poor man.

TROMP, Maarten Harpertszoon (1597-1653)
Dutch sailor

Admiral Tromp was a hero to the people of the Netherlands. By defeating the Spanish and Portuguese fleets he did much to break Spain's hold over the Netherlands and bring about the creation of an independent Dutch nation in 1648. Soon after this, Tromp and his comrade-in-arms Admiral Ruyter (page 212) took on the English in the wars that flared up as a result of trade and naval rivalry. He engaged the English in a long series of skirmishes in the Channel and North sea, before being killed in a fierce encounter with the English Admiral George Monck. On one celebrated occasion, so the story goes, Tromp sailed his flagship up the Channel with a broom tied to his topmost mast, as a mark of his determination to sweep the seas clean of his enemies!

TRUMAN, Harry S. (1884-1972)
American statesman

When President Franklin D. Roosevelt (page 209) died in April 1945, Harry S. Truman, as Vice-President, suddenly found himself in the seat of power, and faced with perhaps the most awesome decision in world history – whether or not to use atomic weapons against Japan. His military advisers reckoned that thousands more American soldiers would die and the war might last for at least another year if Japan had to be invaded. Truman therefore authorised the dropping of atomic bombs on Hiroshima and Nagasaki on the 6th and 9th of August 1945, and within days the Second World War was ended. Elected directly to the office of president in 1948, Truman went on taking decisive action in world affairs. He launched the Marshall Plan, named after his secretary of state, George C. Marshall, which was a huge programme of economic aid to help European reconstruction after the war. He took the lead in forming the North Atlantic Treaty Organisation for defence (NATO), in the light of growing tension between the United States and the Soviet Union. And in 1950 he committed the United States to the Korean War. Hardly less dramatic was his dismissal of the American commander-in-chief in Korea, General Macarthur (page 155), when the two men disagreed on strategy. 'If you can't stand the heat, stay out of the kitchen' was one of the sayings attributed to this tough and strong-willed president.

TURGENEV, Ivan (1818-83)
Russian novelist

Ivan Turgenev was a friend of Flaubert (page 92) and Zola (page 256) in France, and was the first great Russian writer to become well known outside his own country. His novels and other stories are about Russian life and society as he knew it, and the way he portrays his characters, all inter-acting upon each other, looks forward to the plays of his fellow-countrymen Chekhov (page 54). *Fathers and Sons* is the best-known of Turgenev's books.

TURNER, Joseph Mallord William (1775-1851)
English artist

J. M. W. Turner was dead before the Impressionist movement in France officially began. Yet his own paintings are marvellous impressions of light and atmosphere. He loved to paint as though looking directly into the sun, and to portray sunrise or sunset either as a blaze of crimson and gold, or through a veil of cloud and mist.

Snow, sleet and rain were other conditions of weather that he conveyed in great sweeps and washes of grey and white. Turner travelled widely in Europe and selected favourite places and scenes, such as Venice, that he painted many times. Some of his paintings are large, dramatic oils on canvas. Thousands more are delicate water colours. Some are hardly more than abstract impressions of colour and form. Turner was a law unto himself, and one of the most remarkable artists of any age.

TUTANKHAMUN (about 1337-1319 BC)
Egyptian pharaoh

Tutankhamun succeeded Akhenaten (page 7) to the throne of Egypt when he was about ten years old, and died, or was murdered, eight years later. His actual reign was of little significance, but over 3000 years later his name suddenly conjured up wonder and excitement round the world. Nearly all the other tombs of the pharaohs had been plundered down the ages. Tutankhamun's had remained intact. Only in 1922 was it discovered by the British archaeologist Howard Carter, in the famed Valley of the Kings by the river Nile. The burial place consisted of four underground chambers, filled with treasures that the ancient Egyptians believed the dead man would want to take with him on his journey to the after-life. Most breath-taking of all were the golden coffins, one inside the other, and the golden mask protecting the mummified body of the dead pharaoh. No other single discovery has shed so much light upon the marvels of ancient Egypt, or restored to the world such fabulous treasures. These are now housed in a museum in Cairo.

TWAIN, Mark (1835-1910)
American novelist

Mark Twain was the pen name of Samuel Langthorne Clemens. It was a sound that rang in his ears from his days as a riverboat pilot on the Mississippi, as a member of the crew called out the depths of the water. 'Mark Twain' meant 'two fathoms'. His two famous books are *Tom Sawyer* and *Huckleberry Finn*, delightful stories of boyhood life on the Mississippi river when it was still the frontier to the vast, empty American West, and two of the classic works of American literature.

TYLER, Wat (about 1350–1381)
English peasant leader

In 1381 Wat Tyler and his companion Jack Straw led a big revolt by peasants mainly from Kent and Essex. They were angered by attempts at forced labour under the Feudal System, following the catastrophe of the Black Death a few years before. The peasants marched on London, looting, burning and killing. A meeting was arranged between Wat Tyler and the young king Richard II. Tyler was then stabbed to death by the Lord Mayor of London. Richard prevented even worse rioting by promising many reforms, and the now leaderless peasants dispersed. With the worst of the danger over, the king went back on his word. But the long-term effect of Wat Tyler's revolt was to end the Feudal System, which tied peasants to the land as serfs or vassals of the local lord.

U

UCCELLO, Paolo (about 1396-1475)
Italian artist

Perspective – the technique of creating an accurate sense of distance on a flat surface – was something that interested painters of the early Renaissance period in Italy. Paolo Uccello experimented a great deal with problems of perspective in his work. Three of his most famous paintings are of battle scenes, commissioned by the rich and powerful Medici family of Florence. In them Uccello combined the shapes and colours favoured by the older medieval gothic style of painting with new effects of perspective and distance. The result is three of the most interesting and attractive paintings of the whole Renaissance period.

V

VALERA, Eamon de (1882–1975)
Irish statesman

Eamon de Valera was born in the United States, and his father was Spanish. He nevertheless played a vital part in the events that brought about Irish independence after centuries of unhappy union with the rest of Britain. He was in the thick of the fighting during the Easter Uprising of 1916, was taken by the British and very nearly executed. After Ireland secured independence in 1921 (except for the six counties of Ulster), de Valera founded his political party called 'Fianna Fáil' (Soldiers of Destiny), and in 1932 became prime minister of the Irish Free State. In the years that followed he made big constitutional changes, kept the Republic of Ireland neutral during the Second World War, and was President of the Republic from 1959 to 1973. But even such a skilled politician as de Valera could not solve the question of a unified Ireland.

VANCOUVER, George (1757–1798)
English explorer

George Vancouver sailed with Captain Cook (page 63) on two of his great voyages of exploration to Australia, New Zealand and the Pacific ocean. In 1791 he embarked on his own expedition, sailing eastwards round the Cape of Good Hope and across the Indian ocean to Western Australia. From there he headed east again over the Pacific, to reach the western coast of the North American continent. He charted the coasts of California, Oregon and British Columbia in Canada. He gave his name to Vancouver island and the city of Vancouver.

VASCO DA GAMA (about 1469-1524)
Portuguese explorer

Just under ten years after his fellow countryman Batholomew Diaz (page 76) reached the southern tip of Africa, Vasco da Gama followed the same route down to the Cape of Good Hope. He then continued up the eastern coast of Africa, passed between the mainland and the large island of Madagascar (Malagasy) and headed east across the Indian ocean to Calicut on the south-west coast of India. Vasco da Gama and his companions were tired and sick after their long and often stormy voyage, but the local people were hostile and they quickly had to fight their way out to sea again. Many died of exhaustion and scurvy on the journey home. However, Vasco da Gama returned to Calicut in 1502 with a small fleet of warships, captured the port and established a trading post. Thus he opened up the East to European trade and exploration, almost at exactly the same time that Columbus (page 61) opened the way for Spanish and Portuguese colonisation of the Americas.

VELASQUEZ, Diego Rodriguez (1599-1660)
Spanish artist

Velasquez spent most of his life as court painter to the Spanish king Philip IV. By then the 'Invincible Armada' had come to grief in fire and storm, and the long period of Spanish decline in world affairs had begun. Velasquez captured something of this austere mood in his many paintings of the Spanish court. He also conveyed with more depth and understanding than any other painter the sombreness and the dignity which are marked features of the Spanish character. One of his masterpieces is a painting called *The Maids of Honour*, showing a group of the royal children, and one of the famous court dwarfs that feature in so many of his paintings. What adds interest to this famous work is the inclusion of Velasquez himself among the group, and the images of the king and queen reflected in a mirror. Another of his great paintings, this time celebrating a Spanish victory, is *The Surrender of Breda*. This shows the two commanders, victor and vanquished, meeting in a typically Spanish mood of dignity and honour.

VERDI, Giuseppe (1813–1901)
Italian composer

Giuseppe Verdi recovered from the early death of his wife and children, and the miserable failure of one of his first operas, to become Italy's greatest composer and a much-loved national hero. He lived through the period known as the 'Risorgimento', when Cavour (page 48) and Garibaldi (page 101) were leading the fight for a free and independent Italian nation; and his own stirring operas were closely identified with the spirit of the times. From a purely musical and operatic point of view, Verdi started with the older 'bel canto' type of Italian opera, where all the emphasis was placed on the singing, and gradually built up his operas into masterpieces of both music and drama. *Rigoletto, La Traviata* and *Il Trovatore* are three of the famous operas that show him firmly on this creative path. Verdi was already 60 years old when he finished the grandest of all grand operas, *Aida*, intended for the opening of the Suez Canal. He was over 80 years old when he composed his last two operas, based on Shakespeare's plays, *Othello* and *Falstaff.* In many people's opinion these are the finest of all. Verdi also wrote a Requiem Mass for the death of a close friend. Though it is meant as a religious work, the sound and drama of opera surge through it.

VERMEER, Jan (1632–75)
Dutch artist

In the 17th century a Dutch school of art grew up that specialised in painting house interiors. Finest of these Dutch interior artists was Jan Vermeer. His paintings usually have one or two figures, carefully posed among the items of furniture. Vermeer's placing of the figures themselves, and the composition built up among tables and chairs, curtains and carpets, together with the fall of light coming through windows, gives these paintings a beautiful mood of repose. They are also a valuable source of information about Dutch and Flemish styles in clothes and furnishings of Vermeer's time.

VERNE, Jules (1828–1905)
French novelist

Jules Verne was a pioneer of science fiction. His famous books are *Journey to the Centre of the Earth, Twenty Thousand Leagues Under the Sea, Around the World in 80 Days*; and one that is not so well known, but is most original, *The Chase of the Golden Meteor*. When Verne wrote these novels, the Space Age was well over 50 years into the future. There was no radio or television, no telephone, no motor cars. Trains and ships were driven by steam. But his stories are full of imagination and excitement, and are an interesting reflection on what scientists of the time were doing and thinking.

VESPUCCI, Amerigo (1454–1512)
Italian explorer

Amerigo Vespucci helped to fit out the ships for Columbus's (page 61) third voyage across the Atlantic, then made several voyages himself to the Americas. He made claims, about sailing right down the coast of South America almost to the Antarctic, and to having found many strange animals and plants, that historians now either doubt or dismiss altogether. But he did establish that the new lands across the Atlantic could not be a part of Asia, as Columbus believed, but were part of a truly 'New World'. Hence they were named after him: Amerigo – America.

VICTORIA (1819–1901)
British queen

Queen Victoria reigned longer than any other British monarch. She was crowned in 1837, aged 18, and remained on the throne for 64 years. As a young woman she was beautiful and high-spirited. In 1840 she married her German cousin, Prince Albert of Saxe-Coburg, and they were very happily matched, raising a large family, until Albert's sudden death in 1861. Victoria never really recovered from the shock and sadness of this event. For years she withdrew from public life, and lost much of her early popularity. Then she became increasingly stubborn over affairs of state, favouring some prime ministers (Disraeli, page 78), disagreeing with others (Gladstone, page 105), and trying to take a bigger part in government than was expected of her as a constitutional monarch. Nevertheless, by the time of her Diamond Jubilee (60 years as queen), she was a venerated figure, symbolising a period when Britain became the first great industrial nation and controlled a very large empire.

VIRGIL (70–19 BC)
Roman poet

Virgil, or Publius Vergilius Maro, composed the *Aeneid*, the most famous poem in Roman literature. It is called a 'secondary' epic, because it was written down and intended to be read, rather than recited like a 'primary' epic. The *Aeneid* is based on the epics of Homer (page 124), dealing with events of the Trojan War, including the famous episode of the Wooden Horse of Troy, and after. It was also intended as a hymn of praise to the Emperor Augustus (page 17) and to Roman civilisation, since the hero, Aeneas, is represented as the ancestor of Augustus and founder of the whole Roman race. Virgil is also remembered for the *Georgics*, a poetically written book about Roman agriculture.

VOLTA, Alessandro (1745–1827)
Italian scientist

Two Italians led the way in the modern science of electricity. Luigi

Galvani first did some experiments in which he made the legs of a frog jump when they formed an electrical circuit with a copper and an iron plate. He believed the electricity came from the animal's body. His colleague Count Alessandro Volta believed, on the contrary, that the electric current was generated by the contact of the copper and iron, and that the frog's limbs jumped in response to this. Volta was right, and he went on to make the first electric cell, or pile, of copper and zinc discs in a salt water solution. By linking a number of his cells he then produced a battery with a much stronger electrical charge. The voltaic pile and battery opened the door to the great age of electrical science and to the use of electricity in other branches of science. Improved forms of Volta's electric batteries and cells are still used in numerous appliances and machines, ranging from torches and radios to motor cars. The volt, as the unit of pressure or force in an electric current, is named after him.

VOLTAIRE (1694–1778)
French philosopher and writer

'I disapprove of what you say, but will defend to the death your right to say it.' So wrote Voltaire to a friend, thus summing up his passionate belief in free speech and personal liberty. In 18th-century France there was still no real freedom of speech, and Voltaire – the pen name of François-Marie Arouet – was often in trouble for speaking or writing his mind. On one occasion he was imprisoned, and he was later expelled from the country. Nothing, though, could silence him for long. In essays, plays, novels, he ridiculed or openly attacked what he regarded as stupidities or injustices in society. The Church was a special target for his satire, with its doctrines that no one was supposed to question, and the power it wielded within the French state. In one of his most celebrated works, the novel *Candide*, Voltaire also mocked at the misguided optimism of much 18th century philosophy, when he saw so much that was still wrong with the world. Towards the end of his life, Voltaire was accepted by his countrymen as a great writer and thinker. Ten years after his death, the society he had long attacked was swept away by revolution.

W

WAGNER, Richard (1813-83)
German composer

Richard Wagner saw himself as far more than just a composer. From quite early on in his life he wanted to create an entirely new art form, in which music, drama and poetry would be blended together as never before. He inherited from Mozart (page 170), Beethoven (page 24) and Carl Maria von Weber a German style of opera, closer to his tastes than either of the older-established French or Italian styles, and from that point began working towards his own 'Art of the Future'. *The Flying Dutchman, Tannhäuser* and *Lohengrin*, with their powerful orchestration and deeply thought out plots and libretti, marked his progress. Wagner finally achieved his aims in a truly stupendous stage work called *The Ring of the Nibelungs.* It contains four separate operas, which continue an epic story of drama and tragedy taken from old Norse and Teutonic myths. The characters and events are all linked by an unfolding, unbroken series of motto themes, or 'Leitmotiven'. The entire work takes nearly 17 hours to perform, and it took Wagner 25 years to complete. Two of his other giant operas, or music dramas as he called them, are *Tristan and Isolde* and *The Mastersingers of Nuremburg.* Wagner's influence on music, drama, poetry and philosophy was immense. His own life was as amazing as his work. He spent most of it borrowing money so that he could live in luxury. He had numerous love affairs. Above all, there were his dealings with the strange King Ludwig of Bavaria, who gave him most of the money needed to build his own festival theatre at Bayreuth, specially for the first complete performance of 'The Ring'.

Wagner was married to Franz Liszt's daughter, Cosima, who encouraged him in his work.

WALPOLE, Sir Robert (1676–1745)
British statesman

Sir Robert Walpole was a member of the Whig Party, which in general terms held liberal ideas, compared with the landowning Tory Party. He was an astute politician, who controlled British affairs, during a period of relative prosperity and peace, for 20 years. Because of the way he governed, at the head of a small team of cabinet ministers, he is regarded as Britain's first prime minister, though the office of prime minister was not officially recognised until 1905. Also, his London home was 10 Downing Street, which he bequeathed to the nation, and has long been the prime minister's official residence. What brought about Walpole's downfall was an event known as the War of Jenkins's Ear. A Captain Jenkins claimed that he had an ear cut off in a skirmish with some Spanish coastguards in the West Indies. He actually showed the ear to the House of Commons. Walpole was urged to go to war with Spain. The war went rather badly for Britain, and he resigned.

WASHINGTON, George (1732–99)
American soldier and statesman

George Washington, more than anyone else, created the United States of America. His family came from England and he inherited prosperous estates in Virginia. He proved himself a good soldier in the last war between British and French colonists in North America, but for many more years lived peacefully at home, working the land. He was, however, aware of the tensions building up between the American colonists and the king and government in Britain, mainly over the issue of taxation, and in 1775 was a delegate to the Congress that met in Philadelphia. There he was chosen to recruit and command an American army. Washington had the task of making a decent fighting force out of raw recruits, many of whom did not want to fight outside their own state. He was also kept short of food, clothing and arms. But when war came the next year, he showed his true greatness as a commander. The gravest crisis was the winter of 1777, when Washington had to hold his half-starved army together at a place called Valley Forge. He succeeded, and with help from France, brought about the final surrender of the British forces under Lord Cornwallis at Yorktown in October 1781.

His job done, Washington resigned as commander-in-chief and modestly returned to his estates. In 1789 he was recalled to become the first president of the new republic, and was then persuaded to serve a second term. Thus he had led the American colonists to victory in their War of Independence, and founded the United States of America by his leadership.

WATT, James (1736–1819)
Scottish engineer

James Watt was an instrument maker at Glasgow university when he was asked to repair one of Thomas Newcomen's (page 177) old steam pumping engines. This led to Watt's life-long interest in steam power. The greatly improved the design and efficiency of stationary pumping engines, designed new types of engine to drive machinery, and introduced such mechanical features as the flywheel to maintain a flow of power, and the 'governor' by which the speed of an engine was automatically used to control it. Watt might not have got very far on his own, but he had the good fortune to meet a Birmingham manufacturer and businessman named Matthew Boulton. The two men formed a partnership which became one of the cornerstones of the Industrial Revolution.

WEDGWOOD, Josiah (1730–95)
English manufacturer

Josiah Wedgwood was one of the greatest names in the age-old craft of making pottery from hard-baked clay. There was already a long-established pottery industry in the Staffordshire district when he was born. He brought the craft to perfection with his invention of new methods of glazing and other improvements. Wedgwood's ceramics were so highly admired that the most famous English artists of the day, Sir Joshua Reynolds and Gainsborough (page 100), drew patterns and designs to apply to them, and examples of his work are now highly prized.

WELLESLEY, Arthur, First Duke of Wellington (1769-1852)
British soldier and statesman

'I don't know what they do to the enemy, but by God they frighten me!' was one of the Duke of Wellington's remarks about his troops. Another time he called them 'the scum of the earth'. He was a tough, cold, haughty man, nicknamed the 'Iron Duke'. His troops may not have liked him, but they fought superbly under his command. Arthur Wellesley first saw service in India. His great days came with the Napoleonic Wars. In 1808 he commanded the expeditionary force sent to Spain to aid the Spanish guerrillas in their fight against Napoleon's (page 172) army of occupation. At the battles of Albuera, Badajoz, Salamanca and Vittoria he defeated some of Napoleon's best troops and commanders. That campaign, called the Peninsular War, earned him his title of Duke of Wellington. He returned home, thinking the war with France would soon be over. But when Napoleon in his turn returned from exile in 1815 and raised a new army, Wellington was recalled to service. The great clash of arms between Wellington and Napoleon took place on 8 June 1815 at Waterloo, near Brussels. Wellington, who was supported by a Prussian army commanded by Marshal Gebhard von Blucher, admitted it was 'a close-run thing', but the day ended in Napoleon's final and total defeat. As a mark of the nation's respect Wellington's London home, at Hyde Park Corner was given the address 'Number 1, London'.

Wellington's own latter years, when he entered politics and became prime minister, were not such triumphant ones. As a Tory he opposed much-needed reforms, and mobs attacked his London home, Apsley House, on more than one occasion. He was, however, accorded a hero's state funeral and laid to rest in St Paul's cathedral next to Admiral Nelson (page 176).

WELLS, Herbert George (1866-1946)
English novelist and historian

H. G. Wells was one of the first great writers of science fiction, with such classics of their kind as *The First Men on the Moon, The War of the Worlds* and *The Time Machine*. Many of his shorter stories are just as remarkable for their imaginative, sometimes quite frightening treatment of scientific ideas. Wells wrote other quite different novels, such as *The History of Mr Polly*, that are full of gentle humour and give an interesting view of ordinary life in Edwardian England. In addition, he produced a fine work of scholarship with his *Outline of History*. This is the modest title for a book that traces the whole history of the Earth as a planet in space, to the rise of human life and civilisation. Another of his books, *Kipps* was made into a successful musical comedy called *Half a Sixpence*, which was later filmed.

WESLEY, John (1703-91)
English religious leader

John Wesley was an evangelical Christian – someone who believed in going out into the world to preach and convert others, rather than staying in a church. He first went with his brother Charles to the American colonies, to try and convert the Red Indians. The venture was not a success, so he returned to Britain, to begin his real life's work. Each year he travelled on horseback and in all weathers thousands of kilometres round the British Isles, preaching mainly to people in the new factory towns of the Industrial Revolution, who knew nothing of comfortable, middle-class Church life. Wesley himself was a Church of England clergyman, but those whom he converted were impressed by his moral way of life, or 'method', and formed the separate Methodist Church. In the 19th century Methodists, and those associated with them, inspired many of the social and political reformist movements of industrial Britain.

Charles Wesley wrote around 6,500 hymns, including *Hark The Herald Angels Sing*.

WHITTLE, Sir Frank (born 1907)
English engineer and inventor

Jet propulsion works on the scientific principle that every action has a reaction. If we blow air into a balloon and then release it again, the balloon races about as a reaction to the escaping air. In a jet engine air and fuel are ignited, and the escaping gases of combustion at the rear of the engine make it move in the opposite direction with an equal force. Frank Whittle drew up plans for such an engine in 1930, but it was not until 1941, after the start of the Second World War, that his first experimental jet fighter was tested. By then, Ernst Heinkel and other German aircraft designers were also working hard on jet propulsion, and it was the German Luftwaffe that flew the first operational jet combat aircraft. Whittle, though, was almost certainly first in the field with the whole idea, and he has lived to see jet engines, based on his original designs, power many of today's civil and military aircraft, including the supersonic *Concorde*.

WILLIAM I, The Conqueror (1027–1087)
English king

The Vikings or Norsemen of Scandinavia invaded and colonised large parts of north and west Europe during the early Middle Ages. Duke William of Normandy was descended from them. He was also related to the Saxon king Edward the Confessor (page 85), and upon Edward's death in 1066 landed with his army near the present town of Hastings in Sussex to claim the English throne. His landing was resisted by Harold, Earl of Wessex, who had already taken the crown, and came hurrying south from his victory over another Norse invader. At the battle of Hastings Harold was killed, his army routed, and William the Conqueror was crowned King of England in Westminster Abbey on Christmas Day 1066. He quickly put down all further resistance in England, subdued the Welsh and Scots, and imposed his authority throughout the land by building many strong castles in what is called the Norman style of architecture (called Romanesque in Europe as a whole). The earliest part of the Tower of London, known as the White Tower, dates from this time. William also established throughout England the Feudal System, whereby all land was shared out among his lords and barons, who in their turn gave protection to the local tenant-labourers, or vassals, who worked the land for them. And he drew up a complete and detailed survey of the land – who owned it and how it was used – in a document called the Domesday Book. The preparations for William's invasion, and the battle of Hastings, were pictorially recorded in a beautiful tapestry made at Bayeux in Normandy, and which is still housed in the town.

WILLIAM (or WILHELM) II (1859–1941)
German kaiser

When William II became emperor, or kaiser, of Germany in 1888, the nation's affairs were still largely in the hands of its founder, Count von Bismarck (page 28). The young kaiser was proud and ambitious, and two years after his accession he dismissed Bismarck and took over the direction of Germany's policies. He built up the army and navy, established close links with German-speaking Austria-Hungary, and started to acquire overseas colonies in an attempt to rival the empires of Britain and France. In response to what was often called the kaiser's 'sabre rattling', Britain and France to the west of Germany, and Russia to the east, entered into a series of military alliances. The end result of these power politics was the First World War. William took no active part in the war itself, though he was soon dismayed by the course of the fighting, with its terrible casualties on all sides. With the armistice of 1918 he was forced to abdicate and was exiled to Holland.

WILLIAM III (1650–1702)
English king

William of Orange was the central figure in the event in British history known as 'The Glorious Revolution'. He was the Stadholder, or governor, of the Netherlands, and married to the English princess Mary. In 1688 he was invited by a group of high-ranking Englishmen to become king of England in place of James II, whom they feared might re-establish the Roman Catholic Church and authority throughout Britain. William accepted the invitation, and landed with a small army at Torbay in Devon. That was enough to make James give up the throne and flee. William and Mary then became joint British sovereigns. He went on to defeat the Catholic supporters of James at the battle of the Boyne in Ireland. The massacre of Glencoe between the scottish clans also took place during his reign. Generally, however, William was not much interested in British affairs, being more concerned with the defence of his own country against Louis XIV (page 151) of France. Nor was he a very popular figure in England. He had, all the same, played a vital part in establishing a protestant English monarchy, and so helping the steady move towards a constitutional monarchy linked to an elected parliament.

WILSON, Thomas Woodrow (1856-1924)
American statesman

Woodrow Wilson was President of the United States during the First World War. America's entry into the war in 1917, and the big part American troops played in the final Allied victory of 1918, earned him a place at the Versailles peace conference. He presented to the conference his famous 'Fourteen Points', which were his plan for international co-operation and peace, and for a form of world government, to be called the League of Nations. He returned home believing he had achieved his aims. However, Wilson was a Democrat, and Congress was then controlled by the rival Republican Party, whose members refused to agree to American membership of the proposed League of Nations, on the grounds that the United States should not involve itself further in world affairs. Wilson made a tremendous effort to change American public opinion in favour of his ideas, but failed. The League of Nations was established, with its headquarters at Geneva in Switzerland, but without American membership was not strong enough to fulfil its aims. However, Wilson's ideals were revived in the United Nations, formed after the Second World War with full American support and now a major world organisation.

WOLFE, James (1727-59)
English soldier

The Seven Years' War of 1756-63 was, in part, a fight between Britain and France over their empires. Britain had two brilliant military commanders on her side, Robert Clive (page 59) in India, and James Wolfe in Canada. Wolfe was a rather sickly looking man, but had proved himself a tough and tenacious officer fighting the Highland Scots in the Jacobite Rebellion of 1745. The prime minister, William Pitt the elder (page 192), chose him in 1759 to try and capture the city of Quebec by which France controlled the whole area of Canada along the St Lawrence river. The city stood on a high point of land commanding the river, called the Heights of Abraham. It could not be attacked with much hope of success by day. Wolfe, therefore, sent his men down river in small boats and had them scale the rocky side of the Heights of Abraham, all under cover of darkness. By daybreak he had over 4000 men directly facing Quebec. The French gave battle, during which both Wolfe and the gallant French commander, the Marquis de Montcalm, were killed. But at the end of the day the British had captured the city and with it gained control of Canada.

WOLSEY, Thomas (about 1472-1530)
English churchman and statesman

Thomas Wolsey, the son of a country butcher, rose to a position of great power in Tudor England. His success story began during the reign of Henry VII, but it was with the accession of Henry VIII (page 118) that he really achieved power and fame, as Archbishop of York and Lord Chancellor. When the pope made him a cardinal he even had dreams of becoming the pope himself one day. Cardinal Wolsey lived with much pomp and luxury, and tried to take a big part in European affairs. He arranged a famous meeting between Henry VIII (page 118) and Francis I of France at a place called the Field of the Cloth of Gold, in connection with the political situation between France and the Hapsburg emperor Charles V (page 52). It achieved nothing in the long run. His luck then turned completely against him when Henry wanted a divorce from his first wife, Catherine of Aragon. Wolsey failed to secure this from the pope, largely for political reasons beyond his control. Consequently he was dismissed, then arrested for treason. He died soon after, otherwise he would almost certainly have been beheaded.

WORDSWORTH, William (1770-1850)
English poet

William Wordsworth, who became Poet Laureate, was a leader among the English Romantic poets. He disliked what he regarded as the formal and artificial styles of 18th-century verse, and believed that true poetry must be simple and sincere. Along with this went his Romantic love of nature and the open air, and he spent most of his life among the lakes and rugged hills of the English lake district. Wordsworth wrote one group of poems, the *Lyrical Ballads*, with his friend Samuel Coleridge One of his own most famous poems is the sonnet 'Composed upon Westminster Bridge'. His biggest and perhaps finest work is the long autobiographical poem called *The Prelude*.

WREN, Sir Christopher (1632-1723)
English architect

Sir Christopher Wren was the greatest English architect of the Baroque period of architecture, when many buildings, such as the Palace of Versailles, were designed on the grandest scale. He also belongs to what is called the Classical Revival period of English architecture, which continued the Italian Renaissance use of Classical Greek and Roman styles with their columns, pediments and arches. Wren's greatest period of activity followed the Fire of London of 1666. He drew up a master-plan for the complete rebuilding of the city, which would have made London one of the most spacious and grand cities in the world. The plan itself came to nothing, but its centrepiece was built. This is St Paul's cathedral, which replaced the old gothic cathedral burnt down in the fire. It is modelled quite closely on the plan and decoration of St Peter's, Rome, and more especially on Michelangelo's (page 164) great dome. Wren built over 50 other churches in and around the City of London, many of them noted for their beautifully elegant spires, and designed the Monument that commemorates the Fire itself. He also designed a large part of the Royal Naval College at Greenwich, a new wing to Hampton Court Palace, and several fine buildings in Oxford and Cambridge. His own tomb in St Paul's cathedral bears the Latin inscription, which says, 'If you seek his monument, look around you'.

WRIGHT, Frank Lloyd (1869–1959)
American architect

Frank Lloyd Wright revolutionised ideas about the design and appearance of houses. He used the new materials of the 20th century – plate-glass, new kinds of concrete, steel – to build houses that harmonised with their natural surroundings, instead of just being erected upon a given spot. He studied the site for a house very carefully, using the natural contours, where possible, to produce floors at different levels, and choosing materials that blended well with their surroundings. Above all, he did away with the age-old practice of dividing a house into compartment-like rooms, creating the 'open plan', so that people could move about a house with the greatest ease and freedom. Wright also designed some remarkable large buildings, again using materials to match the special function of the building. He knew also how to use materials to give buildings maximum strength. A hotel he built in Tokyo was the only large building to survive a bad earthquake. With Le Corbusier (page 144) and Walter Gropius, he did much to create the architecture of our age.

WRIGHT, Wilbur (1867-1912), **and Orville** (1871-1948)
American aviators

The most significant date in the history of aviation was 17 December 1903. On that day, at Kittyhawk, North Carolina, Wilbur and Orville Wright took turns at flying the form of glider they had equipped with a petrol-driven propellor engine. The longest flight they achieved lasted only 59 seconds, and only covered a distance of 262 metres, but they were the first men to fly in a heavier-than-air machine. By 1905 they had already improved their flying machine so much that they could guide it in a wide circle over a flying distance of 38 kilometres. The history of aviation, as we know it today, had begun.

X

XENOPHON (about 430–355 BC)
Greek soldier and historian

As a military commander, Xenophon fought against the Persians, and saved his army – known as the 'Ten Thousand' – by leading them in a famous retreat into the mountains, from thence to the shores of the Black Sea and through Turkey all the way back to Greece. Xenophon then settled down on a country estate and became one of civilisation's first great historians. He wrote a history of Greece itself, and some memoirs of Socrates (page 218). Other works of his throw a valuable light on Greek culture and society.

XERXES I (about 519–465 BC)
Persian emperor

The great enemies of the Persian Empire, which flourished from about 550–350 BC, were the Greeks. King Darius (page 70) campaigned against them and was defeated at the battle of Marathon. When he died, his son Xerxes took up the fight. In 480 BC, he led an army of nearly 200,000 men – the largest fighting force yet assembled – from Turkey and across the Hellespont, in order to attack Greece from the north. The Spartan king Leonidas and 300 of his warriors put up a heroic defence at the pass of Thermopylae, but could not long prevent Xerxes's armed multitudes advancing upon Athens. The Greeks set fire to the city, abandoned it, and took to their ships. Xerxes called up the Persian navy to finish them off, but at the battle of Salamis, not far from Athens, he was defeated and returned home, beaten by the Greeks like his father.

Z

ZEPPELIN, Count Ferdinand von (1838-1917)
German airship designer

The first of Count Zeppelin's airships, or dirigibles, flew successfully in 1900, and a few years later they were put into commercial service. Early in the First World War, Zeppelin airships were modified to carry bombs and were launched on several air raids against London, though their size and slow speed made them very vulnerable to gun fire and aircraft attack. Zeppelin died during the war, but his designs continued to be used through the 1920s and 1930s, when several famous airships were built. Biggest and most famous of all was the *Hindenberg* which made several transatlantic crossings.

ZHUKOV, Georgi (1896-1974)
Soviet Russian soldier

Marshal Zhukov master-minded nearly the whole of the gigantic Soviet war effort against the invading Germans in the Second World War. In the winter of 1941, when the German Wermacht had dealt the Red Army a series of near-fatal blows, he still managed first to prevent the capture of Leningrad in the north and then launch a counter-offensive on the Moscow front that very nearly broke the German lines. During the winter of 1942-3, Shukov delivered the counter-attack that cut off the German 6th Army in Stalingrad and so brought about one of the turning points of the whole war. With the Germans in full retreat, Shukov then co-ordinated the huge Soviet offensives that ended, in April 1945, with the final battle for Berlin and complete Soviet victory in the East.

ZOLA, Emile (1840–1902)
French novelist

Emile Zola's childhood was tough and poor, and he wrote mainly from bitter experience about poor people struggling against the odds in a brutal and unjust world. His most famous novel is *Germinal*, and in this and his other major works he made a very powerful impression by the conviction of his writing and the fact that he did not gloss over any aspect of life, however grim. Zo was already one of the most famous writers in France when a political scandal blew up over the trial of a French army officer named Dreyfus. The Dreyfus Affair became the focal point for all French political feeling. Zola joined the liberal side of the arguments with a celebrated newspaper article headed *'J'accuse'* in defence of Dreyfus and against that he said was the corruption and arrogance of the army. He was prosecuted for this and had to leave France for a time.